THE LONG FUSE

THE LONG FUSE

AN INTERPRETATION
OF THE ORIGINS OF WORLD WAR I

SECOND EDITION

LAURENCE LAFORE

University of Iowa

WAVELAND

PRESS, INC.

Long Grove, Illinois

For information about this book, contact:
  Waveland Press, Inc.
  4180 IL Route 83, Suite 101
  Long Grove, IL 60047-9580
  (847) 634-0081
  info@waveland.com
  www.waveland.com

Cover photo: UPI/CORBIS-BETTMANN

To the Memory of
Troyer Steele Anderson

Contents

Maps

THE LONG FUSE

Truth and the Historian

WORLD War I has become a fashion and a fad. Musical comedies are written about it, and high school students collect old helmets and anecdotes about the strange behavior of generals. What was once called The Great War has retreated far enough into the past to seem an oddity and to lose its force, in our consciousness, as a living memory or an enduring influence on our lives. It is being interred in the same moldering but monumental tomb as the Napoleonic and Civil Wars, a subject for amateur autopsies, a passionate hobby among buffs who collect its relics with the same degree of zeal that philatelists apply to the early stamps of British Guiana.

Such souvenir-hunting has nothing to do with the work of historians, whose professional purposes may be said to be approximately the opposite of those of the curio collector: the reconstruction of events past with a systematic effort to divest it of the picturesque and to see it with fidelity as contemporaries saw it in order to understand their motives and purposes. But to see it, too, with wider vision and greater accuracy, since the historian enjoys the broader view of retrospect and a larger abundance of documents. Retrospect, to be sure, produces narrowness as well as breadth. It has been repeatedly observed (and indeed has become a creed with some historians) that historians can see the past only through the distorting lenses of the present and therefore can never see it true, and this is, of course, correct. But if he is at all competent the historian is aware of this, and he is also aware of the comparable, but very different, ophthamological limitations of other historians in the intervening seasons. Each age contributes a different set of defects of vision, but it also, by that very fact, contributes new perceptions as well. Historians are always, as it were, using telephoto and wide angle lenses simultaneously as they focus on their subjects, and it is possible to argue that each sees a little more, and a little more accurately, than his predecessor.

The assertion may be optimistic. Myopia is often aggravated by fashion or circumstance so that the historian of a given age may be so preoccupied with the issues of his own world that he tries to see the past as an explanation for them. During and immediately after the second world war, for example, there was an understandable impulse to explain the first in terms of the historical forces that seemed to have climaxed in the awful anti-hero, Hitler. Distinguished English-speaking historians viewed practically all the events of Germany's past as a sort of preparation for the ferocious aggressiveness of Germany's present. Such recurrent short-sightedness has afflicted the viewers of all past events, and in a larger way has prevented, and always will prevent, lasting agreement on such problems as the cause and nature of the decline and fall of the Roman Empire (if indeed it *did* decline and fall), or the War of the Roses, whose rights and wrongs are still, five hundred years after the event, ardently and sometimes hysterically argued between adherents of the Houses of Lancaster and York. But varieties of interpretation, at any given time misleading, still may contribute to enlightenment, as surely as the accumulation of objective facts. The vocation of professional historians is precisely this: to revise past views in the knowledge that they will never win but that, with each new monograph or essay they move further from defeat in the game of discovering truth.

Since no historical analysis is final, reappraisal is a duty. Since "relativism", the notion that the past can be seen only from the distorted standpoint of the present, may lead toward illumination of a true state of things as well as its concealment, it is useful that each generation see how the new developments of its time may adjust the focus of the instrument through which past events are seen.

What follows is an essay in such an adjustment. One of the great developments of our day has been the epic, if still very incomplete, emancipation of the African and Asian lands from colonial tutelage of European powers. A leading element in this has been the complicated interplay of nationalisms, the tired nationalism of the Europeans retreating, gracefully or sullenly, before the comparable but more vigorous emotions which the Europeans inadvertently but inevitably exported to their colonies. Before 1945 it was very rare for anyone to see in World War I an episode, or a cause, of this vast remodeling of the world. But what has happened since 1945 undoubtedly lights new aspects of the intricate events that happened before 1914. Colonial empires played relatively little part in determining the suicidal decisions that led to the devastating events of 1914 to 1918. But a generation that has observed the ways in which elementary economies and politically inexperienced societies can contort the destinies of what used to be called the "civilized" nations run by Europeans and their descendants, may in retrospect now discern a set of historical phenomena, perhaps materials for a new theory of history. The effects of nascent nationalism, still unresolved, in areas recently emancipated politically, may properly be projected into our view of Europe in the early twentieth century.

We know now that such relationships can shake the world; and it is the purpose of this book to suggest that one set of such relationships shook, and in the end destroyed, the world of European Powers in 1914. The peoples and places that caused the explosion in that year were located not overseas but within the boundaries of what geographers had rather arbitrarily named Europe. But they were nonetheless colonial in their situation, and their struggle for independence was the model and antecedent of the world struggle that has developed since 1945.

World War I is the name given to a very complicated series of events. They were, considered together, the most important events of the past hundred and fifty years, and along with those of the French Revolution and the Protestant Reformation the most important of the last millennium. The war destroyed men, treasure, and empires and contorted those that survived; it gave birth to new and unexpected forces; and it greatly speeded the development of many tendencies already in course. It demolished institutions and ideas that in 1914 had been, although already weakening, still strong, such as the Russian and the Austro-Hungarian empires, and monarchy and aristocracy. It demolished equally institutions like the German Empire and ideas like anarchism, which had seemed imposingly vigorous. It gave impetus to forces already born whose destiny had been still uncertain and whose reputation still doubtful: democracy, the self-determination of nations, the rights of women. It enormously speeded secular shifts of power already in the making, most notably the rise of the United States of America to economic and military pre-eminence, and the corresponding decline of the capacity of the Great Powers of Europe to control their own destinies. It decimated a generation of future leaders and producers, and for thiry years shook the political poise and interrupted the economic growth of Europe. It inaugurated an era in which colonial empires, which seemed powerful and permanent in 1914, were to disintegrate. It precipitated the Russian revolution and released communism as a world force led by the Soviet Union. Far from removing the causes of future war—the Allies proclaimed that as their aim—it wrecked the insufficient but not ineffective systems and habits that had provided peace in Europe for forty-five years before its outbreak. And it did all these things in four years; its most spectacular consequence was the effect it had upon the *timing* of history. It reduced Great Powers, unprepared in psychology or in policy, to permanent weakness, and it thrust the United States, also unprepared, into a position of world responsibility.

What caused it? The question is unanswerable, for the war was many things, not one, and the meanings of the word "cause" are also many. To discern the cause of any event, even a single and simple event, is to advance a definition of the word. To discuss causes at all is to move from the historian's world of concrete things, statutes, treaties, battles, and mobs, to the shadowy and metaphysical landscape of the philosophers.

The essay that follows singles out for emphasis a particular group of circumstances and chains of events that preceded the outbreak of the first World War, the effects of the emerging nations of central and southeastern Europe upon the established Great Powers. To argue that they form *the* cause is to gamble with semantics and with the philosophy of history. Other causes—the changing balance of military power in Europe, the growing social tensions within European nations, the shrillness of chauvinists and the stridency of a semiliterate press and public, Anglo-German rivalry, Franco-German hostility, Russian expansionism, colonial conflicts, commercial competition—all these have been studied and restudied. All of them were causes of what became the first World War. But the war, that vast phenomenon, grew out of a single international event, which was the conflict between the Habsburg Monarchy and the kingdom of Serbia. Had Austria-Hungary been differently constituted, had Serbia posed a less lethal threat to it, there would have been no Austro-Serbian war in 1914; and if a general war had come later, it would have been fought on different terms and taken different forms. It was the system of alliances and the changing balance of military power in Europe that converted a Balkan dispute into a world war, but it did not cause the particular war that happened to be fought.

For a hundred years and more, Europe, the prosperous and stable Europe of the west and the north, had suffered from the complexities of the lands and peoples of the east and the southeast, whose difficulties have intruded themselves on Great Powers and have, by magnetic attraction, drawn Great Powers into conflict. Here are illuminated, in a sort of gigantic microcosm, the problems of conflicting and emerging nationalisms, the problems of economic and political immaturity, the problems of attempting solutions by means that worked in the West and which were the only means that anyone knew to apply to new nations.

There were deep and abiding sources of conflict in the rest of Europe. But to a surprising degree they were intertwined with the turmoil of the nationalities in Austria-Hungary and the Balkans. If the Germans pushed Austria into war in 1914—and there is much evidence that they did something of the sort—they did it largely because they apprehended that a general war was someday inevitable and that, if it had to be fought, this was the most favorable time to fight it. But the thing that made general war seem inevitable to the Germans was the existence of the Franco-Russian alliance, which they viewed as a form of encirclement ultimately directed against them; and the Franco-Russia alliance was, indirectly anyway, the product of Austrian and Balkan developments a generation before. In tracing almost any of the circumstances that were most critical in 1914, one is led back to the national conflicts of Central and Southeastern Europe.

It is perhaps artificial so to make selections and emphases. But the study of history is always a study of patterns, of sorting out different hypotheses, of imposing different sorts of order on the confusion of raw facts, of finding in the present new clues to the past. The history of the history of the causes of World War I demonstrates these propositions.

Until the moment when German troops crossed the Belgian border and entered the frontier villages on the early morning of August 4, 1914, the conduct of the affairs of state that led to the invasion had been in he hands of diplomats, politicians, and military advisers. At that moment the events of the recent past were transferred to the hands of others, of publicists and propagandists. For four years an unconscionable volume of self-defense and corresponding vilification was poured forth. None of it was accurate, let alone complete. Official publications—the *British Blue Book*, the *French Yellow Book*, the *German White Book*, the

Austrian Red Book, the *Russian Orange Book*—sought to demonstrate, by a judicious selection from the archives, the moral purity of each nation and its allies and the depravity of the enemy. The selections were by necessity small, and by reason of their purpose highly misleading. Judicious omissions were sometimes supplemented by falsification. Legends were accepted in the belief that the end of victory justified an incautious credulity for rumors.

The belief was sound. For every nation the necessary sacrifices imposed by war had to be justified by belief in the guilt of the enemy for starting it, and the necessary energy had to be ignited by enthusiasm and hatred. There is no doubt that this was true; modern wars are fought largely by emotion and by the creative power that emotion, properly directed, can release. Where the conviction of the public about the righteousness of its cause faltered, as it did in Russia, the nation at war collapsed into an appalling tangle of distraught individuals. Leaders elsewhere, whose moral and legal obligation was to prevent precisely such a calamity, were shrewd and skillful enough to promote the calling forth of hatred. The public response was gratifying.

When the peace treaty was at length written, it became expedient for quite accidental reasons to include in it, in passing, the statement that "the Allied and Associated Governments affirm and Germany accepts the responsibility of Germany and her allies for causing all the loss and damage to which the Allied and Associated Governments and their nationals have been subjected as a consequence of the war imposed upon them by the aggression of Germany and her allies." So thoroughly had the opinion among the Allied and Associated governments been convinced of the responsibility of Germany and Austria-Hungary for deliberately starting the first World War that the statement passed almost unnoticed in Britain, France, and the United States. But in Germany, where precisely the opposite view of the origins of the war had been implanted and received with precisely the same degree of passionate acceptance, the passage was regarded not only as wholly untrue but as further evidence of the ineffable hypocrisy of the enemy states. The discussion of moral guilt for starting the war, instead of fading away when the war ended, was renewed with greater intensity than ever. Instead of being fought by publicists, the battle of "war guilt" now became the concern of whole armies of historians. The flow of literature was torrential. No historical subjects except the American Civil War and the French Revolution had ever been examined with this exhausting thoroughness. Regular periodicals devoted to the causes of the war were established, and flourished. Day-by-day accounts of the crisis were followed by hour-by-hour and, literally, minute-by-minute accounts. It was clear, for example, that the sequence of receipt and dispatch of diplomatic telegrams was very important, and there were erudite articles computing the time required in different capitals for decoding.

In the 1920's in Britain and America, there was a contagion of breast-beating. What was called "revisionism," one of whose forebears was a sullen economic expert on the British delegation at the Peace Conference named John Maynard Keynes who dramatized both the economic and the moral defects of Allied policies, became popular. Moved by embarrassment at the hysterical excesses of wartime propaganda, and faced with what seemed incontrovertible evidence in the impressively edited collections of German documents that the German Republic was bringing out, British and American historians discovered that the Germans had certainly not been guilty of *planning* a world war and that the conduct of the Russian, the French, and even the British governments conspicuously failed to demonstrate any single-minded devotion to the preservation of peace.

Then the approach of a second World War, and the startling evolution of a new Germany that was not only openly but boastfully aggressive, caused a species of counterrevisionism to emerge. Historians began to apprehend everywhere that there was something deep and rooted in the German people and the German state that led them to undertake wars of aggression.

The river of literature subsided. There were now more immediate subjects of interest, and it seemed that almost all that could be said about 1914 had been said. From the mid-thirties on, there was a rapid decline in writings about 1914.

But the river did not dry up. There appeared, a few years after the end of the war, the immense and imposing work of Luigi Albertini, by all odds the most compendious, reliable, and closely reasoned of all treatments. Albertini had not merely studied the documents and memoirs—studied more of them, since more were available—than had earlier scholars. He had also interviewed many of the statesmen, starting in 1919, and had asked them embarrassing questions.

The trend of Albertini's conclusions was to some extent in the fashion of the times: he found the Germans unquestionably guilty. Not by any means solely guilty, not guilty of planning a world war years in advance, but unquestionably guilty of urging Austria to attack Serbia at the known risk of a general war.

This interpretation of 1914 is now generally held among those who write about it. Indeed, the reinculpation of Germany has since been carried much farther than it was by Albertini. On the fortieth anniversary of the crisis, for example, the Regius Professor of History at Oxford published in *The New York Times Magazine* a commemorative article in which he said that it had been finally and definitely "proved that the War was caused by deliberate German aggression." The single fact produced in support of this assertion by Professor Trevor-Roper would not seem final or definite to a close student of the chronology of events, but his attitude is nonetheless illuminating. Seven years later, the distinguished German historian Fritz Fischer published a history of German policy before and during the war called *Griff Nach der Weltmacht*. In it he said that he was not concerned with the allocation of guilt; still, he allocated it, concluding that the German leaders "bear an important portion of the responsibility" for the European war.[1] In demonstration of this, he produced new

---

1. P. 97. Fischer's book appeared in the English translation in 1967, under the title *Germany's Aims in the First World War*.

evidence of a damning sort, and argued with considerable force that a policy of willingness to embark on preventive war had been decided before the crisis, based on a wildly optimistic appraisal of German chances for victory. Austria-Hungary, he said, was to a large extent pushed into war at German insistence. His book occasioned much discussion and some shock in Germany.

Professor Fischer's treatment of the crisis is brief; most of his materials have been used before and subjected to different interpretations. Anyone who has read his account must admit that the Germans were, at least, frivolously willing to contemplate the possibility of a "preventive war" and were exploiting the occasion for a "grab at world power"; still, his treatment is very narrowly of the German side of things, and a wider survey indicates clearly that the Germans were by no means the only people who were prepared to risk a war and who had expansionist programs in their minds. Russians were also ready to grasp at world power. And the fact remains that it was the crisis of Austro-Serb relations that brought these and other ambitions and alarms into open conflict. The question of the guilt of individuals and nations dissolves, as Fischer admits, into an ocean of general responsibility.

By now, after more than fifty years, it is possible to view the question of war guilt as a fact, and not a purpose, of history. The controversy is by now a topic deserving historical analysis. It is time to write a book explaining why historians in the past have been so beguiled by it. The historian dealing with 1914 can by now say that a great many European statesmen in 1914 were irresponsible in their attitude toward the possibility of war, and can try to explain why, without making judgments on their morals. One most important consideration to bear in mind is this: Irresponsibility, even for those Germans who devoutly believed that they could win and that a general war was both necessary and desirable, was limited by the fact that they did not know what was going to happen once the war started. They did not envisage four years of horror; they did not envisage social revolutions and the collapse of Europe.

Or at least, very few of them did. One of the few, oddly, was the German chief of staff, Helmuth von Moltke, who is said to have feared that a general war would mean the annihilation of the civilization of Europe for decades to come. He was approximately correct; still, he was prepared to urge measures that he knew would bring a general war. And this is the sign of another limitation. Moltke, although an indifferent chief of staff, was an obedient subject and a patriot; and he believed that, once war threatened, the safety of Germany required certain measures that would bring it closer. The soldiers' job was to make sure that war was fought on favorable terms; Moltke was obeying the imperatives of his position.

Statesmen, like soldiers, obeyed the imperatives of their offices in a system of competing and frightened national states. When the catastrophe took place, they were held responsible, reasonably enough. But the responsibility was the monopoly of no man and no nation; rather it inhered in the offices and institutions, in the system of European states and its shortcomings.

"War guilt" is an historical phenomenon, one that came into existence only after the public discussion of responsibility began in August, 1914. Like the war itself, it belonged to a species of familiar phenomena which, because of unforseeable circumstances, assumed a scale so vast as to create a new order of magnitude. But no one who was making the decisions in 1914 knew that either the war or the question of responsibility for starting it was to introduce a new dimension into history.

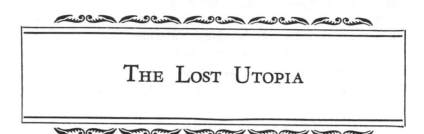

CHAPTER ONE

THE LOST UTOPIA

IN 1871 the Europeans were making over their world. Most of them believed that they were making a better world. There were still those who looked back with longing to the compact age of their great-grandparents, when noblemen and bishops and kings had elegantly presided over lands still peopled by placid peasants and pliant townsmen, and when the absolutes of men's beliefs had been comfortably clear. But even among conservatives the more lucid knew that that age had never existed except in the nostalgia of those who had survived the French Revolution, and that the attempt to recreate it required a radical and not a conservative act of political imagination. There were those, too, who thought the new world could be made a good world only by a second violent eruption of society, in which the remnants of past ages—noblemen, bishops, and kings—and their new partners, merchants, bankers, and manufacturers, would be dispossessed and destroyed. But most Europeans believed that such nostalgia was absurd and such disruption unnecessary.

They thought that mankind had progressed in enlightenment, n humanity, in reason, to a point where the old might be peace-ully and usefully absorbed into the new. They understood that the means to untold affluence were at hand. They believed that with it the planet might ultimately produce a civilization of perpetual peace and progress, guided by the light of exact knowledge that was rapidly being revealed to mankind. It was a time when there was extravagant, if unsurprising, confidence in the proposition that human knowledge is the same as human wisdom; and Europe was engaged in an orgy of self-instruction. By the sun of what was vaguely called "science," all things were to be illuminated: the secrets of the universe made known, superstition dispelled, the nature of human existence revealed, the means to a richer and wiser world fashioned. The sun was only just rising, but already its light had begun, dramatically and unarguably, to bring these miracles.

There was no doubt of it; it was true. Never before had an age believed with such warrant that all ages before had been Dark Ages. Evidence of a change different from all previous changes in human history was visible at every hand. Trains ran, while only two generations earlier it had taken the men of Napoleon's day as long to travel from Paris to Rome as it had taken Caesar. The railways were the spectacular symbols of a vast and revolutionary wealth that included, as well, steel, textiles and chemicals, and houses. And they had their counterparts in the abstract realm of knowledge. The debate over the origin of humans and the nature of matter that had lasted since men first used abstract ideas was now ending. Darwinian biology was recognized by forward minds as providing at least the outlines of genetic truth; the physicists, the anthropologists, the chemists, the sociologists, were not far behind. It was difficult for any educated young person in 1871 to resist the belief that all the man-old secrets, the secrets that had led their ancestors to invoke Zeus' thunderbolts to explain the weather, and witchcraft to explain illness, would presently yield to science. So much had already yielded, and at a pace incredibly hastened in living memory.

And, as was natural and appropriate, political ideas and political facts were changing to accord with this stupendous forward leap of means and learning. The progress here was less consistent, but it was palpable. In France, still as always the forum of learning and progress in Europe, the regime of Napoleon III that had fallen the year before—in defeat and humiliation before the victorious Prussian Army—had shown the world what statecraft allied to science could do. In less than two decades it had, by judiciously applying new ideas and new technology to social policy, begun the creation of a modern economy and a modern society. It had already equipped France with prosperity—not the old prosperity of good crops and a quiet commerce in spices, but a new prosperity of capital investment: spreading railroads, rising capital, and expanding factories, apartment houses, department stores, steel bridges, banks, and a sensational display of public buildings. Napoleon III, whatever else he had done, had tried to free his state of the shibboleths of the past, the dark tyrannies of tradition and stagnation and a fate-ordained separation of the society into poor and rich. And in Prussia, his nemesis, an imaginative group of generals had shown what science could do for statecraft in the very realm where Napolon III had failed to apply it: the Prussians had seen, and acted on, the new opportunities that railways and metallurgy opened to armies. The Prussian triumph of 1870 was the victory of an otherwise poorer and smaller state that had applied the resources of the new age to military planning over a richer and larger state that had applied them to everything else.

There were a thousand other examples. In financial and economic policy, for example, which was as much Great Britain's specialty as war was Prussia's, a new instrument for economic growth, the corporation, was being developed at precisely the moment when outdated restrictions on the freedom of businessmen were being abandoned and the remarkable fecundity of a flexible policy of creating money through the use of credit was being perceived.

The applications of science to policy were for the most part— except perhaps in France and Prussia—haphazard. But they were working. And thousands of men were dreaming—and debating —about ways to make the application systematic, to perfect philosophic theories by which the state and society could be more precisely and more rapidly adjusted to the possibilities of progress. Though their view of the obstacles differed, all the progressives had common enemies: tyranny, illiteracy, priests with their obscurantism and their mysticism, aristocrats with their tradition and their special privileges; kings with their despotism; peasants with their obstinacy and their backwardness—the survivors of the old order that harassed the birth of the new. But most of them thought that the old order was already peacefully dying.

There was no doubt about it: a new world was being made. Even the leaders born to an older tradition, the Emperor Alexander in Russia, Chancellor Bismarck in Germany, Count Cavour in Italy, had moved ahead to policies whereby states and societies might profit through the adjustment to the new science, the new learning, the new ideas. Modern ideas were triumphing everywhere. Europe would soon be organized on a rational basis, its political and social symmetries would reflect the symmetry of nature and the universe. And it was going to happen, was happening, faster than anyone could have imagined ten years earlier. All that was needed now was hard work and common sense and education, and in the lifetimes of men already born the rising sun would light a Europe of perpetual peace and progress.

The International System

The political system under which this fruitfulness would develop was already in existence. It wanted, of course, much adjusting. But this could and would be done, it seemed, even where the older was most deeply entrenched.

The constitutional order thus seemingly destined to emerge as universal in Europe consisted of a series of states of varying size and character that shared—or would share, when the process was done—certain common characteristics. They were *sovereign*: that is, they were free; their duly constituted authorities were subject to no foreign power or control and, as long as they behaved according to the rules of law and constitution, to no internal control either. Sovereign states were equal in legal theory: each was a corporate legal person, a *unit,* and each was free of foreign control. And they were—though this was a condition of fact or of hope rather than of law—*national*: the populations of Denmark, Holland, and Sweden; of Britain, France, Spain, and Portugal; of Russia and Rumania and Greece; and now, too, of Germany and Italy were each predominantly of a single nationality, which meant that they were mostly united to one another by bonds of language and culture and tradition or, if by nothing else, in a common acquiescence in their national kinship.

The fact that most of the European states were national states greatly strengthened them; it gave them a strong and growing foundation of unity, a sense of fellowship among their citizens that, it might be hoped, would always transcend the divisive forces within, struggles between parties and classes and factions, those normal and (the Liberals at least thought) wholesome differences that bred a fecund interchange of ideas and in the end produced progress itself. The national state, itself strengthened by the underlying unity of its citizens, in turn strengthened that unity by providing leadership and defense for the national welfare. And if the state *did* correspond in its geographic limits to the limits of a nation, it added a new dimension to freedom. It not only procured and protected the freedom of the individuals who were its citizens; it guaranteed them against a particular form of oppression: rule by foreigners.

The notion of freedom, for which Liberals and many others strove, possessed then two aspects: freedom for individuals and freedom for nations. And the national state was exactly designed to protect and assure both; the state by its structure protected individuals; by its existence it protected nations. Perfected, it would lead to a world in which the brotherhood of free men would be achieved through a brotherhood of free nations. So many Liberals hoped, and such was the vision of the Italian liberator Mazzini. Such was the project of Napoleon III. Such was the hope of millions of Europeans. For those who dreamed of progress to the good world, the instrument that history had placed in their hands, the national state, seemed almost too good to be true. They were right; it was.

There were dangers in this system, however great its merits. If freedom for nations required that national states be sovereign, sovereignty opened the door to abuses. The sovereign state, un-controlled, might become uncontrollable. Its necessary right to defend itself was difficult to separate from power to attack its neighbors. Armies were necessary to defend freedom; but armies could attack. And even in the absence of attack, strong armies could give to their masters a peacetime capacity to bully others, to disarrange the mechanism of stability.

Against this menace defenders of the system discerned two safeguards, one a matter of doctrine and one a matter of diplo-matic practice. The doctrine was this: wars were made by hungry men, by arrogant men, by ignorant men, by oppressed men, by men with special interests to protect and special axes to grind. In the new world that was being made, where eventually everyone would be free and well educated and where the old vested in-terests of aristocratic armies who had made a faith of military virtues would be dispossessed, *and where all nations were free from foreign rule or oppression,* and where free trade and economic growth had made everyone secure, the causes of war would vanish. When the new world was complete, there would be no cause for war. Everybody still thought armies were necessary, and many people still held the chivalric code of warrior morality. Some of those who, like Bismarck, were most forward in attacking the Church as a rival to secular power, and in attempting to legislate security against poverty, were also the most ardent ad-herents of large armies. But even some militarists believed that prosperity and education would improve the chances for inter-national stability.

The second safeguard, the diplomatic practice, had several aspects. One was simply the professional skill of diplomatists—

the men who were trained in the handling of international relations. It was their business to keep Europe stable, and even under
the handicaps of the old order they had been remarkably successful much of the time. Diplomats were like plumbers: they stopped
leaks before the house could be flooded, they opened clogged
drains before the effluvia could produce epidemics. And modern-
minded people said that if the diplomats were serving a government
based on the will of the people, the enlightened, educated,
prosperous people who could have no interest in war, their skills
would be all the more efficacious.

There was another and more reliable safeguard, which was
international law. There had always been rules and procedures,
largely accepted and agreed to, that governed the relations among
governments. In the last few generations these rules had been
expanding and taking on a more formal quality. They were constantly being applied by courts, they were constantly being defined
by treaty and agreement. International law was coming more and
more to list the things that governments could and could not do
in their dealings with foreign nations: they could not confiscate the
property of foreigners without due process; they could not invade
the embassies of foreign states; they could not seize the ships of
foreign nations. And since the Treaty of Vienna in 1815, there had
arisen still more precise and helpful notions of international
responsibility which had taken on at least some of the qualities
of law. It had been recognized then, and was still recognized,
that the peace of Europe was a matter for the concern of all European countries. There were certain categories of actions that were
widely recognized as threatening the peace and security of all
states, and such actions were not supposed to be undertaken
without prior consultation with the other governments. It was
improper, if not positively illegal, to attack or invade the territory
of another state; it was improper, if not illegal, to annex territories, in Europe at least, and perhaps in the colonial sphere, without asking the permission of everybody else.

Such actions by governments were deemed to be a threat to the general security; they might affect the vital interests and security of others to the point where general war would ensue. Their impropriety lay in this, and so it was thought proper that they be prefaced by consultation with the rest of Europe. But it was neither necessary nor feasible to consult with all the governments of Europe. It was the Great Powers who had to be consulted; they were thought to occupy the position of a directorate, a sort of executive committee, of the European polity, and special responsibility was recognized as a political modification of the legal theory of equal sovereignties. There was a very serious gap here between legal theory and the reality of power and politics, and it was to widen and in the end to take fatal forms when the requirements of Great Powers clashed with the requirements of small sovereign states. But the distinction was clearly necessary, and no one saw it as inherently dangerous. In 1871, the Great Powers were Germany, Britain, Austria, Russia, Italy, and France. The state of greatness was formal; it was reflected in the fact that Great Powers exchanged ambassadors (who legally represented the sovereign powers) while lesser powers exchanged only ministers (who legally represented only the foreign ministries). It was true that in 1871 there were two other powers besides the official Great Powers which, because they had once been "great," still exchanged ambassadors with the others: Turkey and Spain. But these were not now regarded as constituting part of the directorate.

The Great Powers were the spokesmen and leaders and responsible authorities for what was vaguely but incessantly called the Concert of Europe. The name was significant, and it summarized an idea of community responsibility and of common interest in stability that tempered, in both fact and law, the separateness and the sovereignty of states. The Concert of Europe was born of the Napoleonic wars, though its origins were ancient. It reflected the realization, widespread in 1815, after a generation of bloodshed and disorder, that some collective responsibility for order was necessary. It embodied the undoubted fact that Europe *existed*—bound by its heritage from Rome and Greece, by its Christianity, by its technological superiority, by its tight geographical position, into a unity that might, in its parts, be highly various but whose parts were closely interrelated.

The Concert had begun to break down in the 1820's, however, and it had broken down calamitously in the decade that preceded 1871. Since 1859, no fewer than four major wars and several minor campaigns had been fought in Europe. Piedmont and France had attacked Austria without consulting anybody; Prussia had successively attacked Denmark, Austria, and France without sanction of the Concert. It was clear that collective responsibility must be rebuilt. It seemed possible that it might be, now that the great unsolved problems inherited from the Treaty of Vienna—the disunity of Italy and Germany—had at last been resolved. There were many and determined efforts to undertake the reconstruction of the Concert.

But it was not only, and not chiefly, the skill of diplomats and the sense of community upon which Europe relied for the main tenance of what were called "peace and stability." There was also a countervailing system, the *existence* of sovereign states which was seen to contain within its very nature a sort of built-in mechanism for stability. This was the "balance of power."

The balance of power was, as a phrase and a conscious idea, almost four hundred years old by 1871, but events had given it new meanings and a new importance. In its essence it was very simple: a strong power inclined to aggression would be restrained by a fear that many others would come to the aid of its victim. The reason why others would come to the aid of a victim was also simple: if one power grew too strong, it would be a threat to all the others; if one victim could be successfully attacked, then others could likewise be attacked, one by one. An attack against any country was *in fact,* as it was in the theory of the Concert of Europe, an attack on the ultimate safety of all.

These were the safeguards that statesmen and politcians believed to offer guarantees that the system of sovereign states could be held in equilibrium and made to work for peace and stability and not for disorder and war. Mankind—or at least, provisionally, Europeans—could now march ahead toward the age of gold, *la belle époque* as the French were to name it after it had been destroyed. The insttiutions necessary to it were, like the science and the resources, in being. All that was needed was to perfect them.

The Anomalies of the European System

So in 1871. Nor were these hopes delusive. The solid foundations for progress did indeed exist, as did the means and the will to build upon them. It was no delusion to say that the golden age was coming, or that in comparison to all previous eras the decades ahead would be decades of unimaginable growth, of mounting riches to challenge the ancient dreams of Croesus, of ingenious application of human science and wisdom to the problems of a changing society, of incredible increase in education and in knowledge of the secrets of the universe, and of peace.

But the political dreams and hopes ended in despair. Within a decade after 1871, the renewed strength of conservatism, its direction and its program altered, had been revealed. Not only were the Liberals of the early seventies disappointed; many of them were converted. And more were forced, by the erosion of their own position, into radical and socialist positions. The Liberal consensus was releaved as tenuous, and Liberals moved progressively to the right and the left, toward the aggravation of old social conflicts and the revelation of new ones.

The very existence of social classes, increasingly inclined to regard one another with suspicion and animosity, belied hopes for a tranquil future or for steady progress. The people who actually ran governments in 1871 were almost always gentlemen, in the worst sense: haughty aristocrats to whom the notions of progress and of human equality were threats and insults. They were already obsolete and were rapidly becoming more obsolete, so that the system they controlled was subject to more and more violent attacks from other classes simply because they did control it.

A cynic, or at least a realist, might, already in 1871, have seen other oddities and flaws in the symmetrical picture that presented it-self to the hopeful. Marx and Engels saw them and denounced the system. The great Liberal John Stuart Mill perceived the ironic fact that the spread of political freedom and of industrial growth, for all their rewards and riches, had produced a sort of human degradation on a scale and of a kind, if not an intensity, that Europe had not known before. Another kind of realist might see that the unanimity with which Europe apparently was building a common political system based on the rule of the people was illusory, and that even where they ruled—perhaps especially where they ruled—the people were showing themselves no less inclined to bellicosity than did their aristocratic predecessors. For example, public opinion had been a most potent force in hurrying France along the road to war in 1870. The people, demanding a political victory over the upstart Prussia and threatening vengeance on their leaders if it were not achieved, had helped to push the harried politicians at Paris into making outrageous demands on Prussia.

There were other problems, which inhered in the international system and which everyone recognized without, perhaps, grasping the vastness of the questions that they raised.

The first was the very unevenness with which Europe had pro-gressed toward the perfected system of nation states that the hope-ful regarded as the ultimate outcome of its development and the ultimate guarantee of order. It was plausible to say that in the west and the north the nations had evolved into clear national units, each with its own state, and that the rest of Europe must inevitably follow. Neither part of the statement was true; *and the facts of state sovereignty, the very safeguards that were built against changes in frontiers and of the state structure, would help to prevent its be-coming true.* In the recent past the resolution of national issues had been achieved only by violence, by drastic changes that had affected every aspect of European life. The unification of the Germans in their empire had involved three wars and the infliction of defeat and deep humiliation upon the French, as well as many lesser

35

changes. Stability meant rigidity, and rigidity meant the perpetuation of a system that was as yet only partly composed of mature national states.

There was, for example, Ireland. Ireland was part of the United Kingdom of Great Britain and Ireland. It had no separate existence and so no standing in international affairs. It was in theory wholly a domestic concern of the British state. But while opinions might differ, even among Irishmen, as to the extent to which the Irish were a nation, there was no difference of opinion about their ability to threaten the stability of the United Kingdom. They had done it on several occasions, most spectacularly during the long war with France from 1793 to 1815, when they had colluded with the French enemy to furnish a very real threat to Britain's national safety. And the Irish, like many other groups in Europe, were in 1871 becoming more, not less, nationally conscious. Voices were being raised to demand the salvaging of the dying national tongue and the refurbishing of the splendid national culture, and were already numerous and strident in demanding self-government. Suppose Ireland revolted in civil war, which it seemed perpetually on the verge of doing? Its cause could scarcely help but be espoused by Britain's opponents among the nations. If those opponents were sufficiently resolute they might, as the French had done seventy-five years earlier, undertake to provoke a national rising. Then Ireland, an inchoate nation without legal standing, would become very much an international issue.

Great Britain was the oldest of the national states, and among the most solid. Its national government had taken shape a thousand years earlier. It was a model and a prototype for the states that formed the European State System. But in Ireland it contained a subnation that was capable of threatening catastrophe both to Great Britain and to the System.

The complexities on the continent were much greater. France, by far the most homogeneous of any Great Power, was an admirable example. Its numerous subnations, the Bretons, the Flemings, the Basques, the Catalans, the Provençaux, were, to be sure, reconciled and assimilable, if not quite assimilated, to the French nation. But until the year 1871 it had contained another subnation which illustrated a widespread sort of problem, different from the Irish but similarly threatening. This was the Alsatian minority who inhabited the easternmost province, the lands rich in industry and agriculture on the west bank of the Rhine. Alsace had once been part of the Holy Roman Empire of the German people, although it had been attached to the French crown in the seventeenth century. Its inhabitants were for the most part of Germanic origin, and many of them spoke a dialect of German. In 1870 they were reconciled and assimilable, if not quite assimilated, like the other subnational groups within France. They were certainly overwhelmingly loyal to France; despite their origins and dialect, they thought of themselves as French.

But other Germans did not. For them, Alsace was a German land snatched from German control by a brutal aggressor—Louis XIV —two hundred years earlier. The inhabitants and the culture were German. It was, moreover, a land of great strategic importance: its western border marched with the crest of the Vosges hills that commanded, on one side, the heart of France and on the other the valley of the Rhine. It was the natural western border for Germany, geographically and ethnically. The Germans, having created for themselves a national state and having beaten the French in 1871, reclaimed their lost province. Which, having been restored to Germany, instantly and achingly became a lost province of France.

Alsace was accompanied in its change of nationality by half of Lorraine, the region that lay to the north and west of it. Like Alsace, Lorraine had once (and much more recently) been part of the Holy Roman Empire; like Alsace it was strategically important, for it contained the city of Metz, which was the strongest fortress of Europe, guarding the principal military avenue between France and Germany. But Lorraine was almost wholly French in population; its Germanic character, if it had ever had one, had been largely lost; its population retained only a few traces of German language or tradition. Among the Prussian advocates of its annexation were some of the military: they believed that Metz was vital to prevent a future French attack on Germany and they also believed that its loss by France would make easy a future punitive expedition against France, should the need arise. There were important iron deposits in Lorraine, too, but these apparently played little part in the Prussian decision, for the ores were of an inferior sort, and it had only just been discovered that it was possible to use them for steel. Bismarck and the political directors of Prussia were convinced that Metz must be German—the very completeness of the defeat of the French state made it hard to resist the temptation to prey upon its territories, and to the injury of Alsace was added the insult of Lorraine.

The Germans hoped (although without much assurance) that the French would adjust to this loss and accept it as final, as states had over and over again in the past accepted the loss of border provinces to their neighbors. But any Frenchman in 1871 could have told the Germans that this hope was illusory. There were two things that made Alsace and Lorraine, from the moment of their amputation, quite different from the loss of, say, Schleswig-Holstein by Denmark in 1864 or the Austrian loss of Lombardy in 1860, and they illuminated the nature of the new Europe. France was pre-eminently *the* great Continental power. For a thousand years it had been a leader of the European states, and for a thousand years it had perceived, and successfully averted, the threat to its position that must come with the creation of an equally strong and united Germany. Now the pre-eminence was past—that was bitter enough, and perhaps so bitter that it could not be wholly accepted for generations. But acceptance, in any case difficult, was made impossible by the loss of the provinces. They were the symptom, the symbol, the geographical reminder, of humiliation. And there was more: whatever their origins, these provinces were integrally part of France. In places where national unity was absent or undeveloped, provinces might be regarded—as they had been generally regarded in earlier centuries, when national states were loosely organized and their subjects had little authority or concern

38

in the conduct of affairs—as counters in a game whose stake was power. Now, for France, provinces were not counters, they were parts of a body. It was not merely on the French side of the new frontier that anguished memories were alive after 1871; it was, no less so, on the German side. The Reichsland, as the Germans called the recovered regions, bristled with sedition. Many of its million and more inhabitants were irreconcilable, and they posed a problem not only for Germany's international relations but for its domestic tranquility.

No one really doubted that the time had come when Germany must be united. Even Napoleon III had recognized it as inevitable and thought it, in some form or other, desirable. A system of national states required a German state, just as it required a French or a Spanish or an Italian state. The system could hardly work when the disunited Germans were forever fighting against it. But Alsace and Lorraine demonstrated the hazards of trying to perfect the system of national states. The Germans might convince themselves that the new lands were a natural and necessary part of a new Germany; the French might make an effective case for saying that their loss prevented any possible Franco-German amity and promised a perpetual sore spot within the new empire.

Almost nowhere in Europe, even where national frontiers were accepted as final and natural, did the political lines follow lines of nationality. And indeed such lines were rare: national groups overlapped and mingled everywhere. And even where clear ethnic lines existed—there was one *within* Switzerland, where the Alpine pass of Saint Gotthard divided a purely German from a purely Italian canton—they rarely lay on the political frontiers that had been mostly arrived at by complicated bargains and accidents in the remote past. The European states were irretrievably assymetrical. And as the solidity of states and the stability of the System increased, these disparities were increasingly difficult to rectify. Every successful effort to rectify them in the past sixty years had involved a war.

The disparities were much rarer and less important in the west and north than in the south and southeast. In the former regions, at least, the states possessed a majority of citizens whose allegiance was unfaltering even if their nationality was not homogeneous, as it was not with the Scots or the Welsh, or the Bretons and the Basques in France, or in Belgium and Switzerland where national allegiance was the triumph of an idea over the facts of nationhood. In the east the disparities were enormous; nowhere beyond the Rhine was the process of the coalescence of solid national states anywhere near even that degree of completion that had been reached in France. Even where, as in the Russian Empire or in Greece, there was a majority who shared a national identity, there was also always *either* an Ireland of intractable aliens or an Alsace of intractable fellow-nationals exiled by a frontier. While conditions differed drastically with different peoples, the welter of mingled nationalities in the east and southeast could almost all be sorted out into one of these two kinds of problems, an Ireland or an Alsace.

In 1871, it did not occur to the most inveterate believer in national freedom that all of these national groups could or should be made sovereign nations. In this the position of the doctrinaire devotee of freedom and the realistic devotee of the existing order differed only in degree. Bismarck, who now presided like a sort of secular Zeus over the constellation of European states, was satisfied that the sorting out of peoples had gone quite far enough and that any further changes of frontiers or sovereignties (now that his own Germany had emerged free and united) would be pure romanticism. A man like Gladstone, the Prime Minister of Great Britain, was by reflex opposed to such a position; good Liberal that he was, he encouraged the struggles of oppressed nationalities for freedom; he was consistent to the point of wanting to do something even for Ireland. But even Gladstone, so sympathetic to the Poles, the Irish, the Italians, and the Greeks in their national struggles, would scarcely have advocated independence for the Slovaks, even if he had heard of the Slovaks. For in Central and Eastern Europe a political map drawn along lines of clearly defined nationalities (which did not in any case exist) would have been a Persian rug of petty princedoms. It would have brought to Eastern Europe precisely the chaos of small, conflicting, backward states that the consolidation of the Western nations had, over a period of centuries, painfully overcome.

For this was the problem, a problem in timing. In the West, almost nobody had thought of nationality at all, whether as a good thing or not, whether as a suitable basis on which to build political institutions or not, until *after* the states had been formed. Spain and Portugal, Holland and France, England and Sweden, had been created by governments that fused their subjects—or most of them—into a national unit. This was the lesson of the complaisant subnations, the vestiges of the national patchwork, in France: they had been associated with France as a political unit before people thought that states and nations ought to be coterminous, and they had lost their will to nationhood. Little was left of Breton nationality except a picturesque *patois* and a sentimental memory, and efforts to re-evoke it failed. France had once been almost as varied as Southeastern Europe, but it was no longer, and it was the existence of a powerful state that had made the change.

But consciousness of nationality had come late, east of the Rhine and south of the Alps. *It had come after the creation of the modern states,* which were here supra-national. For not more than a hundred years had the curious, almost mystic, sense of brotherhood among the dark, forgotten peoples of the East been stirring. By 1871 it had been converted for many of them first into an awareness, then a philosophy, then a fact, and finally a demand. Unresolved, disunited, unassimilated, the peoples were growing conscious of what they called their destiny.

There were the Rumanians, the sons of a village culture that traced a tenuous link, through its Latinate dialects, to a Roman past. Although provided, mainly by the enthusiasm of French priests doing missionary work along the Danube, with a Latin alphabet, a grammar, a literature, and a sense of cultural pride, the Rumanians had no political past in the last five centuries; they had no aristocracy—their aristocracy was Greek—they had only the heritage of Christianity, and of memories and dialects that survived among the impoverished peasants. But Rumania, in 1871, had been re-born; it made good, in two small provinces of the Turkish Empire, its claim to be a nation and later its claim to freedom. Beyond the borders of the little principality still lay the majority of Rumanians —or at least of people who might, suitably instructed, become Rumanians. They were ruled, or misruled, by Turks and Russians and Hungarians. Rumania had its Alsaces in abundance.

What was true of the Rumanians was true, in varying degrees, of some twenty other groups of people in Eastern and Southeastern Europe. Some, like the Greeks and the Serbs, already had made a state: free but incomplete from the point of view of national com-pleteness. Others, like the Slovenes, had never had a state and as yet were barely stirred by national longings. Others, like the Ruthenes, were only vaguely and uncertainly set off from neighbors and kin. Others, like the Ghegs and the Tosks, were only names for obscure, sparse nomadic tribes. Some, like the Wends, had shrunk to obscurity and almost oblivion, contentedly unaware of destiny in their Prussian fatherland. Others, like the Friulians, were almost wholly unconscious of their own existence. But some had great pasts and flaming national aspirations, and a few of these were of sufficient magnitude to cause, in 1871, a real and present problem of the largest order.

The most important was Poland. Poland fell into the category of Irelands, but on a vastly larger and more complicated scale; and since it lay within the borders not of one but of three coun-tries, it shared, too, the qualities of an Alsace-Lorraine. The Poles were an ancient, proud, and highly civilized people who had once been masters of the largest territory in Europe. They were Roman Catholics, and they had shared and contributed to the intellectual glories of the European Renaissance. Despite the gulf between an aristocracy that was still medieval in its powers and prestige and a peasantry that was wholly voiceless and not entirely free, it was a remarkably homogeneous nation. A century before had taken place the shocking process, completed over twenty years, of destroying the Polish state. Poland was the exception to the rule: Poland had formed its state and its nation on the Western pattern, and then it had been destroyed, forcibly degraded to what had always in modern times been the plight of the Serbs and the Rumanians. Divided among Prussia, Austria, and Russia, the Poles had never ceased to be a dangerous threat, larger and more immediate than the Irish or the Alsatians, to the domestic solidity of Prussia and Russia. In Russia, they had three times within living memory— most recently in 1863—revolted. In Prussia, infiltrated by German townspeople in their cities and a German aristocracy on their land, they remained sullenly hostile. In Austria, Catholic and conservative Austria, their landlords retained their ancient privileges and a degree of local independence, so that Austria was much the least hated of the Polish overlords. But for all three Powers there was a constant fear of troubles that might lead to dismemberment. In all three there was suspicion that one of the others might work on its Polish population to its own disadvantage.

For the three empires that shared it, however, Poland was more a unifying than a divisive force. They were drawn together by common fears, demonstrating the fact that in Eastern Europe stability and a system of national states were incompatible. That had been vividly demonstrated in the Polish revolution of 1863 when Bismarck, implacably supporting the Russian repression at a time when the conscience of Liberal Europe was aflame with eagerness to assist, had won the gratitude of the Russian Emperor to the point where he had granted, as a sort of gift in return, his blessing to Bismarck's venture against the French in 1870. Poland, which did not exist, was one of the most important facts of international relations.

And Poland was, too, the touchstone that caused respectable Europe, the Europe that accepted the System, to split. On one side were the conservatives who, like Bismarck, felt that the sorting out of Europe into national states had proceeded far enough. On the other were those who cherished human and national freedom and the conviction that the System must be complete and consistent; a respectable English Liberal might never have heard of the Slovaks and might smile at the thought of a national state for the Slovenes, but concerning Poland he could have no doubts. For him the completion of the System required a Poland; the System could not assure peace while Poles were languishing. But the freeing of Poland could assuredly not be achieved without war. Liberals in public life privately deplored; Liberals in private life publicly denounced. But Poland and peace, essential to one another, remained incompatible.

The conservatives in 1871 had more than practicalities on their side. They saw, more clearly than those who looked for the freedom of all peoples great and small, that the difference in timing of national development had become a difference in kind. Eastern Europe could not be sorted out, not possibly. It was too late for that. Stability and order, and the chance for fruitful development, required that the tangled peoples live within great empires. Such empires, four of them, were in existence—Germany, Russia, Austria, and Turkey. Together they included almost the whole of Eastern Europe. Together they might, by a united support of the conservative principle, defy the divisive forces of liberalism and nationalism and bring peace and progress and reconciliation to the East.

But the conservative position had its weaknesses, and the more realistic among the leaders saw them with agonizing clarity. There were two in particular that had long caused trouble. The first was simply that the empires could not act harmoniously; their interests overlapped, their ambitions clashed. For a hundred years Russia had been assaulting Turkey, driven as if by a hereditary psychosis toward Constantinople, which was the Turkish capital and which the Russians had dreamed of for five hundred years as the center of their culture and their religion and their imperial destiny, only temporarily fallen under strange and infidel sway. The Turks had progressively lost province after province to the Russians. Nor were the Turks and the Russians the only disputants among the

44

empires that were supposed to maintain the stability of the East. There were rivalries between the Austrians and the Prussians, who had long contested for the leadership of the German peoples until, at last, the Prussians won in 1866. There had been occasional, if less violent, frictions between the Prussians and the Russians, which even Bismarck's tact had not obliterated. And—this was the most intractable of the international conflicts—there were rising tensions between the Austrians and the Russians, inherent in their common interest in the lands to the south but dating, in their most bitter form, from the curious events of the past twenty years. In 1848, Austria, like every other Continental country west of Russia, had seen a complicated and dangerous uprising against its institutions, and the restoration of order had required a Russian Army, generously offered by the Russian Emperor, Nicholas I. He had a right to believe that his assistance would earn Austria's perpetual gratitude but when, less than five years later, he found himself embroiled in an absurd but bloody war with the French and the British, he turned in vain for repayment of his investment. "We shall," the Austrian Chancellor said, "surprise the world by our ingratitude," and proclaimed Austrian neutrality in the Crimean War. The world at large was not surprised, but the Russians were. There were solid reasons for Austrian neutrality: the Crimean War was not one in which they could reasonably engage without high cost and great peril. But from that event dated persistent friction —hatred and disdain on the Russian side, suspicion and fear on the Austrian.

Such rivalries and frictions might, with time and effort, be appeased, and Bismarck believed that he could appease them. What was less easily cured, if it was curable at all, was the condition of Turkey. Turkey was the Sick Man of Europe. Compared even to the other empires, its great European holdings were a tangle of conflicting, discontented nationalities and religions; this might have been, as it had in the past, a fortifying fact; sensible people might reasonably have discerned the need for an arbiter and a policeman to keep the peace among the ten or twelve national groups in the Balkan peninsula. But two things prevented even sensible people from reaching this conclusion in 1871. The first was the frustration the Turks had encountered in their efforts to reform their state. This was due in part to the rigidities of the Islamic and Ottoman tradition, but the rigidities were in themselves the product of outside forces. There was never time, between Russian attacks, to reorganize the Empire, to bring up to date the antique institutions, to face the pressing problems of state.

The second source of weakness was the spreading and by now inflamed consciousness of nationality among the Balkan peoples. It had started in the eighteenth century; by now it was far advanced, with real injustice and maladministration buttressing a purely intellectual preoccupation with, for example, Serb history, Serb language, Serb religion, Serb culture, Serb greatness, Serb independence, Serb grievances, Serb *destiny*. And if the Serbs had their destiny, so did the Rumanians and the Greeks and the Montenegrins. And so *might* the Bulgars and the Macedonians and the Ghegs and the Tosks and the Vlachs. And so indeed might the Turks themselves—a conspicuous minority in their Balkan lands, as badly misruled by the sultans as their fellows and anguished by the vision of a destiny that lay not in the future but, it seemed, in the past.

The decay of Turkey was far advanced by 1871, and it accounted for the few exceptions to the statement that all of Eastern and Southern Europe lay within the confines of the four empires. Montenegro, tiny and mountainbound, had escaped its rule. Serbia had won self-government after 1815, and so, a decade later, had the Greeks. By 1871 there was a Rumania. (Rumania and Serbia were still technically not sovereign.) All four were small and crude and, by the standards of the Great Powers, impotent. But they had two sources of strength: first, their driving, mounting hatred of the Turk, inflamed by professional agitators, that combined with a passionate solicitude for their brothers still languishing under Turkish rule in adjacent provinces. And secondly, they had the power to seek friends among the Great Powers, which might be expected to welcome friends (even though small and unreliable) and bases of operation in the Balkans.

Liberals and realists might conclude in 1871 that the existence of Greece, Montenegro, Rumania, and Serbia presaged the destruction of the Turkish Empire in Europe. They might see that their existence would lead, as their birth had led, to violent conflicts among the other Powers—the independence of Greece had involved, among many other vicissitudes, a dramatic confronting of French and British and Russians that threatened war among them and led to endless bad feeling. Conservatives might fear that the existence of the Balkan nations would destroy that very unity among the great empires on which their premise depended, and might writhingly seek to elude the threat. And a very shrewd observer might note that the four little states meant that the conservative dream was outdated: it was too late, now that they existed, to order the development of Eastern Europe on imperial lines. Once Turkey had begun to disintegrate, the passion for national freedom could not be quenched. Or at least it could be quenched only by a united effort of which the empires were incapable.

Eastern Europe had already, to the delight of Liberals and the alarm of conservatives, entered upon a path of development that superficially resembled the West's, the development of a system of completed national states. But the case was different, as the conservatives saw. The development was not producing Englands and Hollands; it was producing an array of states the size of Luxembourg, simulacra of the utmost backwardness and awkwardness and with no experience or restraint or wish for the preservation of stability.

The burgeoning of national feelings and ambitions was the weakness of the empires and the nemesis of conservatism. Nothing in 1871 was more dangerous to the existing order. But by a paradox it was conservatives themselves, even in the Eastern empires, who were already feeding the flames or spreading the contagion. And for a strange and conflicting set of reasons.

The first and basic reason was the insecurity of conservative regimes and conservative parties. For almost a hundred years the world had seen a spreading campaign for political rights for ordinary people. *Some* rights—the extent and the nature varied—were being demanded everywhere, and everywhere some had been granted by 1871. Most often they took, or threatened to take, the form of demands for a legislature elected by the vote of a large part of the people. Control over it by conservative people—whether they were Liberal businessmen grown moderate with success or people conservative by reflex or people ideologically attached to the old order—was endangered: radicals could almost always make more appealing promises to voters. Even where there was no strictly political problem, as in Russia, there was the threat of revolutionary action.

In 1871 the political tendency most noticeable to contemporaries was this: Europe seemed to be moving faster and faster toward progressive ideas and toward the sweeping away of old institutions. And people who saw value either in the preservation of the old institutions or in a very gradual adjustment of them were finding it more and more difficult to explain to and convince the citizens of their good intentions and their serious purposes. They seemed, always, to be saying: Vote for us and we shall safeguard special privileges for ourselves. In an age when ordinary people, literate people, living in cities and open to ideas, were more and more a political force—*the* political force—conservatives of every sort were obliged to find a political platform to appeal to them.

And ironically this platform could only be nationalism. Conservatives were compelled to find reasons why ordinary people—voters or potential voters—should preserve such institutions as the Army, the established Church, the Monarchy, the Aristocracy. These were the essential keystones of the old order, and they were, naturally, unpopular with radicals. So conservatives hit upon the only *appealing* thesis that could be sold, as it were, to the voters: the old institutions were the embodiment and safeguard, not (they publicly proclaimed) of the existing social order, but of the nation. They were the essential part of its tradition.

THE LOST UTOPIA

It was Bismarck who had discovered the formula: give the people a democratic legislature to satisfy them, and glorify the nation, of which they are members, to flatter them. Then the old institutions can be preserved.

Once this platform had been invented, its popularity spread. By 1871, conservatives were seizing from startled Liberals the platform of nationalism. But for them it was not, as it had been for Liberals, a program for the emancipation and fraternity of all nations; it was, dangerously, a program for the aggrandizement of their own nation. And this was ironic, for until now conservatives had fought nationalism, as they had fought all ideas of freedom, and had sought to save a cosmopolitan Europe. That was to be expected—it was their natural role, for there was a sort of freemasonry of power and privilege and fear among the upper classes, the monarchs and noblemen and the wealthy. Frederick the Great, who was now being transformed into a hero of German nationalism, had disliked to speak his own language, preferring French as less barbaric. The dynastic relationships, the common use of French, the common culture of elegant people, the common horror of the French Revolution, had made conservatism international in the first half of the century. Nationalism had flourished *against* the old order; now conservatives were kidnaping and deforming it for their own uses. And in the multinational empires of the East, the conservative strongholds, the easy and accommodating cosmopolitanism of an earlier day began to be transformed into a narrow nationalism that made the empires in the end ungovernable. It also made them mutually hostile.

Nowhere was this tendency more evident than in Russia. In 1871 a man named Nicholas Danilevsky formulated a program for what was called pan-Slavism, a doctrine based on the assumption that a common racial ancestry and an ethnic similarity in their languages formed a bond of brotherhood, or ought to form one, among all Slavic peoples. It had been evolved, largely by Slavs in the Austrian Empire, before the middle of the century. By 1871 it had been adopted by an important intellectual movement in Russia

49

and was undergoing amendments: not only ought all Slavs to feel a sense of brotherhood; they ought all to form a free political union or confederation, and they ought to accept the leadership and patronage of mighty Slavic Russia in this task. Danilevsky proposed a fraternity of eight states: Russia itself (nothing was said about the very diverse sorts of Slavs who composed Russia and who in many cases disliked their membership in it: White Russians, Little Russians, and, most spectacularly, Poles); Bulgaria (the Bulgars were in Turkey); Czechoslovakia (the Czechs and the Slovaks were in Austria); the South Slavs or, in their own tongues, Yugoslavs (they were partly in Austria, partly in Turkey, and partly in Serbia and Montenegro); Constantinople (where there were, in fact, no Slavs and never had been, but which was the font of Slavic culture); and three countries which lay surrounded by or bordering these five but were not Slavic themselves: Greece, Rumania, and Hungary.

This was nationalism with a vengeance. It was both incredibly ambitious—its realization would have brought Russian dominance in 1871 almost to the limits, and in some places beyond them, that the Soviet Union reached in 1948—and incredibly artificial. It was nationalism wildly extended beyond the usual definition to comprehend the notion of race. But it was influential as an *idea* in Russia, where ideas were already seething with lethal ebullience. Important people were sympathetic to it, both because it coincided with the ambitions of Russian policy and because it was a revolutionary program that strengthened instead of menacing the monarchy and the existing order. And while nobody even in Russia envisaged its immediate achievement—which would have required the destruction of Austria and Turkey and Germany—it became a goal and an ideal and a useful lever with which to harass rivals and encourage the friendship of the other Slavic peoples. The possibilities, both for domestic consolidation and for foreign success, were enormous. It was not surprising that influential circles in the Russian government should pay attention to the drastic views of M. Danilevsky.

In Britain and Germany, comparable developments, more decorously expressed and less wildly novel, were taking place. In both countries the conservatives were beginning to use the appeal to nationhood, to national rights and grandeur, to secure popular support. And where these led, other conservatives soon followed. The logic was too great, the method too easy, to resist. The thunder of the radicals was systematically stolen.

But there were more threats to the dream of a Europe neatly organized into brotherly national states than the problem of the Eastern nationalities and the conservative appropriation and distortion of the nationalists' program. There was, more subtly and perhaps more profoundly, a threat that existed in the very nature of national states. This was the threat of insulation.

The greatest boast and justification of national states was that they could do things that no other kind of state could do. They were free enough, flexible enough, secure enough, to accomplish the achievement of the new world that conservatives and Liberals alike hoped to build. And for the attainment of that world there was one thing that everyone except the most retrograde agreed to be necessary: education. Modern society and national greatness, both economic and political, required literate citizens. It took education to operate the new factories; it took education to make elections work. A British statesman, urging a system of state education after the law in 1867 that gave the vote to factory workers, remarked, "We must educate our masters." From every point of view, humanitarian, economic, and *national,* education was indispensable. It was the admirable system of schools and universities in Prussia, many people said, that was responsible for its military and political triumphs in the past decade. And education had long been a slogan of the Liberals: To be free, it is necessary to be literate.

Education was spreading. French and Prussian school systems were already extensive, if not quite universal, free, or compulsory. Britain was, after a long lag, enacting in 1870 a bill that looked to making at least primary education generally available. In Scandinavia, literacy was mounting rapidly. But education had unexpected consequences: it imposed national uniformity on all who lived within a nation's borders. Instruction meant instruction in the national language; literacy meant literacy in the national language. It meant reading the same textbooks and newspapers as one's fellow citizens, and thus absorbing characteristic national attitudes. In border provinces where the nationality lines were cloudy, education clarified them. Sometimes, as in conquered Alsace or in Ireland, there was resistance, but in the West it was as yet inchoate. By 1871, it was clear that education meant that the nations were growing more separate, the boundaries more sharply defined. This was acceptable alike to conservatives, with their new fondness for nationalism, and to Liberals, with their passion for tidiness. But it meant that one more balance wheel of the international order was disappearing. The peasants of southern France now could read, and what they read was what was published in Paris. For Northern and Western Europe, this meant an increase in the *separateness,* and therefore misunderstandings, among nations. In the Eastern empires it often meant the imposition of alien tongues, changes of cultural tyranny, and resistance.

All these developments were explosive, and what was beginning —though just beginning, in 1871—to explode was Europe itself. It was moving outward, carrying its traders and its settlers and its missionaries and its proconsuls to the rest of a world that, except for the semi-European western hemisphere, was vastly and increasingly its inferior in power and wealth and—most important of all—its capacity for organizing things. For two generations the political expansion of Europe had been almost at a stand-still, after the staggering loss of the Americas between 1776 and 1824, and after Liberals had discovered that colonies did not really benefit the mother country. But in 1871 the grounds existed for another outward push: the new confidence in their destiny, the new power and wealth, the new national ambitions provided them. And a shrewd observer like the British conservative leader Disraeli would note that there was political capital to be gained for his party by promising to build a new empire, by telling the British workingman that, while he might at home be the underdog, he was, to the world at large, very much a master, a ruler, an aristocrat, who governed the distant lands that formed Britain's empire and greatness. And a leader as shrewd as Disraeli noted, too, that such grandiose visions would lead to competition with the other nations of Europe and that such competition might also serve a worthy and glorious end: the strengthening of British national spirit, an impetus to British creativity. In just such ways had the grandeurs of the Elizabethan age been achieved.

There were, then, paradoxes that grew out of the ideal of a Europe of free men in free nations, living together in prosperous serenity, and it was having strange and unsettling effects in Eastern Europe. The symmetries were impossible to achieve; the ideas of nationality were being diverted into peculiar channels. The problems of border provinces and minorities were growing more, not less, serious with each step that was taken toward the perfection of national states. But there was still a chance, in 1871. Despite the Irelands, despite the Alsace-Lorraines, despite the disputes in regions far removed from Europe, despite the new and bellicose dreams of the Danilevskys, there was still a chance that the system might work. No system was ever perfect; compromises might be reached, assymmetries accepted. If even a rough approximation could be achieved, then the skill of the diplomats and the Concert of Europe and the balance of power might yet triumph, the disintegration of European Turkey might be rationally governed, to secure the order and tranquility that would permit to ripen the rich fruit of wealth and culture, freedom and knowledge, that lay so invitingly on the horizon.

It might have worked, even with the anomalies of the Russian and German states and the decay of Turkey, if it had not been for the unresolved nationalities of Central Europe. There, presiding over a tangle of conflicts and aspirations, lay one of the Great Powers of Europe, one of those states responsible for the preservation and ordering of the system of national states; but this was a

Great Power that was not itself a national state, and was incapable of behaving as one. The European order was based now, in 1871, upon the assumption of nations: and Austria was not a nation.

CHAPTER TWO

THE AUSTRIAN ANOMALY

THE European System of national states required that a line be drawn between international and domestic affairs. In international affairs the sovereign state was deemed to be a unit, speaking with a single voice. Beyond this unity foreigners might not with propriety look; domestic affairs and differences were none of the business of outsiders. Governments were to concern themselves only with governments, never with the private citizens or private quarrels in another state.

The principle was unreal in 1871 and always had been. There had always been Irelands and Alsaces. Groups sympathetic to particular foreign states had always existed, and the foreign governments naturally patronized them. Great states had always meddled in the affairs of small ones, and such meddling was within limits accepted as a proper exercise of the responsibilities of greatness. With the rise of political parties, foreign policy became involved in party disputes, and a change of party sometimes meant a change of foreign policy. Bismarck, for example, always distrusted Great Britain as a possible ally because he thought its parliamentary and party system might make one administration abandon an alliance formed by its predecessor. As public opinion and popular participation in government proceeded, the idea of a sovereign state speaking with a single voice, the heritage of an autocratic age, was imperiled by newspaper debates and pressures, by articulate minority groups, by organized economic interests. Each might affect the conduct of affairs by its own government; each might sponsor the interests of a foreign one.

Despite these large exceptions the System, indispensably founded on the false distinction, proved in general workable for many years after 1871. It was so because of patriotic sentiment; in a famous phrase, politics must stop at the frontier. For most citizens, loyalty to their state put a limit to the extent that their interests and debates might distort foreign policy. The safety of the nation demanded support for even a government whose policies they disliked. This built-in mechanism was strikingly illustrated in the French Republic, which had the greatest multiplicity of parties and the most violent factional rancors in Europe, and a ministry that changed on an average of once a year. Nevertheless, Frenchmen more often than not united in defense of the state in its international dealings, and the transient foreign ministers had a policy as remarkable for continuity as for the skill and fervor with which they pursued it. The same was true, with aberrations, of all the Great Powers and most of the smaller ones.

To this generality, as to all others about the European System, Austria-Hungary was the exception. The Habsburg Monarchy was, in terms of law and practice, a Great Power. But it was a Great Power that *consisted*, as it were, of the very anomalies that were troublesome side issues for other Great Powers, the Alsaces and the Irelands. The other Powers were constructed upon a foundation of nationality. Austria-Hungary was not. Major threats to the stability of the System came in the end, by 1914, from the magnetic or divisive forces exercised by minorities in national states. Austria-Hungary consisted entirely of minorities.

The fact was universally recognized as an oddity; increasingly, it was also recognized as a source of grave weakness to the Habsburg state. What was less generally recognized was that the internal oddities had drastic effects upon external behavior. For

Austria-Hungary the neat distinction between domestic and foreign could not, in the last analysis, exist. It could not act as a national state; and it was impossible for its neighbors, themselves affected by its peculiar composition, to act toward it as they could toward a national state. It was this situation that brought about the outbreak of the first World War.

Austria-Hungary was not the only important European Power so composed. The same was true of the European portions of Turkey—the Ottoman Empire, to use its correct name. But the Ottoman Empire was in a very different position from Austria-Hungary, and its capacity for producing disaster was less direct. Its partition might have been arranged by the European Powers—more easily, perhaps, than that of Poland a century earlier—if they had wished to partition it; Turkey was scarcely in a position to offer resistance to their united efforts. Their efforts never *were* united; one of the principal reasons was that many Austrian statesmen thought partition of the multi-national Ottoman Empire would threaten the existence of their own multi-national empire, which adjoined it. Austria-Hungary's own diversity became a principal bulwark of the Ottoman Empire. And Austria-Hungary was far from the condition of military or diplomatic helplessness of the Ottomans. It remained a major military power. While Great Powers might be excused for decorous meddling in the affairs of small ones, Austria-Hungary was by 1914 unique in being a Great Power in whose affairs small ones meddled. The System provided no procedure for handling such a situation.

The intricacies of the national composition and internal politics of Austria-Hungary, the Habsburg Monarchy, were very great. It is difficult to present a simplified version that does not do violence to some vital fact of the situation. Since the history of mankind since 1914 had been so largely shaped by those intricacies, it is worth considering them in what might at first appear superfluous detail.

The Habsburg Monarchy in 1871 was emerging from a decade of violent and painful adjustments, the nature of which was scarcely less portentous than the inherent peculiarities of the society that had produced them. In 1860 it had been defeated by the combined armies of the French and the Piedmontese and had been obliged to abandon its richest province: Lombardy, in the Po Valley. It had also lost its dominance in the rest of Italy, including the two Italian states, Tuscany and Modena, over which branches of the Habsburg family had ruled. In place of Habsburg dominion, which had lasted with interruptions for three centuries, there was a new kingdom of Italy, entirely independent and periodically hostile to the former overlord.

Disunited Italy had been, throughout modern times, one sphere of Habsburg operations and one source of Habsburg power and prestige. Disunited Germany to the north had been another. The Habsburg monarch had been the traditional leader of German, as of Italian, affairs. After the loss of the Italian position, that in Germany was likewise lost. In 1866, Austria was attacked by the rival German kingdom of Prussia and decisively defeated. As Piedmont had undertaken the organization of Italy in 1860, so Prussia now undertook the organization of Germany. In 1866, Prussia and Piedmont had, logically, been allied. By the Peace of Prague the Habsburg ruler lost not only his role in Germany but an additional province in the south, Venezia.

By 1867, then, Austria had ceased to be either an Italian or a German power. But—and this was both fateful and characteristic—it had not ceased to contain either Italians or Germans. The remaining territories contained both in abundance, though in different frames of mind. In the surviving provinces of Tyrol and Istria were over half a million persons of Italian language and culture, many of them increasingly discontented under Habsburg rule and drawn toward the new Italian kingdom. On the other hand, the very core of the Habsburg monarchy was German—the capital, Vienna, and the heartland provinces of Austria, Salzburg, Styria, Carinthia, and most of the Tyrol near it, were entirely or predominantly of German language, culture, and tradition. German Austrians were well represented in many other provinces:

in Bohemia, Moravia, and Austrian Silesia to the north, they formed perhaps a third of the population. German was the language of government and, in the army, of command; the Habsburgs spoke it natively; much of the aristocracy was German in composition and outlook, and so was the great majority of the urban and professional middle class in many provinces. Though there was now a Germany, independent, united, powerful, and alien, Austria was itself also partly German.

It is difficult now to realize quite how drastic a revolution the events of 1860–66 worked in the destiny and nature of Europe. Far more was involved than the loss of Habsburg provinces, far more than the loss of influence in neighboring lands. There had taken place nothing less than the transformation of the oldest throne in Europe from a position of ill-defined leadership transcending boundaries throughout the whole of Central Europe from the Baltic to the Mediterranean to a state, superficially like other states, contained within clear boundaries. The Habsburgs had represented since the thirteenth century the lingering tradition of imperial overlordship, inherited from the Roman *caesars* whose title (in the German form, *kaiser*) they still bore. Their tradition was one of perennial opposition to the ideas of sovereignty and of national states. Now those ideas had become the foundation of European order and the Habsburg Monarchy was confined within borders, but within those borders the basis of government and loyalty was still the archaic allegiance to a crown and a dynasty, not to a nation. On the map, the Habsburg Monarchy was now definable, and it looked like another state. But it was not. It was still, battered, shrunken, and transmogrified, the Holy Roman Empire of the Middle Ages.

After 1866, internal changes were necessary, but there was no example and no guidance to be found in history or in the experience of other European states. Nobody knew how a country like Austria could be governed. Later, imaginative and indeed inspiring ideas were to be proposed. But at first, the only thing that anybody could think of to do was to surrender to the demands of

59

one of the minorities, which sought to create a national state *within* Austrian territory. This was done in 1867, and the anachronism of the Habsburg Monarchy was further transformed into a political monster of a sort never seen before.

The national state that was created within the Monarchy was Hungary, ruled by the Magyar people. The Magyars were in several ways remarkable. They were the most important nationality whose members resided entirely within the Monarchy—in contrast to the Italians, Germans, Rumanians, Serbs, and Poles, most of whom lived outside it. They had had a long history of independence before coming under Habsburg rule in the sixteenth century, and even afterward they had succeeded in protecting, with interruptions, their ancient and special privileges of self-government. They had, in 1848, ferociously and successfully revolted against the government at Vienna, and their revolution had been suppressed only with the aid of armies kindly provided for the purpose by the Emperor of Russia. In the years after that, the Austrians had tried to divide the ancient Hungarian kingdom into provinces and to govern them, like other provinces, from Vienna. The Magyars resisted fiercely. After the disaster of 1866 it became urgently necessary to make concessions, previously debated. The kingdom of Hungary was revived and permitted to fashion a constitution for itself. The Emperor assumed the double-barreled title of King-Emperor. A unique arrangement was made under which two independent states, Austria and Hungary, were united by the person of a single ruler, by a common army, by a treaty (renewable at ten-year intervals) regulating their commercial and financial relations, and by three joint administrative institutions, for defense, finance, and foreign affairs, which were, in theory anyway, responsible to a joint parliament consisting of representatives from the separate parliaments of Austria and Hungary.

This ingenious scheme accentuated the difference between Austria-Hungary and the other Great Powers. There was, to be sure in theory, a single foreign policy for the Dual Monarchy, carried out by a "Joint Foreign Minister." But the foreign minister was in practice responsible for his decisions not only to his King-Emperor but to *two* prime ministers, as well as to the delegations of the two parliaments. The pressure of the European System was such that in most situations the Habsburg foreign minister behaved much like other foreign ministers, but the conformity to pattern was misleading. It was harder to inaugurate new or important policies in Austria-Hungary, or to take action at times of crisis, and the difficulties grew as the years passed. Moreover, each of the two governments that were supposed to have a single foreign policy themselves presided over countries whose composition was strange and inharmonious. A wise or bold foreign policy for *either* Austria *or* Hungary would have been increasingly difficult to achieve.

Hungary, which consisted of more than half the land area, although much less than half the population, of the Dual Monarchy was governed by the Magyars, who regarded it as their state. Not all Magyars were politically privileged; in effect, the country was run by its landowners, a singularly narrow-minded class, ferociously patriotic, many of them indifferent to the fate of other nationalities. The Magyars, privileged and unprivileged, constituted about 40 per cent of the population of Hungary. The rest, mostly less prosperous and sophisticated, was composed of varied minorities. Over them the Magyars exerted a growing tyranny, aimed at a policy of Magyarization, which meant in practice the forced teaching of Magyar in schools, the forced use of Magyar in administration and courts, and discrimination against non-Magyars in all spheres. Hungary was, in a way, a national state, but it was a national state with more than its share of both sensitive chauvinism and national minorities.

The Magyar governing classes were afflicted from the beginning with a number of prejudices and policies. They were, in the first place, and not without some reason, fiercely hostile to all Slavs. They were of Finno-Ugric origin—in their language and tradition wholly alien from the Slavs, Germans, or Latins who surrounded them. Amid the many Slavs who lived near, or within, the Hun-

garian borders, they regarded themselves as a sort of besieged
island. They were disposed to hatred of Russia in particular because of 1848 and because of fear of Russian sponsorship of the
smaller Slav peoples. Second, the Hungarians were inclined to
harass the Austrian half of the Habsburg Monarchy with demands
for further privilege, supported by implied threats of secession.
Third, the Hungarians found a congenial friend in the kingdom
of Prussia, Austria's traditional rival, and after 1870 in the German Empire that Prussia had made and was dominating. The
effect of Hungarian influence on the policy of the Habsburg Monarchy was, therefore, anti-Slav, anti-Russian, pro-German, and in
any case highly distracting.

The other half, what was left of Austria after the subtraction
of Hungary, was much more peculiar than Hungary. It was the
relic, still further reduced, of the old Holy Roman Empire in
which a German dynasty had been overlord of a vast collection of
varied realms. The Germans were the most numerous group in it,
about a third of the total, and the most important in government.
But Austria also contained a large majority of other nationalities.
By no stretch of the imagination could Austria have been called a
national state, even in comparison to Hungary. The Germans
played in some respects a role similar to that of the Magyars in
Hungary, but competition from the other peoples was stronger.

The Germans themselves, unlike the Magyars, were culturally
and linguistically part of a much larger national group which had,
in the German Empire, its own national state. The Austrian
Germans tended to take one of three positions, each of which grew
more clearly defined as the years passed: first, and most usefully
from the point of view of the state, to support the idea of a
supra-national empire whose unifying force was merely the imperial crown; second, to seek to convert Austria into a centralized
state dominated by Germans, on the Magyar model. Third, to unite
Austria (with or without some of the other nationalities) to the
German Empire.

The divisions among the German Austrians, the assertiveness of the other nationalities in Austria, and the structure of the state (which was moderately decentralized, with considerable power exercised by provincial councils) assured that the Austrian half of the Monarchy would evolve in a direction different, almost opposite, from the Hungarian half. In Hungary, the evolution was toward an oppressive control of Magyars; in Austria, toward quarrels, confusions, and mounting demands among nationalities.

The National Composition of Austria-Hungary

To clarify the confusing picture so far presented—it is not possible to clarify it much, since the confusion was not only real but significant—we may list the national groups, with some of their qualities and affiliations, that composed the Dual Monarchy in 1870. The official census did not provide information on national groups within the Monarchy; the figures that follow were based on careful contemporary estimates.[1]

1. *Germans:* 7,315,000 in Austria; 1,770,000 in Hungary. Germans were *native* in most of the old Alpine provinces. They were scattered as landowners, townsmen, and civil servants elsewhere. In Hungary, there was a concentration in parts of the southeastern province, Transylvania.

2. *Magyars:* 18,000 in Austria; 5,490,000 in Hungary, mainly in the great Danube plain surrounding the capital, Budapest.

3. *Czechs:* 4,551,000, mostly in Austria. The Czechs, a Slavic people of ancient culture and distinguished history, had once governed the old kingdom of Bohemia, which now formed the northern provinces of the Monarchy: Bohemia proper, Moravia, and Austrian Silesia. Czech nationalism, fired before 1870, had begun—like Irish nationalism, which it in some ways resembled—to reverse a trend toward assimilation or extinction of the national language, culture, and consciousness. In 1870, however, few if any Czechs envisaged a future outside the Habsburg Monarchy, although they wanted more rights within it.

1. H. F. Brachelli, *Statistik Skizze des Oesterreichische-Ungarnische Monarchie* (Leipzig, 1875); quoted in *Almanach de Gotha* (1876), p. 511.

AUSTRIA - HUNGARY
1871 - 1908

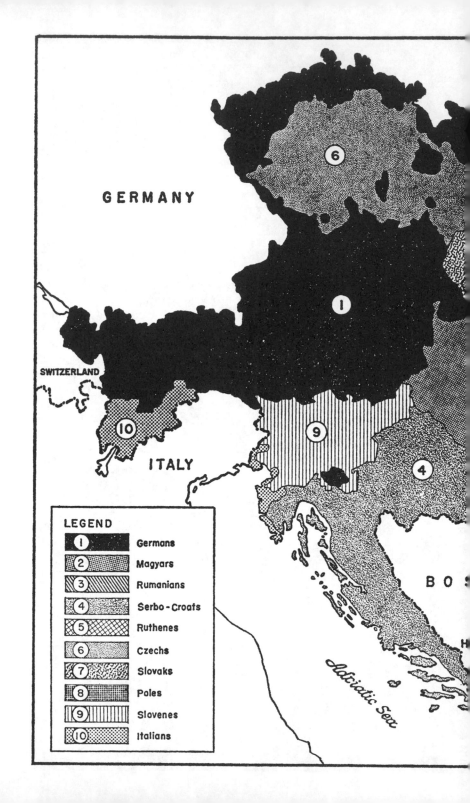

GERMANY

SWITZERLAND

ITALY

BOS

H

Adriatic Sea

LEGEND

1	Germans
2	Magyars
3	Rumanians
4	Serbo-Croats
5	Ruthenes
6	Czechs
7	Slovaks
8	Poles
9	Slovenes
10	Italians

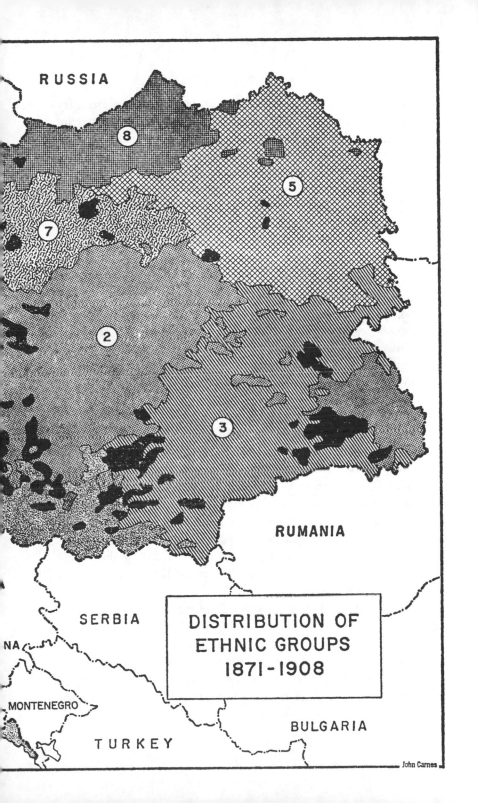

RUSSIA

⑧

⑦

⑤

②

③

RUMANIA

SERBIA

DISTRIBUTION OF
ETHNIC GROUPS
1871-1908

NA

MONTENEGRO

BULGARIA

TURKEY

John Carnes

4. *Ruthenes:* 2,583,000 in Austria; about 500,000 in Hungary. The Ruthenes inhabited the easternmost parts of the Monarchy, the provinces of Bukovina and Galicia. They were culturally and ethnically akin to the Ukrainians, who lived in the adjacent provinces of Russia. They differed from the latter, however, in religion: they were mostly adherents of the Uniate, or Greek Catholic, Rite, in the Communion of the Church of Rome. The religious tie to Rome was the only important source of loyalty to the Habsburgs among the Ruthenes: drastically underrepresented in the parliament, largely rural, backward, and illiterate, they were exploited by the Polish landlords who controlled most of the areas they lived in. Being the low men on the totem pole, they never developed an effective national movement of their own, or an intelligentsia to lead them; but they became more and more sullenly susceptible to the blandishments of Russian propaganda. Russian ambitions and Habsburg apprehensions about the Ruthenian provinces were a source of intractable suspicion and hostility between the empires.

5. *Poles:* 2,444,000 in Austria; none in Hungary. The Habsburg Poles, like the Magyars and the Czechs, had a great national history, a fecund culture, and a remarkably retrograde social system. The rest of Catholic Poland was in Protestant Germany and Orthodox Russia; and this fact helped to assure the loyalty of the Habsburg Poles, for they were able to observe with dread the fate their fellow-nationals in Russia and Germany were suffering. In return for loyalty, the Habsburgs were only too pleased to collaborate with them, which in practice meant assuring the Polish nobles virtual control over their own affairs and their own provinces —and over the Ruthenes.

6. *Rumanians:* 2,892,000, mostly in Hungary. The Rumanians in Hungary possessed, by 1870, a fatherland of a sort, a national Rumania along the borders of the Monarchy. This was now a self-governing principality under the reign of a non-Turkish prince. In 1870, Rumania had not yet begun to exercise much of a magnetic pull upon the Rumanians of Hungary, but it was to do so.

They were mainly Greek Orthodox, and they claimed to be Latins. The Rumanians in Hungary were concentrated in the province of Transylvania. Here, while preserving a village culture, they were mainly subject to the old-fashioned rule of Magyar landowners, and they were increasingly discontented under it.

7. *Serbo-Croats:* 550,000 in Austria; 2,430,000 in Hungary. The Serbo-Croats, forming ethnically a single people, were divided into two very distinct groups by alphabet, religion, and history. There is one Serbo-Croat language, but the Serbs use the Cyrillic alphabet and are predominantly Greek Orthodox, while the Croats use the Latin alphabet and are predominantly Roman Catholic. The Serbs, who had briefly maintained a great empire in the Middle Ages, resided in a wide area of the Balkan peninsula, and while all of them had been at one time or another subject to Turkish rule—and in some provinces had been converted to Islam in considerable numbers—by 1870 they were divided by national frontiers and historical experiences. Besides the million and a half Serbs in the Monarchy, a million and a quarter lived in the Serbian principality, a self-governing state within the Turkish Empire, on the southern border of Hungary. Another million lived in other European provinces of Turkey, governed directly from Constantinople, with varying degrees of corruption, geniality, and tyranny. Over 100,000 lived in the fiercely independent, wholly inaccessible, and almost infinitesimal principality of Montenegro, surrounded by Turkish territory in the mountains. The Serbs, while varying greatly in degree of prosperity and education, were for the most part an oppressed, illiterate people, largely peasant, partly tribal, superbly brave, and decidedly elemental. They possessed no aristocracy and, as yet, little in the way of an intelligentsia; they were, therefore, in 1870, devoid of leaders except for heroic but rather primitive chieftains, one of whom had become prince of the self-governing state of Serbia and was a protégé of the Vienna government.

The Croats, despite their affinities, were in an entirely different position. Unlike the Serbs, the Croats lived entirely within the

Habsburg Monarchy: Croatia was a part of the kingdom of Hungary. Unlike the Serbs, too, they had retained, even under the malign overlordship of the Magyars, their own aristocracy and their own administrative identity. They possessed a capital and urban center, Zagreb, a university, and a civilization that, while also chiefly rural, was markedly more sophisticated—more "formed," it might be said—than that of the dispersed Serbs. Like the Czechs and the Poles, the Croats had as yet produced no important leaders to challenge the rule of the Habsburgs or the integrity of the Monarchy; indeed, they had shown themselves in times past, particularly in 1848, to be among the most loyal of the national groups. But this loyalty had existed partly because they looked to the dynasty as a bulwark against the Magyar pretensions. After 1867, when they were included in the revived Hungary, although with safeguards assuring their administrative autonomy and their own legislature, they found themselves abandoned by the dynasty to the mercies of the Magyars, and their loyalty began to cool.

In addition to these seven substantial national groups, there were a number of smaller ones. The most important were the Italians, to the number of some 600,000 in 1870, whose recalcitrant character has already been mentioned. There were also some million and a quarter Slovaks, a Slavic people akin to the Czechs, who lived in northern Hungary; and the Slovenes, also Slavic and akin to the Croats, to the number of a million and a quarter, who lived in southern Austria, mostly in the province of Carniola. Neither of these two groups had had a national history; neither of them, in 1870, had developed much in the way of national consciousness, although the beginning, especially in Carniola, had been made in 1848. In addition, there were sprinklings of Armenians, Bulgars, Greeks, Albanians, Gypsies, and a million and a third Jews, a majority of them living in German cities and more or less Germanized, but many of them Polish, Rumanian, Hungarian, or Czech.

Several points are to be noted about this picture puzzle of peoples. First, the Italians, the Serbs, the Rumanians, and the

Germans could look across the borders of the Habsburg Monarchy to a national state of their own co-nationals. The Ruthenes could look to Russia, which ruled the Ukraine where their co-nationals lived. On the other hand, the Poles could look to their fellow Poles suffering a much harsher rule in neighboring Russia or Germany. The Croats and the Slovenes might stress—though few of them did before 1870—their affinities with the Serbs of Serbia. The Czechs and the Slovaks were without fellow-nationals outside the Monarchy, as, of course, were the Magyars. To adopt, then, the phrasing of the previous chapter, the provinces inhabited by Serbs, Rumanians, and Italians constituted Alsaces; the provinces inhabited by Czechs and Slovaks constituted Irelands. The Croats and the Ruthenes stood in a situation that combined the most trying features of the plight of Alsatians and Irish.

Second, it should be noted that among these peoples there was a wide variation in the degree of passion and consciousness of national character. There was in 1870—and indeed in 1914—nothing like a general determination to secede from Habsburg rule. In 1870, the Czechs and the Serbs and the Rumanians were only beginning to develop active national ambitions, confined mainly to small groups of intellectuals or politicians. Even in the more developed nation-groups, the Poles or the Croats, there was no tendency to rebellion. Except from the Italians there was no important challenge to the existence of the Monarchy. But there was—and this was vital and to grow more and more so—a very strong disposition on the part of various groups, particularly the Czechs, to seek concessions and advantages within the Monarchy, and to do so without any great concern about the effects their demands might have upon the viability of the state. This was what the Magyars had just done. The system of Dual Monarchy, satisfying to the Magyars, created more problems than it solved for everyone else. It enabled the Magyars to oppress Serbs, Croats, and Rumanians and so greatly weaken their loyalty to the Monarchy. The greatest weakness of the Monarchy in 1870 and afterward arose from the fact that the aspirations of any one of the national groups could be satisfied only at the expense of others, so that any effort at meeting their demands weakened the Monarchy as a whole.

A clear and instructive example of this devolutionary process is to be found in the history of the German population and its programs. At the beginning of the Dual Monarchy, the largest German party had been the Liberals. But liberalism changed, and was supplemented by demands and attitudes that threatened the delicate equilibrium. In 1882, German-Austrian politicians formulated the Linz Program for the Monarchy: it demanded self-government for the Hungarians, the Poles, and the Dalmatians and urged, in effect, the Germanization of the remaining provinces, where lived Czechs, Slovenes, Italians, and others. At about the same time, a German Nationalist Party began to appear, led by George von Schoenerer. It was what would now be called "racist," virulently anti-Semitic and strongly anti-Slav, and it urged the subjection of all the other peoples of the Monarchy to the German population. It was not surprising that this evolution on the part of some German Austrians toward a more strident and impertinent nationalism should provoke fears and disaffection among the other nationalities.

But the Monarchy was still extraordinarily solid, and it was to remain so, beneath a surface of insoluble problems and unseemly disputes, for a long time to come. By 1914, it was being widely described as "ramshackle," and even its own rulers and defenders had grave doubts about its future; but it is debatable whether or not it might have survived indefinitely. As far as domestic affairs went, the elements of strength remained strong, although concealed by long-run threats and short-term quarrels.

What were the sources of the strength of the Habsburg Monarchy? One was undoubtedly inertia, which worked not only to inspire acquiescence but also to make the alternatives to acquiescence appear, to anybody except passionate partisans of violence, distasteful. A state-in-being is difficult to destroy except in times of crisis; its machinery has a built-in capacity for defense that is hard for private citizens to defy. The governments of Austria-

72

Hungary were well aware of this fact and they exploited it, mainly through the development of an ever larger, better, and more *ubiquitous* civil service, which had the advantage of giving its own numerous officials a vested interest in the regime as well as increasing the utility of the state to its subjects. In 1870, there was also a large defensive machinery of secret police, equipped with habits and skills of espionage on seditious activities, which had been inherited from the stormy days of Napoleon and the Congress of Vienna. But this police system was progressively dismantled after 1870, and while it remained formidable, it was never after that date a mainstay of the regime. It was the efficacy of the state, rather than its tyranny, that consolidated the acquiescence that its mere existence provided.

The House of Habsburg was the oldest important dynasty in Europe. The Habsburg crown, associated with the heritage of Rome and the defense of Europe against the Turk, had acquired a deep and mystical significance; it was in the nature of the Habsburgs to rule a supra-national realm, and it was their nature that commanded allegiance. The Habsburgs seemed inevitable and necessary to the area of Austria-Hungary.

The confusion of nationalities in Southeastern Europe had always existed, in varying degrees of mutual toleration, beneath the wide canopies of great empires. The notion of recreating, in miniature, a Western Europe of nation-states amid the very different conditions of the East arose when the minorities of the Turkish Empire first rebelled. The Serbs achieved, and the Greeks received, their states, and Christian princes. So, later, did the Rumanians. The inadequate and misleading analogy of Western states was demonstrated to be, if not exactly workable, at least imposable in the East; the idea behind it took potent hold, even where the institutions were caricatures. The principle that thus, almost inadvertently, emerged from disintegrating Turkey came later to offer a menacing inspiration to the peoples of Austria-Hungary in the face of reason, convenience, and chronology.

But there were basic differences between Turkey and Austria. The most important was religion. The nationalities of the Balkans were mostly Christian, and they had a claim on the sympathies of Christian Europe. For the Great Powers of Europe, the excuse and to some extent the cause for aiding the emancipation of the Balkan peoples had been that they were Christians in revolt against Islam. And for the peoples themselves, religion was deeply entwined with national aspirations and with the smoldering dislike of an alien rule that had lasted with mounting inconvenience and inconsistency for half a millennium. Partly just because of the difference in its religious situation, Austria-Hungary was less vulnerable than Turkey. The Monarchy was overwhelming Roman Catholic; the Habsburg ruler, Apostolic King of Hungary, was the successor of Saint Stephen and of Saint Wenceslaus of Bohemia, and the heir of Charles V. France, no longer the oldest daughter of the Church, had been replaced by the Habsburg Monarchy. Of its thirty-five million inhabitants in 1870, twenty-seven million were in communion with Rome and found their political loyalty reinforced by a religious one. Of the remainder, there were three and a half million Protestants, the majority of them Magyar Calvinists unlikely to practice sedition as long as the dualism satisfied their national aspirations. It was only the Greek Orthodox, mainly Serbs, who constituted a significant body of dissent. And even then the dissent was of a sort different from that of Christians in Moslem Turkey.

There were the civil service, the crown, the Church, to hold the Monarchy together, along with a perception of the unthinkable inconvenience of demolishing it. There were also visible changes in its character that modified, while at the same time complicating, the national issues. The most important of these, very unequally applicable to the various parts of the Monarchy, were economic and social change and the mellowing of tyranny.

The Monarchy was in many respects well governed, prosperous, and progressive. This fact, obscured before its end by the somewhat neurotic atmosphere of despair that engulfed it, and afterward by the venom of its victorious detractors, emerged unarguably from a comparison with its neighbors to the south and east. Vienna and Prague were becoming, by 1870, major industrial centers, and the growth continued rapidly, to be joined by Budapest, Lwów, and Trieste. The Monarchy, financed by the House of Rothschild, had pioneered in railroad-building. The auspices for much of this growth were unfashionable in London and Paris; they were state enterprise and state finance. Pure free enterprise had little appeal to the government or to the businessman in areas where capital, initiative, and a trained labor supply were deficient. But the growth took place, and it was producing an advanced economy, a considerable class of townspeople of middling income and social position, and a further admixture of nationalities in the towns.

Economic growth altered very drastically the balance of society. This was, of course, also true in other countries undergoing a similar growth, and in some places the alteration had effects comparably unexpected and aggravating, notably in Spain, where a highly local industrial society sprang up in a sea of impoverished and primitive agriculture, and in Italy, where the rapid advance of the north was matched by soporific decay in the south. In Austria, a similar regional diversity was accented, and it was vastly complicated by the existence of the Dual system and by the national diversity.

As was generally true in nineteenth-century Europe, industry flourished where previously progressive agriculture and commerce had flourished. On the western rim of the Monarchy, in an arc extending from the Silesian border to the Adriatic, a modern industrial society evolved, as in France, in the middle of a rich agricultural society. The contrast with the backward east was emphasized, and while the backward east of the Monarchy was vastly *less* backward than the east that lay beyond it in Russia, or south of it in Serbia and Rumania, the social gulf within the Monarchy was widened.

This meant several things. First, rural Hungary, increasingly the breadbasket of the Monarchy, had national economic interests definably separate from Austria, imperial in a financial and industrial as well as a political sense, and if Austria could threaten Hungary with bankruptcy, Hungary could threaten Austria with starvation. The economic relations between the two parts, subject to decennial negotiation, became progressively more antagonistic. Second, while most of the peoples remained, in their various ways, agrarian, the Czechs and the Germans were becoming partly urban, and they were providing the new complexities of tension and class conflict that urban societies were everywhere producing. Thus, to national diversity was increasingly added economic and social diversity, and the conflicts that were generated elsewhere here mingled in chaotic profusion.

As economic progress involved peculiar difficulties in a supra-national state, so did political evolution. Hungary remained in some ways rather static, despite the rise of a powerful and rich middle class in Budapest; it retained its constitutional regime without basic alteration; it continued to be a parliamentary government run by the Liberal Party—which meant, in practice, an oligarchy of Magyar landowners. In Austria, more rapidly evolving and spared the dominance of a single nationality, confusion and change were produced. *On paper,* the change was an orderly development toward democracy, and this was by no means wholly theoretical. By the mid-seventies, Austria had a constitution and a parliament, and many of the goals of nineteenth-century reformers had been achieved: religious freedom, private property, civil rights, equality before the law—all were either assured or evolving. The franchise was narrow and peculiar; by dividing the electorate into categories —landowners, chambers of commerce, and so on—a high over-representation for wealth, particularly of noble landowners, was achieved, and the ordinary citizen, at least in the country, was underrepresented, if represented at all. But this changed; a fifth and democratic category was provided in the nineties, and in 1907 the collegiate system was swept away altogether, and the parliament was thereafter elected by universal manhood suffrage.

A very considerable social fluidity, moreover, permitted a good deal of scope for people of humble birth. The civil service, overwhelmingly the largest employer, was open to merit, and mostly staffed by people of varied but unprivileged background. Although the court, in its purely social function, remained exclusively restricted to persons of towering peaigree, the army and the cabinet did not. There was a high representation of aristocracy in the top positions, but it was by no means exclusive, and in Vienna, where politicians and professional people jostled princes on the pavements, a very fair degree of social—and national—mobility prevailed.

But this moderately open and tolerant society broke down both at the eastern edges, where a backward economy persisted, and at the center, which was the Austrian parliament house.

The Austrian constitution took no account, except in the form of the provincial councils, of the national composition of the electorate; it was based on the models developed in nationally united states. There was, as in France and Germany, a multitude of parties. In a national state, a party system makes parliamentary government work, even if it works badly. In Austria, the many parties were divided, not by differing views of the national interest, but into national groups. The consequence was confusion, which grew worse when the franchise was broadened to include, beyond the more or less cosmopolitan privileged classes, the more or less nationally conscious common people. The seventies saw the decline of the dominant party of German Liberals; after that, a majority to support any government was only sporadically available. The peculiar effect of more democracy on paper was less democracy in fact.

Parties proliferated; in the last parliament, elected in 1911, there were twenty-two. All but two of these represented national groups, and most of the larger national groups were each represented by several parties representing different social views; it was rather like a federation of European parliaments. There were, for example, no fewer than five Czech parties of diverse philosophy. But there were also, after the turn of the century, two parties which, while their constituency was mainly among the German-speaking voters,

77

were not national but imperial in appeal and program. These were the Christian Socialist and the Social Democratic parties.

The former had a prodigious growth, especially in Vienna where, in 1897, it captured the city government. Its leader, Karl Lueger, was an energetic, imaginative, and popular mayor; he combined mild socialism with anti-Semitism, Catholicism, and egregious demagoguery.

Socialism and Catholicism are both supra-national, and both of these parties—which rapidly became the largest in the imperial parliament—deplored secessionist tendencies. But their programs nonetheless contributed to them. Both called for drastic changes in the order of society and the structure of the economy; both were hostile to the aristocracy and were no more than tolerant of the dynasty itself. Both demanded far-reaching reforms. And far-reaching reforms did not commend themselves to most of the other groups—to the powerful Poles, for example, who represented a monolithic parliamentary group of landowners, the third largest and much the most loyal of any in the legislature.

The development of Social Democracy and Christian Socialism showed the effect that economic change was having in the regions affected by it; and it showed that economic change, like political change, complicated the problem of parliamentary government. But in effect, parliamentary government, sporadically ventured, had been abandoned. Already by the eighties, government was being carried on in Austria—and on the whole very well carried on— by the Emperor's ministers, appointed by him, dismissed by him (although sometimes as a result of parliamentary demands or pressures), and enacting laws in his name. There was a constitutional basis for this, but it made the ponderous façade of constitutional government a mockery, and it suggested to the reformers, the growing force of Social Democracy and Christian Socialism, that neither democracy nor socialism was likely to be achieved without far-reaching and perhaps extra-constitutional change. Similar thoughts were occurring to political groups whose concerns were national rather than ideological.

Change was much discussed, and had been for a hundred years. Practically everybody who thought about Austro-Hungarian affairs at all, in or out of the Monarchy, prescribed formulas for its reconstruction. None of these formulas envisioned its destruction, although the Italians and some of the Serbs were contemplating their own subtraction. Many of them were sensible and high-minded. But none of them came near, in the state of things existing, to being enacted, and their proliferation merely stressed the extreme difficulty of making any change at all; and this aggravated the melancholy of people who thought change was necessary and increased the panic of people who dreaded it.

The chief stumbling-block—there were hundreds—to plans for revising the structure of the Monarchy was invariably Hungary. If any arrangement designed to satisfy the demands of the nationalities were to mean anything, it must of course apply to the half of the Empire where the demands were most urgent and most just: the kingdom of Hungary. But to formulas that recognized this fact the Magyars responded not only with virulent hostility but with threats. Hungary, they said, was independent, and nobody but its own subjects—meaning the Magyar oligarchy—could reorganize it. The Magyars, thanks to the deal of 1867, had law on their side, and they also had a good deal of bargaining power. The Emperor, the only authority at Vienna who retained any legal power in Hungarian affairs, was fully aware of the problem, but he was by now very old and was inclined to a policy of conservation rather than experiment.

In the twentieth century the problem grew serious. The Emperor tried, with limited success, to blackmail the oligarchy at Budapest with the only real weapon he possessed. When the Hungarian government made more than its customary difficulties about renewing the decennial agreement on commerce, he threatened to introduce into Hungary, by decree, universal manhood suffrage. This would have wrecked the control of the landowners over the government, and it would have endangered, indeed, the supremacy of the Magyars, who would have been a minority in a democratic electorate. The Hungarian government backed down; but it did so with so many threats and such bad grace that no one in Vienna thought of using the weapon again, lest it produce secession or conceivably an Austro-Hungarian War. Thereafter, formulas for change, if they included Hungary, could be contemplated only by extremists. As a result, many loyal subjects developed a violent antagonism to the Magyars, whom they viewed as driving the Monarchy to its doom. The most extreme exponent of this attitude was the Heir to the Throne, the Archduke Francis Ferdinand, who was almost pathologically hostile to the most numerous group of his future subjects. By consequence he was, like many of his view, inclined to be sympathetic to the Magyars' chief victims and opponents, the South Slavs. It was a fateful inclination.

But it was not merely Hungary that presented a problem; an even more unmanageable problem lay beyond the frontiers. The government of Hungary might conceivably be persuaded, blackmailed, or outwitted. The problems presented by the governments of Italy, Serbia, or Rumania could be solved only by diplomacy or by war.

The governments of Italy, Serbia, and Rumania, and—since Russia was inclined at intervals to present itself as the Big Brother of all the Slavs in Austria-Hungary—the government of Russia as well, were problems because of the magnetic attraction that their existence tended to exert upon minorities within the Habsburg Monarchy, which raised the nightmarish prospect of eventual disintegration, precipitated, perhaps, by a coalition of rapacious neighbors. In the late nineteenth century, Austro-Hungarian policy, based upon immense military power and immense prestige, wisely sought to neutralize the potential danger by diplomacy, and did so with success. Italy, Serbia, and Rumania were all made allies of the Habsburg Monarchy, and in exchange for alliance and diplomatic friendship they were dissuaded from patronizing traitors; their governments were, by chance or by plan, in every case sufficiently precariously placed so that their stability depended to some extent an Austrian support. In the case of Serbia, the reigning prince was actually paid a subsidy by the Austrians, and his country was rescued by Austrian arms and Austrian diplomacy from military disaster when, in 1885, it was so ill advised as to entangle itself in war with its determined neighbor, the principality of Bulgaria.

Up until 1900 or thereabouts, this policy weakened, if it did not eliminate, the threat from the southern neighbors. And Austrian diplomacy secured in 1897 an agreement with Russia that neither party would meddle in Balkan affairs.

After 1900, the situation began to change, and it began to change largely because of political changes within the neighboring states. Friendship with Austria became, for the governments at Rome, Belgrade, Bucharest, and Saint Petersburg, less of an asset than a liability. We shall later see in some detail how, in the crucial case of Serbia, this process worked. Here it need only be said that as public opinion came to be more influential, it came simultaneously to be more nationalistic and more ambitious. The neighboring governments became less *capable* of a policy of quiescence toward the "oppressed brothers" in the Habsburg Monarchy. Developing nationalism made noisy demands for an anti-Habsburg policy. Within the Monarchy, its defenders became more impatient of and more frightened by the foreign provocations; and the nationalities concerned became more impatient with Austro-Hungarian rule.

Still, the internal problem was neither acute nor insoluble. This is the crucial fact; Austria-Hungary was still, in 1914, well governed, prosperous, and perfectly solid. No responsible leader, no organ of public opinion, no organized body of any consequence, proposed its dissolution. Many anticipated it; but this anticipation was more conspicuous among its defenders, who were gripped from 1890 on by fear, than among its enemies. Gloom, culturally speaking, was fashionable in Vienna. Frustration, despair, and the fashionable question *What is life for?* were the characteristic topics among Austrian literati. All questions about the future were unanswerable; all plans for reform were doomed to failure. But administratively and politically this *Weltschmerz* made no difference. The civil service was solid and sound, the army was reliable, the crown still commanded enormous prestige. The urgent threat came from outside.

In recent years there has been a great and sympathetic interest in the affairs of Austria-Hungary on the part of historians who perceive that the Monarchy was the only considerable experiment in international government in recent times. One of the best of such historians, Joachim Remak, has persuasively emphasized the strong forces making for stability, often overlooked in the preoccupation with the forces tending toward disintegration, and argued that, in the absence of an unsuccessful war, the Monarchy might well have reformed itself and survived as a model for future supranational states.[1] Strengths there were. But the men who ran the state were more acutely, agonizingly, aware of the external threats. Depression and despair, partly unfounded, informed their actions.

Austria-Hungary was in area the second largest state in Europe. By 1914, it had grown to have a population of fifty million people, ranking third after Russia and Germany. In industrial output it ranked fifth among the European nations; in foreign trade, fourth; in the brilliance of its intellectual and artistic achievements, second only to France. In contrast to its neighbors to the east and the south, it provided stable government, a commendable degree of civil liberty, an efficient civil service, a strong army, and unity, security, and protection for the tangled nationalities that occupied it. In 1848, the Czech leader Frantisek Palacky had remarked, "If the Austrian empire did not exist, it would have to be invented." It was difficult to conceive—and in the event it proved impossible to arrange—any replacement that would provide so satisfactory a way of bringing prosperity and peace to the territories it governed.

It was about to be destroyed, by the actions of statesmen who could find no way to defend a supra-national empire within a system of national states.

---

1. Joachim Remak, "The Healthy Invalid," *Journal of Modern History*, XLI, no. 2, June, 1969, pp. 127-143.

CHAPTER THREE

THE EUROPE OF THE ARMED CAMPS

W HEN Germany was unified in 1871, Europe took on new character. The creation of Germany was the creation of a new and more powerful sun, which lit the mysterious outer spaces and threw onto the European scene itself lights and shadows so different from the old as to make it seem a different place. We must now examine the terms and nature of German supremacy and the way it gave place to a Europe divided into two alliances.

The pre-eminence of Germany assured, while it lasted, a quite unprecedented measure of stability. In the eighties it faded into a second stage where Germany's pre-eminence was less certain and where overseas issues began to intrude into European politics and a period of instability and tension ensued. This was to be replaced by a third phase about 1905, when German pre-eminence had largely disappeared, and non-European issues fell again to second place. The arrangements and impulses that had developed during the first two phases, surviving into the third, were to bring still greater tensions, and eventually to produce in threatened Austria a degree of irresponsibility that detonated a catastrophe.

BISMARCK'S EUROPE
ABOUT 1890

NORWAY

SWED

GREAT
BRITAIN

DENMARK

NETHERLANDS

GERMANY

BELGIUM

FRANCE

SWITZERLAND

AUS

PORTUGAL

SPAIN

ITALY

MONT

Mediterranean Sea

John Cannoe

RUSSIA

ARY

RUMANIA

BULGARIA
EASTERN RUMELIA

EY

ECE

Black Sea

TURKEY

The German Alliance System

Connected with Germany by
Agreements

The *Age of German Dominion*

The stability of the first period, noticeable in comparison with the alarms and excursions (in a very literal sense of those words) that preceded and followed it, was scarcely evident at the time to statesmen struggling with the uncertainties of a new situation. But still the Germans, having secured all the goals they had fought for in the previous decade, were now for a time adamantine supporters of the existing order of things. Their autocratic Chancellor, Otto von Bismarck, had both the authority and the skill to secure its maintenance.

Bismarckian diplomacy need not long detain us. Its breakdown, after his dismissal in 1890, was complete. But some of its mechanics survived, and those played their role in subsequent events: debris, as it were, that cluttered the European stage and dictated, by their now meaningless presence, the crossings, entrances, and exits of the actors. Bismarck's importance, aside from these accidental contributions, lay, so far as present purposes go, in his surprising alliance with Austria and in the resurrection of conservatism as a potent and nationalistic force. This latter phenomenon was mainly the product of domestic politics.

His diplomacy was the product of vital needs and limited opportunities. The chief needs were the security of Germany and international peace. The opportunities were limited, saliently, by: the aloofness of Britain; a Republic of France simultaneously enfeebled and infuriated; a Russia monarchical, conservative, and ambitious; an Austria weakened and distraught; and an Italy seeking to manifest the attributes of a Great Power.

The only real threat to Germany could come from France, and only then from France with powerful allies. It was essential to Germany that no such allies be accessible, and in fact few were. Franco-Italian relations, never very good after Italy was created, were getting worse, and were likely to get still worse. Britain was evidently not going to ally with anybody, certainly not with a resentful and bellicose country that was not only its traditional enemy but whose principal concern would be to drag Britain into an entirely unwanted continental war. Austria and Russia were the powers to be watched. Austria, recently defeated by Germany, might seem a natural French ally; Russia, with which the French had in the past cooperated—the two ends, as it were, against the center of Europe—was a possible ally, though a less likely one because the Russian monarchy loathed the Red Republic at Paris.

Germany, Austria, and Russia were all empires, although of very various sorts, and their rulers naturally supported the principle, vague but comforting, of "monarchical solidarity." A loose understanding was arranged among them and was called the Three Emperors' League. The emphasis on emperors was helpful in keeping Alexander II alive to the perils of republicanism, as represented by France. The League meant little except as a symptom of affable correspondence among the three courts (although it accomplished one thing: it paved the way for a permanent tightening of relations between Austria and Germany). Two crises, both demonstrating its fragility, wrecked it. They are instructive crises.

The first took place in 1875. Its nature and course is still extremely debatable, for its appraisal rests not on documents but on motives. What *seemed* to be happening, however, was clear and illuminating. It *seemed* that Bismarck, having defeated and humiliated the French five years earlier, was alarmed by a simultaneous revival of French strength and stability and the persistence of French vengefulness, and was contemplating another war to banish the French threat once and forever. He probably was not; there is no reliable evidence for it. But the French either thought he was or else thought it useful to say they thought he was. And the effects were precisely what the French hoped. The British and the Russians jointly warned Bismarck against attack upon or further diminishing of France. A France further weakened would have created a German colossus, menacing to Britain and Russia. The balance of power, greatly altered by the creation of Germany, would then have been destroyed. Bismarck was startled and annoyed.

The Eastern Question and the Frustration of Russia

The second crisis was much larger, more serious, and more permanent in its effects; it led by steps to the weakening of the Bismarckian system and, strangely, toward a Franco-Russian alliance. It began in 1876, erupting in the dim, dynamic volcano of the Balkans. There, in the mountain province of Bosnia, inside the Ottoman Empire on Austria's southern border and largely inhabited by Serbs, a revolution took place against Turkish rule. The Ottoman Empire was sufficiently weak and sufficiently unattractive that this provincial insurrection seemed to threaten its existence. As had been happening for a hundred years, whenever the Ottoman Empire faced one of its frequent domestic crises, the European Powers gathered round the bed of the Sick Man of Europe in varying guise, depending on their concerns at the moment, of vulture or physician. As the revolt and the Turkish temper of repression spread, so did the concern of the Powers. In one of their recurrent drives to expansion, the Russians made war on the Ottomans and (not without difficulty) fought their way to the gates of Constantinople, where was imposed, in 1878, a treaty that almost destroyed the Turkish Empire in Europe. It also naturally provided for an arrangement of Balkan territories and sovereignties of a sort the Russians believed would be favorable to their interests.

This war and the remarkable events that followed it are of high importance. The Powers, disturbed by the extensive remodeling of Southeastern Europe that the Russians had singlehandedly undertaken, successfully invoked the principles of international concert and public law to settle a European question. Russia was, as it were, arraigned by Europe for illegal action and summoned before a court of its peers.

The Russians had undertaken, in the Treaty of San Stefano

they had hurriedly imposed upon the Turks, to create out of Turkish territory a new country. It would have been far larger than any of the four existing Balkan states and was to be called Bulgaria, after the Bulgars who inhabited part of it. The Bulgars were a Christian and Slavic people, ethnically close to the Serbs, and the Russians were hoping that the Great Bulgaria they sponsored would in the future be grateful to, and reliant on, its Russian foster father. The Russian Empire would so acquire control of much of the Balkan peninsula, and its influence and possibly its agents would approach the gates of Constantinople and the Straits.

This prospect, so alarming to all other European Powers, coincided with two deep aspirations of Russian imperial policy, one ancient, the other recent.

The first was a sense of destiny, almost as old as the Russian state, in connection with Constantinople and the Straits. Its sources were twofold: first, Constantinople had been the capital and religious center—the "Rome" of the Byzantine Empire, with its Roman imperial heritage, its Orthodox religion, and its Greek culture. Russia had inherited the religion, some of the culture, and the dream of empire, as well as a legal claim to the Byzantine crown. This rather mystical affinity was matched by a strategic one: the huge Russian state had no outlet to the open sea, being shut in by ice on the north and the east, and the land masses of Asia and Europe on the west and the south. The only warm-water Russian ports were on the Black Sea, which led to the Mediterranean only through the Straits, astride which lay Turkey and its capital Constantinople.

The second aspiration was pan-Slavism, referred to in Chapter 1. It was much more recent, this sense of communion with the Slavic peoples of Eastern Europe. The Russians possessed the only free and independent Slavic state, and they were vastly the largest of the Slavic peoples. Some of them (among mystical and upper-class Russians, as least) felt an impulse of almost religious intensity to lead their kinsmen to freedom, just as they felt a religious impulse to re-Christianize Constantinople. In both cases, dividends in power and strategic advantage impended.

The two ambitions fused in the Treaty of San Stefano. The Russians were jubilant. The other Powers were appalled.

The most appalled were the British. For a generation the British public had been having nightmares about Russia, and these had reached the surface in many diplomatic crises and once in war, the Crimean War, in 1854.

British anxieties were ecumenical; Austria's were provincial. The Russian danger to Austria was much more precise. Russia, established in Great Bulgaria, at the gates of Constantinople, and on the shores of the Aegean, would be a threat to Austria. The threat had several heads. First, an extension of Russian power was as distasteful to the Austrians as to everybody else; since the days of Metternich the Austrians, like everybody else, had brooded over the Russian tendency to grow in a westerly direction and had conspired to frustrate it. Since the Austrians were the nearest neighbors, their power position was most gravely threatened by expansion in the Balkans.

Second, the Austrians had interests of their own to the south. These were at least partly commercial—a figurative Austrian highway, and perhaps eventually a literal railroad, to the Aegean. Such an avenue would be gravely compromised, if not absolutely cut, by a Russian-dominated Great Bulgaria.

These two sorts of Russian threats were greatly aggravated by a third sort peculiar to Austria arising from the composition of the Habsburg Monarchy. Some years later, a Frenchman was to observe, "When the Turk departs from the bed of the sick-man of Europe, Austria will replace him in it." Sorel's logic was more artistic than realistic, as suggested in the previous chapter, but the decomposition of Turkey-in-Europe resulting from the assertive nationalism of minorities championed by Russia was a process clearly menacing to the future of the Habsburg Monarchy.

Compared to the Ottoman Empire, and indeed to Russia, the Austro-Hungarian state was a model of efficiency and modernity. Still, parallels were visible. And there was one feature of the situation in 1878 that was novel and particularly harrowing: *Russia was patronizing small peoples and their right to national freedom, in the name of Slavdom and Orthodoxy.* This was to recur significantly to Austrian statesmen thereafter. The policy was only sporadically (and rather frivolously) a feature of Russian activities for a generation after 1878. But the Austrian response to San Stefano was to prove permanently affecting.

The third Power immediately affected by Russian activities was Germany. Bismarck had toward "The Eastern Question," as the problem of the Ottoman Empire was invariably called in this era, an attitude characteristically haughty, detached, and cynical. The matter was one of profound unconcern, he thought, to Germany. It was not, he said, worth the bones of a single Pomeranian grenadier. The statement summarized the sensible view that the Balkans could produce nothing but trouble for anyone who controlled them, and were certainly not a suitable stake for a war into which Germany might be dragged. Bismarck's interest was in maintaining good relations with both Russia and Austria; on this depended the success of the monarchical principle, so appealing to the three emperors concerned, which was, for Bismarck, a tactful way of describing the isolation of the French Republic. It required at least a modicum of good manners on the part of both his friends.

In the present situation it was clear that the Russians had shown very bad manners indeed. There were urgent negotiations among the Powers, and Bismarck invoked the Concert of Europe to rebuke them. Acting, he said, in the role of "honest broker," he called at Berlin a Congress of European Powers to discuss the matter. The Russians were furious; their hard-won triumph, the rights of their brother Slavs the Bulgars, their prestige, their sovereignty, were to be placed in the defendant's chair in a tribune of Europe and to be judged by their competitors and rivals—who happened to be also their peers. It was a very clear example of the conflicts within the European System, between the deep-rooted tradition of a public law defended by the Great Powers acting in concert, and the scarcely less deep-rooted conception of the sovereignty of those Powers. But in this case, the former tradition had the weight of great force behind it, and it prevailed; the Russians, furious but intimidated, came to Berlin and there, with the worst possible grace, disgorged the meal of Turkish territories that they had just consumed.

The Congress of Berlin wiped Great Bulgaria off the map it had so briefly decorated. Instead, there was created a "Small" Bulgaria—a concession to the general feeling that the Bulgars deserved *some* reward for being the principal victims of Ottoman brutality and infidel persecution; and to the Russians, who were unwilling to abandon all remnants of their success. Rumania and Serbia, over which Turkish suzerainty had long since ceased to have much meaning, were now declared to be fully independent, joining Greece and Montenegro as sovereign Balkan states.

To reassure the Austrians and the British about the threat potentially represented by Small Bulgaria and its Russian protectors, "compensations" were provided. The Turks' Island of Cyprus, so located as to furnish strategic control over the eastern Mediterranean, was given as a present to the British. The three northernmost provinces of the Ottoman Empire, Bosnia (where all the trouble had begun), Hercegovina adjoining it to the north, and the *sanjak* (district) of Novibazar to the south, were confided to Austrian control. They remained under Turkish sovereignty, but all three were to be garrisoned by the Austrians, and the first two were to be "administered"; which meant that they would be effectively subject to the Habsburg Monarchy in all political and military concerns that mattered.

There are several aspects that should be noted. In the first place, the attrition of Turkish territory proceeded, and was indeed shared by the Ottoman Empire's principal protectors, Britain and Austria. And secondly must be noted the reluctance of the Habsburg Monarchy to undertake (what it might have gotten if it wanted) outright annexation of Bosnia, Hercegovina, and Novibazar. The security of the Monarchy would have been admirably served by participating fully in the disruption of Turkey and the extension of its own territories to the south, and so would other purposes, including the drive toward Salonika on the Aegean. The best way to frustrate the Russian policy of sponsoring the nationalism of Slavic peoples within the Monarchy by encouraging the nationalism of Slavic states outside it would have been to include as many Slavs as possible *within* the Monarchy, where they would be much less susceptible to Russian blandishments.

As a matter of fact, an almost incredible opportunity for forwarding this sensible policy was about to present itself. Milan Obrenovich was the Prince of Serbia. He was not precisely a paragon of patriotism, and was given to referring to the Serbs as "my damned subjects," having a reasonably well-founded suspicion that they intended to assassinate him. He did not care for the lures of primitive kingship among the pig-herds of his country, and preferred to live in Vienna in a large palace, handsomely subsidized by the Austrian government. Preferring subsidies to sovereignty, he proposed, in effect, to sell Serbia to the Habsburg Monarchy. If this transaction had been called out in conjunction with an annexation of Bosnia, Hercegovina, and Novibazar, the Habsburg Monarchy would have included the great majority of all the South Slavs within its borders. It would have been in a position to dominate the remainder. It would have been in a position to control, and perhaps seize, the avenue to Salonika and the Aegean. It would have had a position of impregnable, overwhelming, strategic dominance and political power throughout the western half of the Balkan peninsula. Nor would the Russians, at that moment, necessarily have objected, if they had been compensated in Bulgaria. Their destiny, they felt on the morrow of the Congress of Berlin, lay in the eastern half of the peninsula. Shortly afterward, they actually proposed to the Austrians a partition along these lines. And the Germans, anxious to conciliate both empires, were favorable.

The Austrians did not act, either in 1878 or later. They cautiously avoided outright annexation of Bosnia, Hercegovina, and

Novibazar. They declined the offer of Milan Obrenovich, despite the ancient and perfectly valid dictum of Metternich that "Serbia must be Turkish or Austrian." It was, indeed, reluctantly and mainly for military reasons that they agreed to garrison the three Turkish provinces in 1878.

This remarkable self-abnegation arose partly from timidity—the Dual Monarchy was not set up for bold acts. But there were better reasons, some foreign and others domestic. The foreign concerns were raised by the prospect that a deal with Russia for the partition of European Turkey would very probably involve the cession to Russia of Constantinople and the Straits and, therefore, the unleashing of Russian power and battleships in the Mediterranean. This was a development that the Austrians themselves would certainly not welcome; and it was one to which Great Britain would probably react with a declaration of war. So large a reconstruction of the European balance would involve endless and shocking reactions.

But these might have been risked and, with boldness and skill, managed, if Austria-Hungary had had the same structure as the other Powers. The territories that would have been annexed through an "active" policy were inhabited by South Slavs, mainly Serbs, aside from a sprinkling of Turks. Annexation would have doubled the number of South Slavs—Serbs, Croats, Slovenes— in the Monarchy. Instead of being a decided, if unassimilable, minority, the South Slavs would have *exceeded* the Magyars, the Czechs, and the Poles in numbers, and would almost have equaled the Germans. Such a prospect would have been regarded with apprehension by everybody, and with consternation by the Magyars. The only possible way to handle so vast an increment of subjects of another nationality would have been to substitute for the unwieldy dualism of Austra-Hungary a trialism: Austria-Hungary-South Slavia. And this seemed impracticable. For one thing, it would have led to progressive demands: quadralism for the Czechs, which the Germans would have undyingly opposed; quinquelism for the Poles—perhaps sexualism for the Italians—

and so on endlessly until the Habsburg Monarchy was nothing more than a heaving mass of incompatible principalities. But there was a much more cogent and unanswerable objection to the suggestion of trialism. It was not only that the Magyars wanted no more equals within the Monarchy; more vitally, much of the South Slav territory that would go to form the third kingdom would be part of their own kingdom of Hungary. Having revived Hungary as a unit, the Magyars were resolutely and flatly determined to preserve it. Its integrity was a matter that was totally unsusceptible to negotiation or even discussion. Trialism was out, and an Hungarian policy, unalterable, was defined: *No More Slavs in the Monarchy.* It was defined by a Magyar, Count Julius Andrassy, who happened to be the Joint Foreign Minister at the time of the Congress of Berlin. It was (subject to a change of degree in regard to Bosnia and Hercegovina) to remain the Magyars' and thus, perforce, the Habsburg Monarchy's, policy until the end.

The Austrian Alliances

So the consequence of the crisis of 1876–78 was to leave the situation fluid, to leave the Ottoman Empire diminished and weakened but extant, to emancipate Bulgaria, and to leave the Austrians anomalously occupying Bosnia, Hercegovina, and Novibazar.

There remained only one possible policy for the Austrians: security through alliance. The positions of the Habsburg Monarchy and of Germany were in this fashion, if in no other, alike: both required peace and the maintenance of existing boundaries, and both had to achieve them through treaties to bind their friends and neutralize their enemies. There the similarity ended; Austria's enemies were legion, and could hardly all be indefinitely neutralized; the Germans conceived only one possible foe, France.

But the similarity of their requirements logically drew the two empires, both dynastically Germanic, together. The similarities

95

were emphasized after 1878; the Three Emperors' League was disrupted by the extreme irritation with which the Russians had responded to Germany's role in frustrating the Treaty of San Stefano. For the moment the differences between Austrian and German needs were obscured by their common alienation from Saint Petersburg. The result was, logically, a treaty of alliance between them.

The Austro-German Alliance, signed in 1879 after some rather tortuous negotiation, remained the basic diplomatic fact of Europe so long as Europe survived intact. About this static alignment revolved the dynamisms of changing societies and interests. It was, as everyone has since pointed out, a reasonable and plausible connection for each. The Germans feared France. The Austrians feared all their neighbors, including even Germany. By securing Germany as an ally, they eliminated the threat of some Germans' inchoate inclination to unite the German Austrians to a Great Germany. With the alliance, the Germanic overtone of the Habsburg Monarchy was converted from a danger to a strength, a bond of union. The Austrians agreed to support Germany if Germany were attacked by France; the Germans agreed to support Austria if Austria were attacked by Russia. But there was more implied than this: a diplomatic bloc was formed, a geographically vast, militarily impressive, strategically impassable unity from the North Sea to the Adriatic, across Europe.

There were other implications, more revolutionary than logical, that did not immediately appear. For one thing, the Austro-German Alliance involved an alteration in the methods of diplomacy. It was almost, if not quite, the first time that a binding, written, permanent alliance had been formed in peacetime between major Powers. The System had previously operated to maintain the peace through flexibility, through sudden shifts to bring the weight of diplomatic alignments against aggressors; that was what had happened, with great effect, at Berlin. Now the element of flexibility was subtracted and it was possible to anticipate—although no one did—the eventual development of competing alliances and so of a rigid European System in which aggression, or attempted expansion, would lead not to the uniting of other Powers against the aggressors but, automatically, to general war.

There was another aspect to the alliance, not novel, but important. Its terms were secret. Europe knew that it existed, but no one outside from the chancelleries of its members knew exactly what it involved—at least not until Bismarck, a decade later, found it expedient to show the text to the Russians in order to allay their fears about it. The secrecy was standard practice, and was natural enough. But when it applied not to an alliance made for a particular object but to one intended to become a permanent cornerstone of European alignments, it introduced a peculiar element into politics. And it foreshadowed further secret treaties.

There was a third implication of devastating, but for a long time uncertain, meaning. The peculiar internal structure of Austria-Hungary made it a different sort of unit from Germany, one more vitally affected by external influences. Because of this the day was to come when the Germans were obliged, sometimes against their will and judgment, to participate in affairs beyond their partner's borders and their own sphere of interests. Germany was tied to a state whose future involved securities of a very different kind from Germany's.

The next steps in the progress of the Austro-German Alliance, however, reflected not the disparity of interests but their temporary coincidence. It was necessary to extend the alliance—from Germany's point of view to neutralize France and construct a system of international security, from Austria-Hungary's to neutralize its neighbors and secure its domestic interests. And a happy configuration of interests permitted these needs to be met to the satisfaction of all.

The most important addition to the Austro-German peace system was Italy, important to Germany because it was a Great Power, and to Austria because it was the most provocative of neighbors. The motives for Italy's adherence were complicated and subtle. They involved domestic political concerns. The Italian

97

Right, newly and precariously installed in office, was ideologically inclined to friendship with the conservative powers and was anxious, despite its ambitions against Austria, to neutralize Catholic Austria's patronage of the Vatican, the irreconcilable enemy of the Italian state. Italy welcomed the prestige of a connection with the titanic powers of Central Europe, and the protection that such a connection would bring. It was hoped by some that the new allies would provide support for maturing Italian plans for imperial expansion. And, most of all, Italy was seeking friends and supporters against the French.

Franco-Italian relations were bad. Italy had ambitions and interests in Tunisia, and the Italians had long contemplated measures to control it. The French occupied it in 1881; the effect was a serious Franco-Italian rift. An invitation to seek consolation and comfort in the Austro-German Alliance was forthcoming from Berlin and Vienna, and, after extensive negotiations conducted in the utmost secrecy, was accepted. In 1882, Italy joined the alliance, which thereupon was renamed the Triple Alliance. The Central European bloc, in appearance anyway a diplomatic monolith, now extended across the continent, a powerful wall against French vengefulness.

A rather similar situation helped to consolidate the allies' relations with Britain and to alienate Britain from France. In 1882, for complicated reasons, British forces occupied Egypt, where France had large interests and ambitions. It was Tunisia in reverse, and thereafter the British were in some measure dependent on the diplomatic support of the Triple Alliance to offset French hostility.

A year later the Rumanian state also adhered to the alliance. The Rumanians were afraid, like everyone else, of the Russian activities in the Balkans. And they had been lured by Austrian support for their ruler's recent proclamation transforming Rumania from a principality into a kingdom.

Serbia, under its egregious ruler Milan (who had also transformed himself into a king), was practically an Austrian pro-tectorate. Rumania and Italy were allies. With Russia, Austrian and German relations gradually improved after the shocks of the Congress of Berlin. It was Bismarck's concern to prevent a Rus-sian-French understanding, and while he is said by some privately to have regarded the Russian Empire with animosity, he was nonetheless determined to maintain its friendship. This had been done by a reassertion, in 1881, of monarchical solidarity, in the form of a revised version of the Three Emperors' League.

The new arrangement was made possible by domestic changes in Russia—there was a new and less experimental emperor, a new foreign minister, and a new and disturbing wave of unrest that indicated diplomatic re-entrenchment. Moreover, the Russians were now convinced that their only hope for expansion southward to the Straits lay in an agreement with Austria to partition the Balkans, and the best chance of doing this lay in a diplomatic alignment with the two great Central Powers. An agreement was arranged, providing that if one of the three empires became in-volved in war, the other two would remain neutral. And it was also provided that changes in the Balkan arrangements inherited from the Berlin Congress should take place only after consultation and agreement.

The situation of Germany and Austria was now, for the six years that the Three Emperors' League lasted, extremely favorable, and peace in Europe appeared more secure than at any time before or since in modern history. France was effectively isolated, but it was relaxing somewhat in its antipathy to Germans as a result of systematic German attempts to conciliate it. The Germans had nothing to fear. And neither did the Austrians. All of the neigh-bors of the Habsburg Monarchy were now also its allies, and it could be expected that while they remained so they would abstain from policies likely to rock the Habsburg boat. This was Bis-marck's triumph, and it was Austria-Hungary's good luck. It was the apex of the Bismarckian system.

The Breakdown of the Bismarckian System

The security of the early eighties proved short-lived, and the root source of its breakdown was, once again, the Balkan peninsula. It is illuminating that the international arrangements and tranquility of the entire civilized world should have been shaken and in the end disrupted by the activities of the Bulgarian state, which was composed of some two million peasants. It was their action that forced open the breaches in European order that could never subsequently be closed. Thus they illustrated the incapacity of the European State System to assimilate a part of the world where the institutions of the national state were anachronisms.

The Bulgars and Alexander of Battenburg, their Prince (another gift provided by the fecund German dynasties to emergent Balkan powers), were harassed after Berlin by two problems. One was the recalcitrant attempts of the Russians to control the country, which the Bulgars ungratefully resented. The other was the tantalizing presence of Eastern Rumelia—a Turkish province, Bulgar in population—on their southern border. Prince Alexander made himself intensely unpopular with the Russians by resisting their attempts to take over his administration. He made himself equally unpopular with other Powers (except Britain, where Queen Victoria was maternally infatuated with him) by upsetting the apple cart in 1885 and annexing Eastern Rumelia, at the insistence of his avid subjects. He beat the Serbs, who objected to their neighbor's aggrandizement—Serbia was eventually saved from extinction only by Austrian aid—and Alexander eventually secured international approval for the union of the Bulgarias. But the Russian antipathy to him proved insuperable. In the end he was *kidnaped* by Russian agents and obliged to abdicate. There was, as usual when the interests of the Powers became engaged in the Balkans, a major crisis. It was finally adjusted, and still another German prince, Ferdinand of Saxe-Coburg-Gotha, was sent down to Bulgaria to replace the abducted Alexander.

These remarkable episodes of Bulgarian history sounded to

civilized ears like farce—and indeed some of them eventually became so, in the form of Bernard Shaw's *Arms and the Man*. Nonetheless, they were of the utmost importance in the history of the world. The Russians had once again been frustrated, this time by the determination of the Bulgars as well as the antipathy of the Powers, in their drive southward through the territories of the Slavic Little Brothers. They were stopped dead—for twenty years they made no further gestures toward Constantinople but turned their expansionist impulses to more easterly spheres. But *because* they were stopped, they were angry. They were angry principally with Austria, which they regarded as the chief source of their frustration. The Three Emperors' League was not renewed. The pan-Slavists directed their attention with ever more enthusiasm to the plight of the oppressed Slavs within the Habsburg Monarchy. While Austro-Russian relations were thereafter to have their ups and downs, there persisted a steady recognition on both sides that each was the other's antagonist; the Russians were for long restrained from aggression to the west and the southwest by fear of a combination of Powers against them—by the logic, in short, of the balance of power; but to the hostility of France and Germany had been added one scarcely less ineradicable, if less consistently displayed; the antagonism of Russia and Austria.

The effect of this grave disruption of relations between their two partners in the Emperors' League deeply troubled the Germans. Nothing could be done for the moment to reconcile the antagonists. But Germany might at least temper their hostility and maintain good relations with both. With skillful manipulation the difficulties were overcome; something called a Reinsurance Treaty was signed in 1887, the year of the Bulgarian kidnaping and the lapse of the Emperors' League. Russia and Germany agreed, in the event that either was involved in hostilities, to maintain "benevolent neutrality." However, since Germany was already committed to assist Austria in case it was attacked by Russia, benevolent neutrality would not be required in case Russia embarked upon an "aggressive" war with Austria.

This was terminological legerdemain, and both parties knew it.

Reasonable men in Germany might suppose that the Reinsurance Treaty was therefore meaningless and basically incompatible with the Austrian Alliance. Bismarck believed that *any* measure that tied Russia to Germany would keep it from an understanding with France and thus safeguard both German interests and the peace of Europe. But in 1890, with a new and brash emperor on the German throne, the Bismarckian theory was abandoned. Bismarck was summarily dismissed from office, primarily because of the clash between his young lord and master, William II, and the aging Chancellor who was accustomed to conduct affairs without interference. The Emperor and his advisers, after due consideration, decided that the Treaty was, by implication anyway, inconsistent with German obligations to Austria, and allowed it to lapse, while at the same time expecting and hoping for a continuation of cordial relations with Saint Petersburg on the basis of monarchical solidarity.

The Bismarckian system was ended with its author's tenure of the chancellorship. There were now two isolated Great Powers, France and Russia, confronting the great bloc of the Triple Alliance and its friends. Their diplomatic fusion was certainly not inevitable, but it became a possibility—the precise possibility that the European System, as managed by Bismarck, had been constructed to obviate. The balance of power made of the new situation an invitation to collaboration between France and Russia. And this prospect had been opened by the ill will of Austria and Russia, which was, in turn, the product of Austria-Hungary's peculiar domestic character.

The *composition* of Austria-Hungary helped to make the Bismarckian system flounder. It was the composition of Austria-Hungary that was to bring disaster to the next shape that the System of European states took.

France Finds an *Ally*

A Franco-Russian Alliance was signed in 1894. Conversations had begun four years earlier. The timing is a very clear indication of the accuracy of Bismarck's belief that in the absence of a German connection the Russians would form a French one. In 1891, there had been an informal agreement to consult and agree with one another in the event that either should be threatened by aggression.

Almost as if by natural law, Russia and France, despite the paucity of common interests in any other sphere, were obliged to draw together against the super-Power that lay between them. The agreement of 1891 was followed by more specific agreements, including in 1892 one for mutual military support in case of an attack on either party by Germany. The structure of Franco-Russian relations remained fragile. The Russian Emperor had been induced, during a visit of the French Navy to the Baltic base at Kronstadt, to stand at attention while his band played the hymn of democracy, *La Marseillaise;* but he could not regard the French Republic, or its anticlericalism, with any more enthusiasm than Louis XVI must, under similar circumstances, have regarded the ideals of the American Declaration of Independence. In this attitude the Germans urgently encouraged him, and on it they counted heavily. In 1894, William II wrote to the new Russian Emperor Nicholas II, "We Christian Kings and Emperors have one holy duty, imposed on us by Heaven, that is to uphold the principle of 'By the Grace of God' we can have good relations with the French Republic, but we can never be *intime* with her . . ."[1] The rhetoric, though inane, was not without appeal to the Russian ruler.

Nor was there any real coincidence of political interests beyond a common wish for security against Germany. The Russians certainly did not, at this stage, encourage French dreams of a vengeful aggression to eradicate the losses of 1870. The French had no interest in encouraging Russian ambitions in the Balkans or in Asia.

Nonetheless, in France anyway, friendship with Russia (the text and even the existence of the formal alliance was secret) provoked wide enthusiasm. And there was one additional point at which French and Russian interest did coincide. The Russians, embarking now upon a vast, planned program of industrial development—the

1. *Kaiser's Letter,* p. 24; quoted in M. Balfour, *The Kaiser and His Times* (1964), p. 189.

first deliberate program of its kind, and the forerunner of the Communists' five-year plans—needed capital. The French, inveterate savers, were willing to invest their savings in Russia. After 1890, French patriotism and prudence alike dictated it; very large loans were made and strong financial links developed.

There now existed in Europe two sets of allies: the balance of power had taken on a new and more coherent form. The alliances made each member more dependent for its own safety and survival upon its ally, and thus supplemented the written texts with a vital concern for the ally's welfare. In time the Austro-German bloc and the Franco-Russian bloc solidified into more than diplomatic alignments; they were ultimately to become the cornerstones of the European System. But this fact was at first obscured and mitigated by distractions.

Distractions Overseas

Beginning in the 1880's, the attention of European governments was diverted increasingly to non-European excursions. In the nineties, it was in Africa and Asia, not in Europe, that contemporaries witnessed the most serious conflicts among the Powers and apprehended the most serious dangers. Russia's chronic expansionism was now directed to Asia; Germany, Belgium, France, Italy, Britain, and the United States were all engaged in adventures overseas. Territories were being infiltrated and frequently annexed. Naturally, there were clashes, including some major ones, the largest being the Boer War and the Spanish-American War. International attention was upon these disputes, and they shaped the policies of all the Powers. It has been indicated how Tunisia and Egypt played a role in European politics. But it must be flatly and emphatically stated that *the flurry of overseas expansion and its accompanying tensions never led to war between European Powers;* no overseas conflict proved insoluble, and none contributed substantially to the outbreak of the first World War. *The vital consideration for the European states remained, as it always had been, the territories, sovereignty, and prestige of the homelands in Europe.* Only these interests were of sufficient importance to provoke a major war. To this extent, anyway, the structure of the national state proved true to its origin and function.

The name of imperialism is given to the phenomenon of the extension of political control by European Powers outside their borders, in Asia and Africa in particular. Its causes, nature, and meaning are highly debatable and need not be here reconsidered. But some things about it are relevant to our purposes. It was accompanied, if not precipitated, by an explosion of nationalism of a new sort and on a new scale. The purpose of building or extending empires, in the minds of some of their sponsors—and of publics aroused on behalf of such ventures—was the enhancement of the power, wealth, prestige, and greatness of the homeland. Men in that era dreamed great dreams; it was not surprising, considering the extent to which horizons had been widened by science and industry. Like the Elizabethan Age, the Victorian Age was a time of virile self-assertion, and extravagant visions took the now acceptable form of patriotic orgies. Men dreamed of fortunes, and frequently made them, but they also dreamed of world empires for their homelands—and frequently made them too. Cecil Rhodes, half-educated, half-genius, half-maniac, and all English, made himself a millionaire in South Africa and wrote a will designed to encourage the reconquest of the United States for an enlarged British Empire. Less imaginative advisers dissuaded him, however, and in the end he produced nothing more dramatic than a program of scholarships to encourage men from the colonies, America, and Germany to study at Oxford.

Rhodes, the imperialist, was a patriot; his imperialism was an *extension* of British nationalism of the old sort. In France, in Italy, in Germany, in Russia, a similar extension was taking place. Consciousness of national unity, coupled with the literacy and the legal emancipation of masses of the people, had bred eagerness for national grandeur, now projected to faraway places. Slavophilism was one form of it, Teutonic racism another. It was all encouraged as

a stock-in-trade of conservative parties and, on the Continent anyway, some Liberal ones. And all the Great Powers (as well as some
minor ones) were affected by it. With one exception: Austria-
Hungary. The government at Vienna repeatedly and explicitly fore-
swore the impulse to acquire colonies. It would have been possible
to do so; Austria was certainly strong enough to insist on a share in
the spoils. It was a rising industrial and capitalist power; its businessmen possessed the same motives to find markets, raw materials,
places for capital investment, that presumably moved the businessmen of Britain, France, Germany, or Italy—they possessed them
in considerably larger degree than the businessmen of Russia. Still,
the Habsburg Monarchy withheld its hand from the African and
Asian plunder. At the time, the Austrian statesmen explained that
this was because they already had enough on their hands; foreigners
assumed it was because Austria-Hungary lacked the vitality of other
states. But it is significant that national zest, so abundantly present
in all other imperialist states, was absent from the Habsburg
Monarchy. If there had been a nation to glorify by a colonial empire, one may guess that public opinion might have wished to
glorify it.

Habsburg destinies were nevertheless powerfully affected. The
juggling of European alignments arising from the imperialist phase
had some permanent effects, although most of the enmities and
friendships were transient. There were kaleidoscopic changes in
the diplomatic picture: two Powers bitterly opposed in West Africa
might find themselves cordially cooperating in North China. There
were sudden reversals too: in 1890, Germany and Britain successfully settled an intense rivalry in East Africa by an exchange of
islands; the British were given a protectorate over Zanzibar in exchange for ceding the miniscule but strategic North Sea island of
Helgoland. The most sinister of African clashes took place in 1898,
when a French force marching east across the Upper Nile region
encountered a British force marching south, at a place called
Fashoda. The meeting evoked real fear of war. The French retreated, in the worst possible humor, and Franco-British relations

struck bottom. But there was no war, and very shortly France and Britain were to be aligned in cordial friendship. On some occasions France and Germany were found operating in unison, notably in the East. On two occasions the imperialist Powers managed to convene for the unanimous and amicable settlement of African disputes.

Such alarms and affinities left only the most oblique of permanent marks. But some aspects of the imperialist struggle shaped the more lasting structure of the European alliance system. Of these, the most important were those affecting Great Britain. The colonial empire was more nearly central to the concerns of Great Britain— or at least to British consciousness—than was true in the Continental states. It may be, and has been, endlessly debated whether the colonies were *profitable* to Britain. The question is meaningless in terms of the late nineteenth century. The colonies were deeply and intimately involved in Britain's government, economy, and national consciousness, and had been for two hundred years; and they were a gauge of dignity and greatness. Earlier in the century, to be sure, there had been influential, almost dominant, schools of thought that preached the cost and the immorality of colonies. After 1880, less was heard from the thinkers of those schools.

At the turn of the century, Great Britain fought and barely won a colonial war—a war, however, not against "natives" but against Dutch settlers—Boers—in the South African republics of the Transvaal and the Orange Free State. The British—the details need not detain us here—attempted to subdue a remarkably ferocious and remarkably disagreeable population that stood squarely athwart the developing routes of African empire and the developing interests of the British settlers at Cape Town. By means that the naïve soldiers of 1900 considered foul, the Boers resisted long and successfully. When they were at length overcome, the dangers of diplomatic isolation had been clearly shown.

They had been vaguely perceived for some time in Britain. For a generation it had seemed prudent to inter old quarrels. The bitter animosities with the United States had been skillfully buried in 1871, in the Treaty of Washington, which prefaced an era of increasing cooperation. It was notable that when the two English-speaking Powers were each engaged, at the turn of the century, in their private wars against the Boers and the Spaniards, each stood as the only friend of the other. And retrenchment had proceeded in other parts of the world. In the Near East, the thankless job of shoring up the Turkish Empire, so long pursued and at so high a cost, was now being abandoned or—more precisely—was being transformed from a positive to a negative form.

These had been straws in the wind; what followed the Boer War was a hurricane laden with a haystack. The signs of the time were in truth ominous. The French, infuriated by the passage at Fashoda on the Nile, had reacted with a venomous jubilation to Britain's humiliating entanglement. The Germans' truculent disapproval of Britain's imperial course had been amply and exasperatingly demonstrated in 1895: following a clumsy assault by British settlers against the Boers, the German Emperor had sent provocative congratulations to the victim, the President of the Boer Republic of the Transvaal, Paul Kruger. Now Germany openly displayed in its press an unconcealed jubilation. The Russian Emperor, although not in public, complacently contemplated an attack on India. Even the kingdom of the Netherlands, not a contender for world power or independent diplomacy, angrily joined the hue and cry.

The consequence of all this was to dampen imperialist ardor in London and to hasten the end of isolation. The British now accurately appraised the perils of standing alone and in every sphere hastened the policy of disengagement, of transferring or sharing responsibilities. In the West, the transfer of power to the United States was sealed in the Hay-Pauncefote Treaty, by which the British conferred, as it were, their legal rights to construct a canal across the Central American Isthmus upon the United States. In 1902, Great Britain made an alliance with Japan, a vigorous, newly westernized state, the only modern and wholly independent power not governed by Europeans. Japan was to serve as a counterweight to Russian scheming in Manchuria. British isolation officially ended.

The Boer War was a major incident in the emergence of Britain from its haughty aloofness. But neither the war nor any overseas consideration determined the side on which the British were eventually to line up. Their most immediate concern was to assure that there *were* sides in Continental affairs, with one of which they might line up. In the case of the other Power whose diplomacy and destiny were mostly directly affected by overseas affairs, Italy, the case was different.

Italy's imperial dreams had risen rapidly in the 1880's, and had as rapidly come to grief. Italian affairs in the early nineties were in the hands of a chauvinist, Francesco Crispi, whose impulses had led to a serious worsening of relations with France—regarded almost as an Italian enemy since the seizure of Tunisia—and to a corresponding enthusiasm for the German and Austrian allies of the Triple Alliance. Crispi undertook to share in the African plunder by attacking the empire of Ethiopia, a venture prudently backed by the British, who saw in Italy a suitable counterweight to French advances toward the Nile Valley. But the Italians fared badly in the venture. Owing mainly to the inadequacy of its maps, the Italian Army found itself chopped to bits at the Battle of Aduwa, in northern Ethiopia, in 1896.

The defeat at Aduwa was as decisive as it was ridiculous. For the first time in living memory, "natives" had inflicted a crushing defeat on a European army. The turning point in Europe's easy dominance of the world was approaching. More immediately, the principal causes of Franco-Italian rivalry—the leadership of Crispi and conflicting ambitions in the Nile—were removed. Crispi resigned under circumstances of contumely so extensive as to discredit his entire policy. Italy was eliminated, for a time, from substantial participation in African affairs; the Ethiopian dream had to be abandoned for forty years. Henceforth, predatory Italian instincts were directed toward the Turkish province of Libya, which lay across the Mediterranean, adjoining Tunisia. Here, the satisfaction of ambitions indicated not conflict but cooperation with the French. Moreover, in the Ethiopian struggle the inutility of the Triple Alliance had been revealed. There was nothing Austria or Germany could do, or cared to do, to support Italy in its most vital concerns of the moment.

For this reason, and for various domestic political and economic reasons, Italy was henceforth inclined toward a gradual and partial accommodation with the French and a gradual and partial alienation from Austria and Germany. In this case, a colonial conflict had, although in a strangely oblique way, contributed to a new alignment in Europe. That alignment was not born out of Aduwa, but was made possible by it. It was, in the immensely less important case of Italy, equivalent to the Boer War in deciding Britain's eventual participation in the European System.

These were the two cases in which colonial struggles had a permanent and important effect on European affairs; one further instance was to take place later, in the Russo-Japanese War of 1905. But these three are isolated cases. Imperialism left barely more than traces on the European situation. It might even be argued that imperialism had served, rather than threatened, the cause of peace. As long as public attention was concentrated on "little wars," which could be lost without vital damage and therefore could be and usually were avoided by concessions, the danger of a head-on meeting, where the really essential interests of Great Powers were involved, was lessened.

After 1901, that danger began again to increase, and in a world where neither the old stabilities of the cosmopolitan System inherited from Vienna, nor the more recently demolished stabilities of the Bismarckian system, had survived to curb it. A decade now passed in which it appeared that the vital interests of each European Power required measures that threatened the vital interests of another. The scene shifts back from the misty horizon of evening isles to the center of Europe and the question of national survival. In this decade it was Germany that played the most conspicuous role, a Germany whose conduct of affairs was much changed from the subtle, conservative days of Bismarck.

CHAPTER FOUR

The "Encirclement" of Germany

It was Germany's principal interest to assure the isolation of France. In 1894, this objective was defeated by the Franco-Russian Alliance. The consequence was to be the isolation of Germany. Many German leaders did not recognize the solidity of the circle that had begun to be formed around them; when they did, they regarded their condition as outrageous, pathetic, and, in view of their power and progress, grotesque; they were inclined to view it as the result of malevolent and aggressive intentions on the part of the Russians and the French. But the facts were different: if it had been Russia, not Austria, with which the Germans had chosen to maintain an alliance, then they might have been faced by the prospect of a Franco-Austrian Alliance and their "encirclement," if less symmetrical, would have been equally real.

Against this exasperating situation the Germans reacted in ways that were calculated to enhance rather than to diminish the dangers. German conduct, from the mid-nineties on, was viewed by foreigners as increasingly boorish and bellicose; bad manners led to suspicions of bad intentions, and ample evidence substantiated the suspicion of sinister plottings. The Franco-Russian Alliance led, too, to a more substantial result in Germany: it obliged the Germans to contemplate and prepare for a war on two fronts. To meet this painful contingency, they evolved a strategic plan that was to have far-reaching effects.

The Aspect of Germany

The sinister aspect of the Germans grew in the minds of foreigners in the years before 1914; after 1914, it was to assume the aspects of a fairy tale with an ogreish villain. The fault was not entirely Germany's. Patriotic politicians and press in Russia, France, and Great Britain naturally stressed the lofty intentions and legitimate interests of their own countries and their friends and allies, and this often meant portrayal of Germany as irresponsible and immoral. Nonetheless, to a considerable extent, the fears and antipathies that the German Empire evoked abroad from 1890 on were, if not always well founded, clearly explicable in terms of German conduct. There were several identifiable sources for German bellicosity and—what was no less damaging—German tactlessness and ineptitude.

The first was the German constitution. This intricate edifice, devised by Bismarck in 1866, had been a purely personal invention, intended to permit the Chancellor to neutralize his domestic enemies, facilitate German unification by bribing its opponents with political favors, and ensure for himself the authority necessary to bring peace and prosperity to his fatherland. Even before Bismarck's resignation, it had proved to be insufficient for changing times, but the very complexities it had been designed to harmonize prevented any serious consideration of its revision.

Germany was a federal empire. Each of the twenty-six states that composed it retained, like an American state, its theoretical sovereignty. The federal government was, on paper anyway, very restricted in its powers, and its institutions were correspondingly few. They consisted of the Emperor and his sole minister and executive agent, the Chancellor, an establishment of civil servants, military and naval commands, and a parliament whose lower house was elected by universal manhood suffrage. It was in the German states that the residual authority was vested; their delegates composed the upper house of the federal parliament, and they were in a position to dominate the federal government. But one fact distorted and shaped the real meaning of the imperial constitution. Among the states, one was so far dominant that it was in a position profoundly to influence, if not control, the imperial regime and in important ways the other states. This was Prussia, which accounted for about three fifths of the territory and population of the German federation. The King of Prussia was also German Emperor; the Prime Minister of Prussia was as a matter of custom also the imperial Chancellor; and the Prussian Army was overwhelmingly the principal element in the German defense establishment.

The result of this situation was peculiar and in many ways unsatisfactory. There were a series of conflicting authorities, troublesome even under the leadership of Bismarck. After his departure, they threatened to become unworkable. There was no clear limit on the authority of the Emperor, who could appoint and dismiss the Chancellor and who considered himself responsible for forming policy. There was similarly no clear line between the spheres of the executive authority and the parliament. The lower house, the democratically elected Reichstag, was authorized (as lower houses usually were) to approve or reject new taxes. But this power did not lead, as it had led in great Britain, to any direct control over the executive authority: the Chancellor and the monarch. All it did was to oblige the Chancellor to assure a parliamentary majority for his budget; this was an harassment, which obliged the Chancellor and his master to show a great interest in election politics but did not result in the supremacy of the Reichstag. There were other potential conflicts. The government of the state of Prussia was in its turn dependent upon the Prussian parliament, and that body was dominated, by reason of an undemocratic voting system, by a minority of the Prussian electorate, a minority in turn dominated by the dour, Parochial, conservative, and half-bankrupt landowners of eastern Prussia. The Chancellor, as Prime Minister of dominant Prussia, was thus sometimes dependent upon the support of its decaying aristocracy;

as Chancellor of Germany he was in some measure dependent upon the democratic Reichstag; in both capacities he was dependent upon an hereditary monarch.

These anomalies were further complicated by the role of the Prussian Army. It had been remarked a hundred years earlier (by a Frenchman) that, whereas most states had armies, the Prussian Army had a state. The making of Prussia had been a military venture. The House of Hohenzollern, which had occupied the Prussian throne since its creation, was by tradition and inclination a party to this tradition, and this gave to the monarchy, and through it Prussia as a whole, and through Prussia, after 1871, Germany, a flavor of soldiery. The "Prussian officer" was a familiar stereotype: stiff-necked, contemptuous of civilians, haughty, reactionary, belli- cose, caste-conscious—and Prussian officers were a very noticeable part of the German landscape. They gave to the new Germany, in the eyes of most foreigners and of many liberal-minded Germans, a "militaristic" character, and few bothered to define "militarism" very carefully. It was assumed, because the army was arrogant and conspicuous, that it was also aggressive and powerful in the affairs of the government. The assumption was not in the beginning—and need not have become—altogether true. But because of the character of the institutions of the German Empire and its ruler, it tended to acquire verisimilitude. Two things were happening: First, the monarchy and a great many private citizens were making a proud connection between the imposing military reputation of Prussia and the welfare, greatness, prestige, and, indeed, inward character of Germany. Second, the Chancellor, faced with the opposition of powerful opponents in the Reichstag, was given to invoking patriot- ism and the glory of the army in order to induce voters to vote for the right parties—that is, conservative parties that were prepared to preserve the powers of the monarchy and the existing social order. Bismarck early made the connection between political stability for his own administration and the invocation of national traditions and nationalism as a sort of electoral platform. The connection grew more immediate and more continuous under his weaker successors. There were several clear illustrations of the process: in the parliamentary elections of 1907, for example, following a considerable growth in the strenuously left-wing Social Democratic Party, the government appealed to the voters explicitly to vote for pro-government parties in order to safeguard the fatherland, the army, the navy, the colonies, and to augument their greatness. The appeal was successful, and it required, in the next few years, a firm government commitment to a large defense budget. The Chancellor, whatever his inclinations might have been, had become a prisoner of his own electoral platform. And the army enjoyed a prestige and a strength that allowed it to develop into something of a font of national leadership.

It must be pointed out that a similar "militaristic" tradition—meaning in this case a close association between the glory of armies and the glory of the nation—was intimately part of the politics of other and less bumptious countries. Even third-rate Powers were given to boasting about their glorious military traditions and to installing generals in office in time of crisis. The appeal of honor was very ancient and respectable, and the demands of an army in the nineties were not generally among those that civilian governments cared to thwart. In France, a prolonged and profound domestic conflict was waged in the nineties and nineteen hundreds about the role of the army in national life, arraying in bitter struggle those who felt that justice and the rights of the individual must take precedence over every other consideration against those who felt that if the rights of the individual conflicted with the dignity of the army, the epitome and defender of the state and society, the army must prevail. This was the Dreyfus Affair, the leading sensation of the *fin de siècle* and a potent if temporary source of French weakness. The army lost; the republic of free men won. But the victory was narrow and, as events showed, impermanent. By 1913, the French Army was once again riding high, once again trumpeting its sacred mission and its sacred honor, and some of its spokesmen were behaving with public irresponsibility about the peace of Europe. Germany was not the only place where the army distrusted civilian rule and liberal values.

Still, the Prussian Army was an intractable and imposing element in the situation, which was aggravated by the inclination of German generals to dream their dreams of conquest in public. One of them, Friedrich von Bernhardi, wrote a book—called, in the English translation, which came out in 1911, *Germany and the Next War*—in which he not only asserted that war was inevitable and that Germany would win it, but that war was positively desirable, purifying, strengthening, and ennobling the nations which waged it. Bernhardi's views had no official standing, but like so many other German utterances they tended to confirm the fears and suspicions so rapidly growing elsewhere.

Then there was the German Emperor, William II. He was, along with the General Staff, to appear to foreigners as the principal author for the first World War. He was portrayed, even before 1914, as an arrogant and foolish autocrat. After the war broke out, the public of allied and neutral countries were informed that he was a bloodthirsty monster.

He was not that, and he was not an autocrat either. But he was, in many ways, foolish and irresponsible, and his public pose was intentionally one of extreme hauteur. His power was limited, but its limits were so ill defined as to permit him to think, and sometimes to act, like an omnipotent ruler appointed by God. He was in some ways a perceptive man. He was warmhearted, sentimental to a degree, egotistical, grandiloquent, impulsive, and, judged by latter-day psychological standards, exceedingly neurotic. He resented Bismarck. He was determined to rule by himself, to be a great, victorious, benevolent leader of his people. He liked to be portrayed on a charger dressed in medieval armor.

It was not surprising that Bismarck should have been fired or that William's Chancellors should have had short tenures, like the next two, or been a courtier like the third, or a scheming and, in the end, futile man, like the fourth. Nor was it surprising that William should have engaged, quite often without informing his Chancellor, in otiose gestures that conveyed to foreigners the impression of a wild and willful design of conquest. In 1895, he had wanted to make a violent gesture of protest against the raid of some

Englishmen into territory of the Transvaal Republic; and after efforts of some advisers to moderate his proposals, he still infuriated the British by his gratuitous wire of congratulations to President Kruger of the Transvaal. Later, he impulsively proclaimed to the Arab world that he regarded himself as the Protector of Islam. Later still, he was to grant an interview to a British journalist in which he conceitedly, and incorrectly, claimed that it was his superior military advice, kindly offered, that had saved the British from defeat in South Africa.

All these, and almost all the rest of his actions, were of a sort calculated to provoke extreme mistrust abroad. They did so at home as well. His Chancellors, however compliant, found it hard to govern. After the newspaper interview—*The Daily Telegraph* episode, which took place in 1908—the most sycophantic of them, Prince von Bülow, resigned. *The Daily Telegraph* episode was a public scandal that shook German confidence in the throne. For a while thereafter, William found it discreet to disappear from public view, and while he was unfailingly consulted, and his advice copiously given, he was no longer the commanding figure he had been. But public appearances were maintained; foreigners and most Germans had little understanding of the extent of his eclipse. He still remained, in the eyes of the world, the responsible authority, the Supreme War Lord, as he later called himself. He had, in fact, no one to blame but himself for the excessive odium that the world increasingly attached to his name.

The odium would have seemed less plausible, and William's leadership of the great German Empire less ominous, had that Empire not been growing palpably greater. Its increasing greatness was accompanied by an increasing satisfaction in greatness which, like any appetite, fed upon itself. Germany, the greatest military power in Europe in 1871, was by 1914 the leading industrial power, and it was a leader, too, in administrative efficiency, in education, in technology, in the handling of social problems, in the growth of its population. It was not surprising that many Germans, congratulating themselves of their own remarkable accomplishments, should have begun to dream dreams of a dangerous sort, or—considering their resources—to translate some of those dreams into reality.

The realities were frightening; they may never, until after the war started, involved any agreed-on plan or plot for extension of German territory in Europe, let alone for a German-dominated Europe. But enough was done to give many people reason to suspect them of privately planning for such purposes.

German Dreams and German Diplomacy

German destinies were perceived to be glorious and were intimately associated in the influential writings of people like the historian Heinrich von Treitschke with armed conquest and the military virtues. Treitschke was a spokesman for a school of deeply rooted Prussian jingoism. Even moderate and liberal writers, like Friedrich Naumann, could project, after the war began, a "Middle Europe"; this meant in practice the creation of a sort of Common Market to include the Habsburg Monarchy and perhaps the Balkans under German leadership. But such ideas suggested a vast destiny for the Germans in Southeastern Europe. There was the violent Pan-German League, small but loud. There were whole schools of zealous chauvinists who wanted to unite all Germans under one flag. This meant, for some of them, not merely the German-speaking citizens of Switzerland and Austria-Hungary but also those settlers in the Americas whose Germandom was both stressed and extensively cultivated. There were the men of the Navy League, who were more specifically alarming. Until the nineties, Germany had not been a major maritime power, and its navy was negligible. By then, however, a scattering of colonies had been acquired, German overseas commerce was growing, and a navy (it was asserted) was required to protect these far-flung interests. This was plausible enough to people at the time, although the logic might not bear very close analysis, since much larger colonial empires, like the Dutch, struggled along without naval protection from their homelands. It was not only suspected by foreigners but imprudently shouted from certain German rooftops that the reason for a navy was quite different: to display and prove the existence of Germany as a world power. Great, vigorous, growing nations had navies; Germany, as the greatest, most vigorous, and most rapidly growing, must have an imposing one. The Navy League was influential, and it had the backing of extensive shipbuilding interests; it struck a deep harmony in the mind of William II and his people.

The Navy League and the Pan-Germanists and the racists were not in any way peculiarly German phenomena. They had their analogues elsewhere—in Russia, with pan-Slavism, and in France, where comparable theorists were absurdly distinguishing between two races of Frenchmen, the one "Latin" and therefore debased, servile, incompetent, lazy, and immoral and the other "Germanic" (or sometimes "Celtic") and therefore imaginative, creative, virile, dominant, and suitable for leadership. In both the United States and Britain (where, indeed, much of this theorizing about the national superiority of certain peoples had originated) there were if anything more enthusiastic supporters of "Anglo-Saxon supremacy" or "the natural superiority of the Teutonic races" or "the white man's burden" than in Germany. Theodore Roosevelt spoke for a whole generation of men in many countries who found a mystical link between national glory, mental health, and deep sea navigation. In important ways each of these competitive notions frightened and aggravated other nations.

The Germans' assorted dreams of glory, however, caused more alarm than those of others. They were coupled with the egregious conduct of the Emperor, who was undoubtedly (if inconsistently) sympathetic to some of the dreamers. And they were coupled with an enormous and superbly effective German Army and a tendency to bullying in the conduct of diplomacy.

The bullying character of German diplomacy in the twenty years before 1914 played a role in deciding the terms on which war was to be fought. In particular, it played a part in determining the side on which Great Britain would align itself, thus emboldening Great Britain's friends to adopt intransigeant attitudes. It intensified, too, the strains of animosity that were being woven into Russo-German relations—although they were still fairly cordial for some years after the turn of the century. The bumptiousness and irresponsibility and grandiloquence, the pan-German hysterics, the successful operations of the navy enthusiasts, were not in themselves responsible for the crisis of 1914. There was a general embitterment of international relations that resulted from German activities. But embitterment does not in itself lead to mobilizations or the crossing of frontiers.

German policy was to be, in one sphere, decisive in its effects; but this sphere was only indirectly connected with the truculence and the jingoism of expansionists. Here was involved a response to a purely European situation. This was the increasingly unrestricted diplomatic support of Germany's ally, Austria-Hungary.

The ways in which such support operated will presently be examined; its background concerns us here. It will be recalled that Bismarck, always cautious in committing German power in problems in which Germany had no direct interests, had been extremely chilly in his view of the Eastern Question. He had been correspondingly reserved in backing any of Austria's varied interests or gestures to the south of its border. He had always deplored both the impetuosity of the Russians and the edginess of the Austrians in the dismal Balkan mess. After his dismissal, the question of the extent to which Germany would give diplomatic support to Austria was in abeyance; there were, to be sure, numerous Balkan problems in the 1890's and early 1900's, but they did not involve anybody's vital interests, for Russia was engaged elsewhere. After 1905, Russian interests began to return to the Balkans and Austrian trepidations again became acute. And there began to be felt the influence of a calculating but slightly deranged grandee of the German Foreign Office, its political director, Baron Friedrich von Holstein.

Holstein has always been regarded by later observers as a Mephistophelean figure, an *éminence grise*. For once, observers have been proved correct. The odd structure of the German state permitted him a larger influence than would have been possible in more tightly organized governments like the French or the British. His own surviving diaries and memoirs, fragmentary but amply illuminating, show him to have been a man with twin passions for anonymity and power, and with a number of other passions as well, including a quite morbid posthumous antipathy to Bismarck and a no less morbid conviction that Germany's fate required an absolutely total commitment to preserve Austria-Hungary as an ally and a Great Power and, to that end, to support whatever adventures the Austrians found expedient.

Holstein, who retired in 1909, left a mark on German policy. But he might not have done so had not his precepts coincided with realities, or at least convincing appearances, that everybody else could perceive. After the Franco-Russian Alliance, Germany was faced with potential enemies in two directions. In the third direction lay its remaining major ally. The unconditional support of that ally, in the face of "encirclement," seemed logical. Within certain limits, it was; it was also fatal.

The interweaving effects of German truculence on the world scene and of this logical support for Austrian interests form a principal theme of the complicated transactions of the first fourteen years of the twentieth century. There were other themes, however, each of which must have its expression and its resolution before the awful coda could be composed.

The Alienation of Britain

Germany was already, in 1894, faced with the diplomatic combination of France and Russia. But the Franco-Russian Alliance would not be fatal in a war if Great Britain remained neutral, and until the end the Germans believed that this was likely. They were wrong; and they were wrong partly because of mistakes they themselves made.

As was remarked in the previous chapter, the unpleasant experiences of the Boer War had climaxed a slow evolution in British opinion and policy away from "splendid isolation." But there was no clear indication what kind of safeguard for British interests should be sought among European Powers, nor which of the two European alliances would be approached. There was a good deal of historical cause, and some contemporary reason, to prefer an approach to Germany. France and Russia were regarded as Britain's natural enemies, Britain and Germany were traditionally friendly, and Prussia and Britain had fought together in the two greatest wars of British history—the Seven Years War and the Napoleonic War. Germany had supplied Britain's dynasty and most of its rulers' consorts, and the German Dowager Empress was a British princess. There were strong cultural affinities, and the Germans, at least before 1870, had usually been regarded in Britain as romantic and poetic folk with picturesque governments, in contrast to the ravening beasts of France and Russia. Queen Victoria had spoken of "our dear little Germany."

This view was grotesquely outdated by the nineties, and the traditional friendship had, even before the Kruger telegram, begun to cool. No one could have spoken of Bismarck's Germany as either dear or little, and there was already by 1890, concern about the rapid advances in industrial production and overseas commercial enterprise, as well as about Germany's colonial ambitions. But German and British interests did not at any vital point conflict.

The Germans were aware of this; they were also aware of several diplomatic realities that set the British at odds with Germany's potential enemies, the French and the Russians. One was Egypt; when the British had, highhandedly, occupied Egypt in 1882, their principal if impotent opponents were the French, who had large and ancient interests in the Near East and the Suez Canal and had always regarded Egypt as a sort of private preserve for their future attention. German support in international councils was required to outweigh French opposition to the Egyptian venture. The Germans counted heavily on Britain's other colonial conflicts with France. They also observed, with satisfaction, the bitter and mounting rivalry of Russian and British interests in the Ottoman Empire and in the Orient.

And a German-British agreement appeared to be possible. There were a number of proposals for a formal understanding, some tentative, some definite. They had begun as early as the 1880's; the last was made in 1901. The failure of these, and other less formal proposals, was partly the result of German coyness. There were some sensible reasons for it. From the British point of view, what was needed was an ally to safeguard British interests in regions where Germany had no great concern, and as a result Germany might be led into a war it did not want against Russia and France; and since Germany, but not Great Britain, possessed a large army, this would have meant that the Germans would be fighting Britain's battles with no visible compensation. As a result of this threat, and of the less well-founded belief that they were in a strong bargaining position, the Germans set terms: if the British wanted an alliance, they were welcome to join the Triple Alliance.

The invitation was unacceptable, and for reasons complementary to those which had produced the German reservations. The British had no interest in Germany's Continental rivalries. Nor were they constitutionally able to accept the secret commitments of the Triple Alliance. The discussions, like earlier discussions, ended in indecision. Each side thought the other was trying to exploit it, which was (naturally enough) true. And the British thought, what was also true, that the take-it-or-leave-it attitude of the Germans was a bullying sort of blackmail.

What was more—and what the Germans did not realize—was that the conditions that had produced these British approaches were changing. For at the very moment when the last unsatisfactory exchanges with Germany were in course, approaches were beginning to be made to France. This amounted to a revolution; both British diplomacy and the situation in which it operated had been revolutionized.

The Franco-British Understanding

The changes in the situation resulted from many things. Some of these originated in France. The French, on the morning after the

Dreyfus binge, were troubled with a serious hangover of domestic conflict, but they were, simultaneously, equipped with a new and extraordinarily gifted set of statesmen and diplomats who were, by ideology and temperament, inclined to do business with Great Britain. These men of the post-Dreyfus age, like the able Cambon brothers, who were to occupy the embassies in Berlin and London, and Théophile Delcassé, who was to have an exhilarating tenure at the Foreign Ministry, inherited and forwarded an evolving French ambition. For some years France had been developing an interest in the rotting sultanate of Morocco, a monumentally inefficient state which adjoined French Algeria on the east and extended southwest along the Atlantic coast. The French yearned for Morocco, and they had been bargaining with the Spaniards and conspiring with Moroccan elements, during most of the nineties, to secure a role of preponderance in its disorderly affairs. Morocco might have been nothing but an incident of the imperialist scramble. By coincidence, it became a touchstone in the much more portentous realignment of European Powers.

The changes in Britain were rather similar in some respects to those resulting from the Dreyfus Affair in France. There had been nothing like the Affair in London; such a thing was inconceivable. There had not even been any change of party; the conservatives held office from 1895 to 1905. But there were other and great changes that accompanied the Boer War and the crisis of imperialism. Victoria, who had reigned since 1837, died in 1901. Her son and successor was a cheerful and, in an elegant way, slightly dissipated character who disliked Germany and his German relatives and who was fond of the Paris of the gilded age.

Edward VII had no real part in making policy, but he could and did exert strong influence to secure the appointment of pro-French and anti-German diplomats to important posts abroad and in the Foreign Office. In 1900, the Prime Minister, the elderly, evangelical Marquis of Salisbury, had divested himself of the Foreign Office, which he had previously held along with the premiership. In 1902, Salisbury retired, too, from the premiership and was succeeded by his nephew, Arthur Balfour, an intellectual representative of an emancipated generation.

John Fisher, a brilliant naval officer and a close friend of the King, was becoming convinced that Germany was a major threat to British security and was developing the plans for a massive expansion and reorganization of the British Navy. He was able to put his ideas into effect, when in 1904, he became First Sea Lord, the highest service position in the Navy.

Salisbury, in accordance with the practice of earlier times, had made his own policies and treated diplomats and members of Foreign Office as agents for executing it. But the growth of the administrative establishment and the determination of the civil servants who now staffed it, gave new power to the bureaucrats. They tended to fashion policy themselves, a tendency that increased rapidly after 1905 when the Liberals chose a somewhat indolent and indecisive Foreign Minister, Sir Edward Grey. The genteel amateurism of the nineteenth century was being replaced by a vigorous and up-to-date professionalism.

It was also being replaced by Francophilia. The younger men who were seizing the initiative in the Foreign Office and Diplomatic Service disliked and distrusted Germany and were correspondingly eager for friendship with France and even Russia. In this they were representative of the new generation of the British ruling class. Like the King, and John Fisher and Arthur Balfour, they were far removed from the earlier leaders who had been hypnotized by memories of Waterloo, or those of the eighties and nineties who regarded the French as arty, volatile, irresponsible, arrogant, scheming, grasping, and immoral. Or, at least, some of the twentieth-century English gentlemen now appearing on the scene might still regard the French as arty and immoral but were themselves in favor of artiness and immorality; they dismissed the other adjectives as irrelevant or inapplicable. It was partly simply because of a changing taste in foreigners that they undertook—without completely planning its outcome in advance —an improvement of relations with the enemy of Crécy and Waterloo. King Edward, nothing loath, was sent in 1903 to enjoy the gastronomic treats of French state banquets. The French (who three years earlier had been engaged in the improbable task of disparaging his mother's personal morals) were charmed by their guest.

These developments reflected a change in the balance of real power in Europe. Germany was growing: it was growing in industrial power, in military power, in diplomatic power. Its population was increasing more rapidly than that of Britain, and much more rapidly than that of France. The successful visit of King Edward to Paris may be taken as a symbol of the progressive relative weakening of both France and Britain, compared to Germany, as Great Powers in a world where greatness was the guarantee of safety and of independence. It was not surprising that relations should abruptly improve.

They presently improved still further, and in ways less ephemeral than a favorable impression made by an engaging but politically insignificant king. A diplomatic agreement was reached in 1904 which settled, without any great difficulty, the more concrete differences between the two countries. The French, at last, recognized and accepted the British occupation of Egypt. The British, in exchange, recognized the particular interest of France in Morocco and promised to refrain from objecting if France felt obliged—euphemistically—"to provide assistance for all administrative, economic and financial reforms which it may require." There were other provisions; British interests were to be safeguarded, and so were those of the Spaniards, with whom the French had been quietly negotiating for some time. All this was secret; for public consumption, certain vexed questions of fishing rights arising out of the Treaty of Utrecht of 1714 were disposed of openly.

The agreements were a triumph for the French, and for the personal policy of Delcassé. Nor was this *entente* the only French triumph. A no less difficult one had been quietly arranged two years earlier, when an agreement of a rather similar nature had been reached with Italy. The Italians, abandoning the disastrous course of Crispi and disillusioned with a Triple Alliance that had served them so ill in their colonial ventures, had been ready to bury hatchets too. They were eying Libya with the same predatory glance that the French were directing toward Morocco. A deal—legally compatible with the Triple Alliance—had been worked out. The French agreed to let Italy take Libya whenever convenient. The Italians agreed, in effect, to let France take Morocco. This had been decided in 1900. In 1902, the Triple Alliance had been renewed. Immediately thereafter, the Italians and the French agreed that they would remain neutral if either were deliberately attacked by another Power. Italy's allies, although unaware of the terms of the agreement, were troubled by the signs of Franco-Italian cordiality. The German Chancellor made light of the matter in public—Italy, he said, was having a harmless flirtation. But in private, while clinging to the same metaphor, he was more definite: Italy, he said, must choose between being a wife and a whore.

It looked therefore by 1904 as if the diplomatic picture that had held with minor changes for ten years was in a state of flux. The Triple Alliance no longer faced the Franco-Russian Alliance in the presence of an isolated Britain. Instead, the Triple Alliance was weakening and Britain was drawing close to France. The change, as far as the Germans could see, was inchoate, but it was menacing. And the Germans decided to clarify it by arranging a crisis, a crisis in which the basic animosities between Britain and France and the basic solidarity between Germany and Italy would be publicly displayed from under the superficial blanket of obfuscating pacts.

Morocco

A crisis was arranged and duly took place, the supreme example of several attempts by Chancellor von Bülow to call things that turned out not to be bluffs.

The Germans had become convinced earlier—when Franco-

British relations were at their worst, in 1899—that the British were strenuously opposed to the establishment of French power in Morocco; they had even thought that this opposition might be strong enough to induce the British to accept an agreement for joint action with Germany on German terms. And they did not think that anything sufficiently basic could have happened to alter the British viewpoint in the following five years. The real nature of the Entente Cordiale was not known.

The German Ambassador in London was assuring Berlin that he considered a "British surrender in Morocco" unlikely, since the remaining French interests in Egypt were much smaller than British interests in Morocco.[1] Meanwhile, the Sultan of Morocco had been asking Germany for assistance in resisting the French, and the Germans were morbidly hospitable to appeals from threatened governments that they hoped to convert into friends. They had gotten in trouble, in 1895, by responding sympathetically, and provocatively, to the plight of President Kruger. Now they were to make another and more grandiose response.

The purpose was to force the British publicly to abandon the French, simultaneously to demonstrate Germany's solicitude for the beleaguered Sultan, and to give an awesome display of German power and prestige in world affairs. The purpose seemed to the rest of the world characteristic of German methods and the product of a carefully planned policy. The first impression was correct but the second was not. The provocation of the crisis was much more the result of a foolish impulse on the part of the Chancellor, who was able to have his way because of the lack of clearly indicated lines of authority in the German government. In the Moroccan situation, the Emperor himself was against the policy; he thought, sensibly enough, that it would be useful rather than otherwise to allow the French to become entangled in Morocco, where Germany had no real concerns. But Bülow wanted a crisis in order to "test" and disrupt the Anglo-French understanding, threatened by the war between France's ally Russia,

---

1. Quoted in Bernhard von Bülow, *Memoirs* (1931), II, 5.

and Britain's ally Japan. The Emperor was forced to provide one. He was enroute for a pleasure cruise in the Mediterranean when a report appeared in the German press saying that he would stop in the Moroccan port of Tangier to pay his respects to the Sultan. He now felt obliged to do so; and the visit was a public intimation that Germany proposed to protect Morocco against French designs. Bülow in Berlin called for an international conference to consider —in effect—French violations of an earlier international treaty regulating the position of the Powers in Morocco. The French were seriously alarmed by what seemed to be a direct German threat; the Foreign Minister, the gifted Delcassé, advocated disregarding the German mutterings, but he was outvoted in the Cabinet and forced to resign.

An odd and hazardous situation now existed. It looked as if the Germans had succeeded in forcing France to dispose of a foreign minister whom they disliked—the real grounds for dislike being obviously not his expansionist policy in Morocco but his success in achieving an agreement with Britain. France had suffered a humiliating diplomatic defeat. In terms of international usages of the time, this was automatically a German diplomatic victory, but in fact it was merely an embarrassment. Nothing had really been achieved by Germany, and (although this was not fully recognized in Berlin) a good deal in the way of good will had been lost by what seemed to be bullying. If Germany were to gain anything from its *démarche* in Morocco, then further steps were necessary. The demand for an international conference, originally intended mainly to impress the world with Germany's insistence on not being disregarded in the disposal of places like Morocco, had now to be pressed.

The conference eventually met, in the Spanish town of Algeciras, in January, 1906. Now for the last time before the war the European Powers met in congress assembled, significantly, to discuss the completion of Africa's partition. The consequences were worked out slowly, during three months under the Mediterranean sun, with confusion, delay, and embarrassment. But when the conference ended, they were clear and stunning. The Germans had lost their game.

The loss was not total. The French had been obliged to accept that the fate of Morocco was a matter of concern for all the Powers: the rules of the System that had emerged from the Congress of Vienna still held. The public law of Europe, so boldly invoked by Bülow, was still valid. But if the Powers had successfully asserted their right to govern the international decision, the decision that they made was precisely the one that Germany had opposed. The French were recognized as having special rights, and they were empowered to organize the Moroccan police and Moroccan finances. The arrangement was described as a compromise, and was accepted by all parties. But the reason that it was accepted was that the Germans found themselves helpless. The French and the British stood together against German efforts to save Moroccan independence, and they were in the end joined by an evasive and embarrassed Italy. Austria alone, and that with trepidations, had backed the German Empire. The outmaneuvering of Germany in an international conference was to remain in German memories: the Concert of Europe was not a trustworthy instrument for the defense of German interests.

Bülow had made a crisis in order to disrupt the Entente Cordiale and to break the forming ring around Germany. He had no real interest in Morocco. In the end, he saved a little in Morocco and lost everywhere else; Germany was not only still encircled, and more tightly than ever, but the fact had been publicly displayed. The Anglo-French agreement appeared now not as a settlement of particular disputes but as something more far-reaching. Italy's unreliability was ringingly announced to the world. And Algeciras demonstrated, too, Germany's fatal dependence on its ally, Austria. And this led in Berlin to a state of mind approaching paranoia; the German leaders convinced themselves, and convinced much of German opinion, that they had been conspired against rather than merely out-witted. Henceforth, consciousness of the iron ring that was allegedly being forged around Germany, became a real emotional factor in German policy. The Germans were genuinely scared.

The Moroccan crisis itself, however, did not bring war nearer in any concrete way. The future of Morocco had been peacefully, if provisionally, settled. Five years later, its condition was to occasion another Franco-German dispute, and that, too, would be peacefully settled. There was no *cause* of the first World War that arose from Morocco. Nor was there any cause for war that arose from the hardening of Britain's alignment with France. That was a cause of German defeat; it was not a cause of the outbreak of war, or even of Britain's entrance into it. But it was a sign of the progressive breakdown of German-British friendship.

The Naval Question

More than anything else, the German Navy had converted suspicion into hostility, and so converted the Francophilia of British statesmen into the Franco-British solidity displayed at Algeciras. At first the symbol was more important than the fact: the first German Navy Bill, in 1897, provided for a powerful fleet of nineteen battleships, to be built over five years; but in itself this would be no serious match to the British Navy. More ominous than battleships was the avowed motive for building them. The Secretary of the Navy, Admiral Alfred von Tirpitz, a close friend of the Emperor and a man of large determination and ferocity, had justified the expense to the German parliament in a speech that alarmed the British. The purpose of navy-building, he said, was not to achieve equality with possible enemies; it was to provide a naval force strong enough to threaten serious damage to the most powerful of the world's navies. That navy (the British, of course) would not dare to attack Germany, for the damage Germany could inflict would be enough to deprive the British of their margin of safety. The argument, called the "risk theory," was sophistical and unsound, but it appealed to the exuberant German opinion of the day. And it confirmed important elements of British opinion in dark suspicions: expanding Germany was looking toward the day when it would openly defy Britain, and was preparing to challenge it on the seas. The effect was exactly the same as the effect of the Kruger episode earlier and the Moroccan episode later: what was basically a German gesture of self-assertion was construed, and indeed could only be construed, as a threat to Britain.

The threat was still symbolic, but it heightened the meaning of the fact when it emerged. At the very moment of the Moroccan crisis, the British were beginning the construction of a new battle-ship called the *Dreadnought*. It was the most powerful ship ever built; so powerful, in fact, that it made all existing battleships obsolete, since its armor, speed, and firepower made it practically invulnerable while converting earlier vessels to easy prey.

The British thought that by stealing the lead with an altogether new kind of warship they would be giving themselves a large margin of safety. They also counted on the fact that the Kiel Canal, finished in 1895, connecting the Baltic and North Seas and absolutely vital to German naval mobility, would have to be completely reconstructed to accommodate ships on the scale of the *Dreadnought*. But instead of giving them an advantage the building of the *Dreadnought* eventually had devastating implications for Britain's naval supremacy. Since it made all other battleships obsolete, it meant that Germany and Britain were almost starting from scratch and that the Germans, might conceivably achieve naval equality.

The naval rivalry was very much on people's minds in both countries. It gave rise to a sensational literature, which tended to give the public in both nations the idea that each was threatening the other. Alarmist pamphlets in Germany said that the British were planning a surprise attack on the German ports and fleet. A whole school of writing, called "invasion literature", flowered in Britain, starting with a brilliant spy story called *The Riddle of the Sands,* by Erskine Childers, published in 1903. The British, by the time the *Dreadnought* was launched, were thoroughly alarmed.

The Germans, similarly alarmed, overlooked one basic fact. No enemy navy, however powerful, could defeat the German Empire; but a victorious enemy navy could defeat Great Britain. The British Isles produced less than half the food needed to nourish their population. The rest had to be imported, and the importation had to be defended against potential enemies by superior naval power or else Great Britain would be perpetually subject to threat of blockade and starvation, and its independence would be lost.

The result was to affect profoundly the balance of power, as seen from the vantage point of London. The new foreign policy, now taking shape, was analyzed by a Foreign Office official in 1907. Sir Eyre Crowe, one of the new, Germanophobe, bureaucrats who were shaping policy, re-interpreted the traditional policies and requirements of Great Britain in the light of the new world situation in which Germany was emerging as the chief potential threat to British security. His memorandum was a basic document in British diplomatic history in the early twentieth century. It was the statement of a creed, and it became a test of orthodoxy.

> The general character of England's foreign policy is determined by the immutable conditions of her geographical situation on the ocean flank of Europe as an island State with vast overseas colonies and dependencies, whose existence and survival as an independent community are inseparably bound up with the possession of preponderant sea power.

So ran the opening sentence. And the memorandum grew even more forthright as it proceeded. Because of England's maritime position, which is both its danger and its safeguard, its naval power will provoke jealousies. To reduce the effect of jealousies, England must seek the friendship of the greatest possible number of nations by supporting all their legitimate aspirations, of which the most basic, of course, is their independence, and the second their freedom of commerce. This means *protecting* the independence of all other countries against predatory neighbors, and this means that aggressors or potential aggressors must be curbed by defensive leagues, sponsored by England.

Beneath the high-minded words, this was simply a statement of the old balance-of-power policy, tried and true but now, as a result of changing circumstances abroad, directed against Germany.

Accommodation was still possible; certainly war between the two was a remote contingency. But the Germans greatly overestimated, from 1906 on, the amount of pressure that would be required to push the British into war on the opposing side.

The Triple Entente

The French shared the German uncertainties about the meaning of Britain's new alignment. The British were coy; they consistently refused to consider an outright alliance with France. They constantly talked about conciliation and appeasement instead of about preparation for war. And they were as constrained as ever in their relations with Russia, which had, in fact, become even worse than usual in recent years. Diplomatic support of France at Algeciras was one thing; participation in a war on the Franco-Russian side was quite another. The best French efforts were accordingly directed toward appeasement of relations between their ally and their new-found friend.

They were promptly and surprisingly successful in this, as in all their ventures. The French record in these years, regarded purely from the standpoint of technical diplomatic skill, is dazzlingly brilliant. Nothing seemed more unlikely than an Anglo-Russian entente. But within a year after Algeciras something like it was achieved.

Conditions were favorable. The French dream could scarcely have been realized so much as three years earlier. What had brought about the change was, ironically, the very development that seemed on the surface to constitute the largest obstacle: Russia's defeat at the hands of Britain's ally, Japan.

The tangled affairs of North China, which had been the forum of Russian expansion since the disappointments in the Balkans in the eighties, cannot and need not here be elaborated. The situation was in its details incredibly intricate, but in its outlines it seemed simple. Two nearby predators, Japan and Russia, eyed the inviting booty of the disintegrating Chinese Empire, while more distant ones rubbed or wrung their hands, according to temperament and interest. Prominent among the wringers was Great Britain, which had conceived the notion of calling Japan into existence to redress the balance of its relations with Russia. An alliance, assuring British neutrality and, by inference, benevolence, in case of a blowup with Russia, was signed in 1902; this first step toward the abandonment of isolation had been, it is interesting to note, an anti-Russian, not an anti-German, measure.

Thus emboldened, and aided by the folly of the Russians and their ponderous military establishment, the Japanese had forced the issue by attacking Port Arthur, in Manchuria, which was a center of Russian interests, property, and influence, and within a year had occupied most of the major centers of Manchuria. The Russians, harassed by the enormous distances and the inadequate transport that separated their centers of power in Europe from the end of Siberia, audaciously dispatched their fleet around the world to cut the Japanese supply lines. En route from the Baltic, the Russians produced a first-rate crisis with Britain by sinking a fleet of English fishing vessels on the Dogger Bank in the North Sea. When they reached Far Eastern waters, their fleet was immediately sunk by the Japanese at the Battle of Tsushima, in May of 1905. Russia crumbled into revolution. An embarrassing peace was arranged at Portsmouth, New Hampshire, through the helpful services of President Theodore Roosevelt.

The Russo-Japanese War and the accompanying revolution in Russia dramatically altered the balance of power in the Pacific; its effects in Europe were more striking still. Russia was suddenly subtracted temporarily from the ranks of the Great Powers. The Germans and the Austrians no longer had to worry about their eastern frontiers; the Russian Army was in a state of shock, verging on distintegration. The British, infuriated by the Dogger Bank episode, were in the worst possible humor. The French were experiencing the most painful moments of the Moroccan crisis, with Delcassé's resignation taking place a month after Tsushima, and they were frantic with alarm about the impotence of their ally.

But the situation redressed itself almost automatically. The shock to Russia in the long run helped to overcome the ancient British enmity. Germany was now looming more conspicuously than ever as the source of danger to Britain. Russian threats need no longer be taken seriously. The situation contributed to the beginning of a revolution in Anglo-Russian relations. For the first time since the sixteenth century, they began to improve and even to exude a certain warmth.

The Russians clearly needed British friendship. The French were working overtime to sponsor it. Moreover, there were emerging influential Englishmen, most notably the British Ambassador at Saint Petersburg from 1906 to 1910, Sir Arthur Nicolson, who pled the cause from a positively Russophile point of view. Russia began to become fashionable in Britain after 1905. There were many causes: the arguments of people like Nicolson, the good impression made by the first Russian venture into representative government after the revolution, a new fad for Russian literature, Russian ballet, and the well-publicized attractions of Russian high society. The basis of it undoubtedly was the fact that Russia no longer had to be feared, and Germany did. In August, 1907, the French dream was at last realized. An Anglo-Russian Agreement was signed.

It resembled, in its terms and content, the Anglo-French Agreement of 1904. Specific problems only were dealt with: the tug-of-war for dominance in Persia was settled by the neat expedient of partitioning it into spheres of influence, without, of course, consulting the Persians, whose survival as an independent nation became a matter of the narrowest margins and of fortunate accidents. Both parties agreed to refrain from activities in Tibet. The Russians conceded Afghanistan to be a British sphere of influence, and the British agreed not to annex it. But, as in the case of the entente with France, the real significance lay not so much in the terms in which disputes were settled as in the fact that a friendly spirit permitted them to be settled at all.

The phrase "Triple Entente" now began to appear in the press. The course of Anglo-Russian friendship was, however, troubled. There were controversies about the ways in which Persia was to be dealt with. There was, most alarmingly, a tendency on the part of the Russians, frustrated in the Far East, to turn their attention to the Balkans and to Constantinople, and the British were by no means so beguiled as to agree to any extension of Russian influence in the neighborhood of the Straits. The Germans, confronted with a Triple Entente, blanched, but they also laughed. The idea of any permanent or profound cooperation between Russia and Britain seemed to them out of the question.

Germany was "encircled." The ring was not complete, the circle not tight. But there were some distressing indications of finality. They had been illuminated earlier by an attempt, at once serious and comic, to break the encirclement by forming a Continental coalition against Britain. In the summer of 1905, at the nadir of the Russian embarrassment in the East, the emperors of Russia and Germany had met in a friendly way on the German imperial yacht during the course of a family gathering at Bjorkoe, in Denmark. The Russian, Nicholas II, was exasperated to a degree with Britain; William II was, as usual grandiloquently prepared for a gesture. He impulsively prepared a treaty of alliance between Russia and Germany; equally impulsively, Nicholas signed it. William announced to his Chancellor that he had created a Continental union by bringing the Franco-Russian allies into union with the Austro-German-Italian combination.

Both emperors had been carried away. Their ministers, when informed of the world-shaking event, soberly pointed out that the text was entirely incompatible with their obligations to their respective allies. Nothing more was heard of a Continental coalition. The division of Europe was too far advanced for monarchs to

GERMANY ENCIRCLED
IN 1914

NORWAY

SWEDE

GREAT
BRITAIN

DENMARK

NETHERLANDS

BELGIUM

GERMANY

FRANCE

SWITZERLAND

AUST

PORTUGAL

SPAIN

ITALY

MONTE

Mediterranean Sea

John Carnes

RUSSIA

ARY

RUMANIA

BULGARIA

TURKEY

Black Sea

The Central Powers

The Entente Powers and others
potentially hostile to Germany
and Austria

reconstruct the international situation by signing secret treaties on a yacht.

With luck or skill the ring might yet have been broken. But when, two years later, the Triple Entente was appearing, the prospect that Britain could be weaned away from Germany's enemies, never wholly delusive until August of 1914, was beginning to enter the realm of what Germany's most astute diplomat was to describe in that still-distant summer as "pious wishes." The Germans' supply of luck and skill was too small to destroy the always precarious connection between Britain and the Franco-Russian allies.

The effect of the events between the Boer War and 1907, then, was to jeopardize Italian loyalties to the Triple Alliance, to lead the British into an uncertain but ominous connection with the French and the Russians, and to solidify the Franco-Russian alliance. There were no Great Powers upon whose neutrality—if worst should come to worst—Germany could count. And this fact in turn had profound effects: it led the Germans to adventurous investigations of an understanding with Turkey; it frightened German officialdom and public opinion and provided cause for grievance and for arguments that the ring must be broken by force, the anti-German conspiracy demolished; it made necessary the preparation of a detailed plan for military campaigns against both the Russians and the French; and it made it indispensable for Germany to defend, and if necessary to shore up, the might of Austria-Hungary and its prestige and posture as a Great Power. The ominous phrase began now to recur with deadly regularity in the German documents, and in German public statements as well: The Habsburg Monarchy must be preserved as a Great Power. If Austria goes, then Germany is lost.

The consequences of this belief were to make themselves promptly felt. To the Near Eastern Question, still not worth the bones of a Pomeranian grenadier so far as any of Germany's national or world interests went, the German Empire was becoming shackled by the chains of circumstance.

CHAPTER FIVE

THE BONES OF A POMERANIAN GRENADIER

WHAT mattered to mankind was what the German Army did. What the German Army did was determined, in the end, by what the Austrian state required. What the Austrian state required was decided by what some angry Serbian officers in Belgrade did. In June, 1903, the officers shot their King and Queen, chopped the bodies into bits with sabers, and threw them out a window into the garden of the royal palace.

It was a singularly messy assassination, and one that shocked Europe. Its aftermath was a great deal more shocking. Like all developments in diplomatic history, the sequence of large events that followed seems to move, when seen in retrospect, in an orderly and majestic fashion. But when seen under a lens at any given moment, the situation was so complex, with so many distractions of a sort that seem unimportant now but at the time seemed vital, with so many uncertainties and so many small decisions required, that only in the vaguest and most inchoate form could the larger meaning of events and decisions be accurately appraised. To illustrate this truism, and because the events *were* important, it is of use to investigate the dismal complexities of the Serbian situation and its international implications.

THE LONG FUSE

Serbia

Serbia in 1903 was a kingdom of about two and a half million people. Its capital, Belgrade, had a population of less than seventy thousand. The country was largely rural and its population largely illiterate. Its principal market and source of supply was the Habsburg Monarchy, which adjoined it to the north across the Danube River, and its most considerable export was livestock, in considerable part pigs, a fact that was to have a terrible importance to the peoples of the world. It had been gradually emancipated from the Turkish Empire in the course of the past century, and had produced two families that led the struggle for freedom and eventually became rival dynasties alternately occupying the throne. One of these, dispossessed for more than half a century, was the House of Karageorgevich, whose scion in 1903 was Prince Peter, an elderly, intelligent man who lived in exile in Geneva and passed his time by translating John Stuart Mill into Serbian. The other was the House of Obrenovich, which was at that time occupying the throne in the person of King Alexander II, a young man of indifferent talents, doubtful morals, and very bad political judgment. He had in 1901 married his mistress, Draga Masin, a widow of even more doubtful morals and the daughter of a lunatic municipal official whom Draga was reputed, probably incorrectly, to have murdered. Their marriage had been ill judged from every point of view. The lady was thirty-seven years old and barren, which meant that there could be no heir to the throne and no future for the dynasty. Her family was disliked and disdained by most of the population. Her morals were a matter of public scandal. Her position as Queen was regarded by a great many Serbs as a national indignity. The marriage had infuriated the government of Austria-Hungary, since it took place in defiance of Alexander's promise to wed a German princess sponsored by Austria. It was coolly received in Russia, for complicated political and dynastic reasons. The King's parents, whose own scandalous relations had already outraged public opinion and contributed to the father's abdication some years earlier, united—for the only time in their lives—in excoriating their son's matrimonial venture.

Alexander's throne was not, in any case, secure. Like his father, he had made himself dependent upon Austrian support, although unlike his father he was inclined to try to secure the friendship of the Russians as well, as a counterweight. He had played a similar game at home, trying alternately to appease the two leading parties, the Liberals, who had supported him and his father, and the Radicals. The Radical Party was the key to the situation in Serbia. It was, like other European Radical parties, democratic and nationalist. It favored a limited monarchy, parliamentary government, and civil rights, and it had, since the formulation of its aims in the early eighties, also cautiously favored the union of all Serbs in a single state, which meant that it was by implication hostile to Turkey and Austria, where most of the "unredeemed" Serbs lived, and friendly to Russia, the anti-Austrian, anti-Turkish, Slavic Big Brother.

In alternating between the conciliation of one party and the other, Alexander had alternately supported and opposed constitutional government, suspending and promulgating constitutions and revising ministries in a fashion both frivolous and imprudent. In the end, it was the Liberals who had turned against him and organized his murder; but he had also alienated the Radicals, who were not inclined to support so volatile and unpopular an ally.

The Russians had intimate connections with the Radicals, whom they supported and patronized, just as the Austrians were inclined to support the Liberals. This was a situation familiar enough then as now in small countries where large competing neighbors strove for advantage. But the composition of Turkey and Austria, with their millions of Slavic inhabitants, made Austria's concern not one of detached desire to secure an international advantage but one of nervous preoccupation with its domestic stability; it also made the Russian techniques of patronage, the encouragement of pan-Serb nationalism, a peculiar danger.

On the other hand, in 1903 and for several years before and after, the Austro-Russian rivalry in Serb affairs was muted. In 1897, when the Russians were becoming ever more deeply involved in the Far East, there had been an Austro-Russian agreement to abstain from activities in the Balkans of a mutually disadvantageous sort. The Austrians hoped that the two Powers would cooperate; they looked for a guarantee that the Russians would abstain from conquest and for an agreement that, if Turkey eventually disintegrated, the area would be divided into an eastern Russian sphere and a western Austrian sphere. The Austrian Foreign Minister, Agenor von Goluchowski, suggested the eventual annexation of Bosnia, Hercegovina, and Novibazar for themselves and the creation of a state of Albania on the Adriatic.

The Russians rejected these proposals as excessively hypothetical. Had they agreed, there might well have been much less trouble in the future. As it was, major trouble was avoided for ten years after 1897 by the agreement to maintain the existing order of things. The Balkans were put on ice.

Thereafter, the Russians were occupied elsewhere. In 1902, the Russian Foreign Minister, Count Lamsdorff, had emphatically and explicitly told King Alexander that Russia was too much involved in Far Eastern affairs to seek anything but tranquility in the Balkans, and that the Serbs should "pursue a policy of peace."[1] This was not to say that Russia was not still engaged in cultivating friends in Serbia. Relations with the Radicals continued to be close and cordial; the Russian Minister at Belgrade still kept an eye on things. Still, Russian activities were passive, and Russian-Austrian relations were for the time fairly harmonious.

This fortunate state of affairs benefited the revolutionary government formed by the assassins of the King and Queen. Serbian opinion, violently hostile to the deceased sovereigns, was not particularly fussy about matters like mass murder (the Queen's brothers, two cabinet ministers, and quite a number of royal guards had also been killed). Most of Europe was stunned with horror, and

1. W. S. Vucinich, *Serbia Between East and West* (1954), p. 37.

the British withdrew their diplomatic representatives in protest. But the imperial governments of Vienna and of Saint Petersburg, while scarcely eager to applaud regicide, were inclined to make the best of a bad situation. They recognized the revolutionary government and the new king, Peter Karageorgevich, who was summoned from Switzerland and installed on the bloodstained throne. In an affable way they hastened to assure him of their support. In return, he promised to maintain good relations with all his neighbors.

The course of King Peter's government ran rough, however. It rapidly became clear that the regime had to be nationalistic if it was to stay in power and to find a cabinet that could command a majority of the parliament, which was dominated by the Russophile Radicals. A parliamentary resolution in 1904 made this obvious. Expressing sympathy for Russian aims in the Far East, it said, "Slavic Serbia naturally considers every Russian success as a strengthening of the Slavic cause."[2] The results of democracy were pan-Slavism and Austrophobia. There was an immediate expansion of clubs and secret societies devoted to the "redemption" of the South Slav brothers languishing in Austria and in the adjacent provinces of Turkey. The government was dependent on Austria diplomatically and commercially; but it was dependent domestically upon doing something definite about its national destinies and the languishing brothers.

The most distressing languishing was in Macedonia. No one quite agreed on where Macedonia was—but wherever it was, it was a problem. It lay under Turkish rule somewhere south of Serbia and west of Bulgaria and north of Greece, and its population comprised a large number of Slavs—whether mainly Serb or mainly Bulgarian was a matter for argument—as well as some Greeks, Turks, Vlachs, and a pair of peoples called, separately, Ghegs and Tosks and, collectively, Albanians. It was, in 1903, in a state of horrid disorder. Here the Serbs felt impelled to take a strong line, partly because the Bulgarians were busily organizing pro-Bulgar terrorist activities, partly because Serb opinion urged it, partly because they were

2. Vucinich, p. 90.

anxious lest Austria-Hungary might contrive to extend its authority on the pretext of disorders. The Serbs hoped for Russian support in some project of "reforms" in Macedonia.

But the Russians, while paternally urging the Serbian government to have faith in their beneficent attitude, were more than ever entangled in the Far East and more than ever inclined to defend their position in the Balkans through agreement rather than conflict with Austria. A few months after the Serbian revolution, the Russians and the Austrians achieved the Mürzsteg Punctation. This agreement, accepted by the Ottoman government, sensibly provided for the policing of Macedonia by the Great Powers, which were to set up a *gendarmerie*. After prolonged squabbles as to what constituted Macedonia (the Austrians strenuously insisted that much of the territory in question was not Macedonian at all but an Austrian sphere of influence, which should not be subjected to international control), the arrangements went into effect, to the mutual annoyance of Serbs and Bulgars, who were largely excluded from nationalist activities in the area. The international control was not altogether a success, but it was the most imaginative idea that anybody had had, either for dealing with the problem of Turkish misrule and native violence in the Balkans or for solving the problem of Austro-Russian antagonism.

The solution was far from complete and even farther from permanent. By the end of 1905, Russia had been defeated in the Far East and had retracted its Oriental horns. The ominous implications for the Balkans were instantly apparent; despite military disaster and domestic revolution, the Russians solaced themselves by a renewal of meddling in Serbian affairs and by a much smaller willingness to cooperate with Austria. In the course of a Serbian ministerial crisis, they urgently supported the elevation of the Russophile Nikola Pashitch as Prime Minister. It may be argued that the Russians were especially in need of some political successes in Europe following their defeat in Asia; but it seems likely that, if they had defeated the Japanese, they might have adopted from strength the policy that they now adopted from weakness.

The Serbs were in increasingly urgent need of their patronage, for their relations with Austria-Hungary were going from bad to worse. There had begun, gradually and almost invisibly, a calamitous downward spiral, with the demands and the provocations of each party precipitating higher tempers, greater fears, and more intense provocations.

The Pig War and the Rise of Pan-Serbism

The most critical of these provocations concerned commercial relations. Since the 1870's the Habsburg Monarchy had arranged, in a series of treaties, to tie Serbia commercially to the Austro-Hungarian market. These arrangements were not economically unfavorable to Serbia, but they led to a quite disproportionate growth of trade between the two, so that by 1903 something like 90 per cent of Serbian foreign commerce, upon which the economy of the country was wholly dependent, was with the Habsburg Monarchy. There was a good deal of Serb resentment against this situation, both on the grounds that it impaired Serbian independence and on the grounds, which were conjectural but turned out to be correct, that the guaranteed market in Serbia for Austrian manufactured goods retarded the growth of Serbian industry.

After 1903, efforts were made to break out of this position of dependence, the first major step being the signing of a customs treaty with Bulgaria in 1905. The Austrians, convinced that the subordination of Serbia was indispensable, responded in 1906 by stopping the import of all Serbian livestock—the largest part of all Serbian exports—to the Monarchy. There followed a desperate commercial struggle, called the Pig War, that lasted with short interruptions for five years. It had enormous political implications; from the point of view of both parties, it was a sort of war for Serbian independence. The Austrians were determined to demonstrate their power to reduce the Serbs to compliance by commercial blackmail; the Serbs were determined to free themselves from the economic stranglehold.

The effects were unexpected. The Serbs, with considerable energy and skill, developed markets for their goats and pigs in other countries—Egypt, Greece, Turkey, and, rather strikingly, Germany. Their manufactures grew prodigiously. Public opinion, solidly united in defiance of the Austrian bully, responded with discipline and even enthusiasm. After the first year, Serbian foreign trade actually expanded over the pre-Pig War level. It was a striking demonstration; it showed that the way to get things done in Serbia was to challenge the enormous neighbor to the north; and its success made the Serbians extremely brash.

There were opposite effects in Austria-Hungary. The government was surprised and angered by its failure and by the audacity of the Serbs. Moreover, the Pig War divided opinion in the Monarchy. The Magyars were extremely dubious about a policy that seemed both imprudent and costly, and one invented by the Germans in Vienna. The Slavic groups within the Monarchy were indignant. Everybody perceived the political implications. What was being fought by Vienna was a war against Serbian—and Slavic—aspirations. Foreign Minister Goluchowski had stated the case explicitly and threateningly. The Habsburg Monarchy, he had said, could "never allow the creation of a Greater Serbia . . ." Such a development would make it impossible to "govern Austria," because "the centrifugal Slav elements would tear her to pieces." "Rather than allow [this or any similar eventuality] Austria would appeal to the sword." It looked as if, as a preliminary measure, an economic sword were being appealed to.

This was quite enough, but there was more. One of the results of the economic subordination was to make the Serbs excessively sensitive to trade routes. There were several vital considerations for them: they did not want an Austrian railroad to be built to the Aegean in the Austrian-occupied Turkish territory of the province of Novibazar to their west; such a railroad would bypass Serbia, hurting it economically, and would also form a sort of commercial barrier between Serbia, Montenegro, and the Adriatic; by contrast, they much wanted a railroad from Serbia to the Adriatic, which would give them a direct commercial outlet to the sea. The Austrians consistently, though somewhat uncertainly, opposed the latter. And in January, 1908, they announced the construction of the former. Once again, no doubt was left about the political implications of what they were doing. And, more remarkably, even less doubt was left when six months later it was decided to postpone the project. The decision was made on the basis of political consideration; the railway would simply not be effective in frustrating Serbian ambitions, it was decided. Baron Alois von Aehrenthal, Goluchowski's successor, remarked:

> . . . even if we are able, by intervention in the Sanjak, to keep Serbia and Montenegro permanently apart we should still not have attained our main objective . . . to make our southern frontiers secure in case Turkey in Europe breaks up. We shall not obtain these secure frontiers until we decide to grasp the nettle firmly and make a final end to the pan-Slav dream.[3]

The appeal to economic swords was now deemed insufficient. The pan-Slav dream, it seemed, could only be ended, and the Monarchy made safe, by the use of other kinds of swords.

The inference was shocking, and it was certainly somewhat exaggerated. But there were increasing grounds for the serious loss of poise that was being evidenced in Vienna. The talent for conspiracy that Serbs had so clearly displayed in 1903 was more and more evident, and it was more and more evidently directed toward pan-Slav and against vital Austrian and Turkish interests. There was, for example, the remarkable little incident involving the attempt to murder the ruling Prince of Montenegro. Montenegro, small, obscure, mountainous, and wholly Serb in population, was at once the chief ally in the Serb national movement and the chief rival for leadership of it. For dark, domestic reasons, Prince Nicholas had made himself unpopular with some of his own people, who decided to kill him. They found aid, comfort, and bombs among influential circles in Serbia, particularly a group called the Yugoslav (South

3. Quoted in Vucinich, p. 229.

Slav) Club. They took their bombs to the Montenegrin capital of Cetinje, but the plot was discovered in time and Prince Nicholas was saved. The Montenegrins suspected, with some reason, the complicity of the Serbian government. In this suspicion they were greatly strengthened by incriminating information provided by an informer, who obligingly gave evidence that the Serbian Ministry of War had supplied the bombs. As it happened, the source of this information was the Austrian Intelligence Service, by whom the informer was employed. He was later unmasked, and the incident did little to make Austria more popular in either Belgrade or Cetinje, but the whole episode did show the extremes to which the Serb nationalists—and perhaps the Serbian government—were prepared to go in pushing their plans for Serb leadership of a South Slav Liberation Movement that would involve Montenegro, Macedonia, and the several provinces of the Habsburg Monarchy where South Slavs predominated. And it was a symbolic prophecy of a plot to be directed against another royal person nine years later in the interest of South Slav Liberation.

The Yugoslav Club was only one of many nationalist societies that were beginning to flourish in Serbia and to spread across its borders. Some of them were born out of the 1903 assassination conspiracy and were led by veterans of that heroic slaughter. Others were mainly student groups. A few were undoubtedly being patronized by the government. But none of this would have been fatal to Austro-Serb relations had it not been for the exacerbations of the Pig War and for the impact that the noisy pan-Serbism was having within the Monarchy. In 1905 there were, for example, two meetings of South Slav politicians in the Monarchy, at Fiume and Zara on the Adriatic, which demanded full rights of self-government for the Austrian Slavs and an end to the dual system that enabled the Magyars to oppress them. It was not surprising that the government at Vienna should begin to contemplate extreme measures.

Extreme measures were about to be taken, and their outcome showed that the Serbs, if unaided, were helpless in the political and military counterpart of the pressures they had successfully resisted in the economic sphere. The lesson was quickly learned in Vienna; there was no point in wasting time on economic pressures.

In the autumn of 1908, the long Bosnian crisis began. It was to illuminate the existing tensions and realities, and to produce new ones.

Bosnia

The architects of the Bosnian crisis were the foreign ministers of Russia, Alexander Izvolsky, and of Austria-Hungary, Alois von Aehrenthal. They were both new to power, having been appointed in 1906. They were both, although in different ways, professionally ambitious. They were both convinced that spirited policies, policies of "movement," were desirable—indeed indispensable both to the interests of their states and to the furtherance of their own careers. The result of their activities was to intensify enormously the conflicts and dangers of the European situation and to bring Europe to the verge of a war that was averted only by the painful retreat and humiliation of two of the parties to the controversy.

It was odd that the events that were to destroy the 1897 agreement, bring an end to the period of relative Austro-Russian harmony in the Balkans, and lead to an irreconcilable animosity between the two empires, had their origin in what seemed to be the most promising effort yet made in the direction of collaboration. So far, in the ten years that it had lasted, the agreement of 1897 had been entirely negative in its effects. But now, quite aside from the presence of the new and bold foreign ministers, there were reasons for change.

In Russia, the reasons were simple and painful. The defeat by Japan had battered both its armies and its prestige. It would be years before Russian military power was sufficient to any large international adventures. For the restoration of the government's authority at home there seemed necessary some gauge of its authority abroad. Despite recent unpleasant experiences, it seemed that the invocation of national unity in a great diplomatic gesture would prove the most reliable of medicines for the curing of domestic maladies. The theory, as events six years later demonstrated, might sometimes be correct; when the medicine finally was administered, after the rehabilitation of the armies, the sickness of internal disunity and turmoil was relieved, although there were side effects that had the unfortunate result of killing the patient. In Izvolsky's case, however, the therapy suffered from the mistaken belief that diplomatic triumphs could be attained without a reliable military force—and the mistake was a bad one.

The Austrian case was somewhat similar. There was a comparable sort of desperation, a belief that an "active" foreign policy was necessary to reverse the slow attrition of Austrian solidity and prestige. The safeguarding of solidity seemed to require the elimination of what the Austrian chief of staff, Baron Franz Conrad von Hötzendorf, called "the dangerous nest of vipers," by which he meant Serbia. Not everybody in Austria agreed with this, and almost nobody agreed on just how the vipers could most conveniently be exterminated, but there was a feeling that something had to be done. And prestige, they thought, also required it. The effects of a passive foreign policy had been to raise doubts abroad as to the Habsburg Monarchy's capacity to take effective action, or any action at all. Once again, the painful parallels with Turkey were influencing opinion. The Austrians had begun to think of themselves as the new Sick Man of Europe, and they thought a demonstration of vigor might dispel the notion. After the action had been taken, one Austrian diplomatic cheerfully and revealingly wrote, "The sick man no longer drags out his existence, but rather has in a few months become a powerful factor in European politics."

The needs were similar and, Izvolsky and Aehrenthal felt, urgent. They also seemed to be compatible. The most telling success that the Russians could hope for, without military power, was the opening of the Straits to Russian warships. This ancient aspiration would mean that Turkey would permit Russian ships to pass freely through their territorial waters between Europe and Asia, converting the Black Sea into a sort of Russian lake open to Russia but closed to everyone else. It would be (though this was of course not mentioned publicly) a new step toward the strengthening of Russian influence at Constantinople. It would give the Russians a "position" in the Mediterranean. The French ally might be expected to acquiesce. The traditional enemy, Britain, might now be prepared to consider it, in view of the recently contrived entente. If Austria could be bribed, bargained with, blackmailed, then . . . So ran Izvolsky's train of thought.

The Austrians had their own ambitions, and they now revived, in altered form, the scheme proposed by Goluchowski in 1897. They wanted to annex Bosnia and Hercegovina. This step might, objectively considered, seem rather pointless, since they already occupied and administered the provinces. It might also be regarded as hazardous and illegal, since it meant upsetting the 1878 Treaty of Berlin, which all the Powers had signed. The official excuse was that, since coming under Austrian control in 1878, the provinces had progressed so rapidly in material prosperity and domestic tranquility that they were now ready to enjoy the blessings of "self-government," which would be bestowed under the beneficient sway of Habsburg sovereignty. The real reasons were, of course, quite different. They reflected the appetite for solidity and prestige. Solidity, it was thought, would be served by formally incorporating the two provinces into the Monarchy. They were overwhelmingly populated by persons of Serb nationality, and as long as they remained technically under Turkish rule, the Serbs of Serbia might hope to acquire them when the day of Turkey's final disintegration came; to that end, a good deal of Serbian propaganda and secret organization had been directed. Prestige, Aehrenthal considered, would also be served, by a "positive" gesture. Some action, any action, that displayed vigor and resolution would bolster the image of the Monarchy as a state still capable of exercising authority and making its weight felt. In fact, it was Austria-Hungary's deep inability to agree on any constructive policy that forced it to adopt a meaningless one.

As early as 1906, Aehrenthal and Izvolsky had been in touch about the possibility of striking a bargain: Austria would support the opening of the Straits if Izvolsky would support the annexation of Bosnia. In the greatest secrecy the negotiations continued. It was agreed by Austria that to keep the Turks and the Serbs and the Montenegrins from making a scene, certain concessions would be made. The province of Novibazar, occupied (but *not* administered) since 1878, would be evacuated by Habsburg garrisons—a drastic change from the 1897 scheme. Certain Austrian controls on the Montenegrin coast would be abandoned. A private deal was arranged with the Bulgarian Prince, Ferdinand, that Austria would support a declaration of Bulgarian independence (Bulgaria was still, like Bosnia, technically under Turkish sovereignty) and the assumption by the Prince of the title of King.

Izvolsky had practically committed himself by the summer of 1908. He had not consulted, apparently, with his colleagues or his sovereign; at least they were not completely in his confidence. He certainly had not consulted with the Serbs, who were bound to be appalled. He seems to have been foolishly overconfident about securing the approval of the Powers for the opening of the Straits, although he doubtless felt that approval for the annexation of Bosnia would be at least as hard to get, so that at most he would lose nothing. In any case, by July of 1908 a general basis for agreement between the two foreign ministers was beginning, in a leisurely way, to emerge. Its completion and execution would require a final working out of details.

The courses of Austro-Russian diplomacy were at this juncture drastically altered by external events. A revolution took place in Turkey.

It is not necessary to inquire in any detail (the reader will be relieved to learn) into the Turkish domestic situation and the *coup* that took place in July of 1908. The government of Turkey was an obsolete tyranny exercised by an unattractive Sultan, Abdul Hamid, who had maintained himself in power and, to the greatest extent possible, preserved his empire by making humiliating deals.

with foreign powers and then, when conditions permitted, betraying them. The revolutionaries, whose name became a phrase of common usage in the English language, were called "Young Turks." They were determined to arrest the decay. They were ardent nationalists, very secular in their outlook (Turkey was run as a Moslem theocracy, the Sultan also holding the position of Caliph, which corresponded roughly to that of Pope in the Roman Church). They were enthusiastic Westernizers and reformers. They were young and able as well as enthusiastic. They promised to rebuild the government and to meet the demands of the Christian populations in the European provinces.

The Young Turk revolution had remarkable effects. Almost no one in the vicinity was pleased; the recovery of the Sick Man of Europe was an upsetting idea to his heirs, the Balkan states. To the Austrians (who might some years earlier have been encouraged by the possible revivification of the fellow sick man, whose integrity they had generally regarded as important to their own), the change in the existing order south of their borders now seemed both threatening (they did not want the Balkan states to profit) and promising (here was an opportunity, now that the situation was fluid, to push the annexation of Bosnia). This step was decided upon in August.

It was desirable to wind up hurriedly the negotiations with Izvolsky. He was taking the waters in Germany in September, and was cordially invited to meet Aehrenthal at a castle in Moravia, in a village called Buchlau. There, over afterdinner drinks, the details of a bargain were agreed to. At least, it was thought at the time that they were agreed to. What was decided was not written down at the time, and subsequent versions differed broadly.

Izvolsky in any event immediately set about to secure, in person, agreement to the opening of the Straits. When he got to Paris, on September 30, he received word that the Austrians would proclaim the annexation of Bosnia a week later. He does not seem to have responded with any overwhelming astonishment, which may suggest that the date had, in fact, been agreed to at Buchlau. But frustration awaited him; while Austria was receiving delivery of the ordered goods, Izvolsky was receiving disappointments. The French were extremely cool about the Straits project, and the British cooler still. The British Foreign Minister, Sir Edward Grey, observed that he would be happy to consider opening the Straits to *all* warships—an assertion that was quite likely persiflage—but that opening them to Russia alone was out of the question. At this point, Izvolsky turned nasty.

Realizing that he would not get the Straits, he also realized that his own position had become hazardous, if not absurd. He had given something for nothing. His own government was startled and perturbed by the annexation. The Turks were in a rage. The Serbs were in a frenzy. The Austrians had won a success that now could only be interpreted as a Russian failure. Izvolsky's reaction was to assert that he had been duped and to denounce Austria as an aggressor and Aehrenthal as a liar. His vituperation knew no bounds. Aehrenthal was of Jewish ancestry, and Izvolsky was an anti-Semite. "The dirty Jew," he cried to the German Chancellor when he reached Berlin, "has deceived me. He lied to me, he bamboozled me, that frightful Jew."[4]

His response was ill judged. He may possibly have been deceived about the timing, but there was ample documentary evidence that he had cordially agreed, and over a long period of time, to the principle. The Austrians had now only to publish the record of his personal negotiations with Aehrenthal to ruin him. Izvolsky's previous willingness to agree to the annexation he now so virulently denounced laid him wide open to a form of blackmail upon which the peace of the world hung.

For war now became a very real danger. This was mainly the result of the reaction in Belgrade, which was even stronger than might have been anticipated. There were howls of rage in the press —and in the streets. There was talk of an invasion of Bosnia. There was the most open expression yet of the sentiment that Austria-Hungary was the implacable foe of all South Slavs and must be destroyed to ensure their freedom and their destiny. There were

4. Bülow, *Memoirs*, II, 440.

impassioned pleas to other powers. The Serbian Crown Prince was dispatched to Saint Petersburg to plead with the Russian Emperor for aid.

It was not really expected that the Serbs would attack Austria. It would have been suicidal to do so, and while there was some thought in Belgrade that martyrdom would have the advantage of bringing the "Serb problem" to the attention of the Powers, and possibly of forcing a "solution" by a general war in which Austria-Hungary would be defeated and destroyed, this was not seriously contemplated. The government, while adopting a posture of martyrdom, anticlimactically modified it with demands for territorial compensations from Austria. Such a demand was at least negotiable. The real danger came from the possibility that the Austrians would take the occasion of the Serbian fervor to attack Serbia. The "Serb problem" would, they seriously considered, find a "solution" through the defeat and destruction of Serbia. There was a good deal of attention given to the possibility of partitioning Serbia between Austria and Bulgaria.

The crisis lasted—officially, as it were—from October of 1908 to March of 1909. During that time an attack on Serbia was the subject of constant debate in Vienna. Conrad von Hötzendorf was violently in favor. He was indeed in favor of attacking everybody in sight; he favored the "solution" of "the Italian problem" through a war against Italy too. His calculations, while wholesale, were not unsound. The attempt to protect the Monarchy through alliances with its neighbors had failed, and if the defeat of neighbors could solve the problems raised by their ambitions, then the time to attack was now, while Russia was still very weak. In January, a newspaper, the *Danzers Armee-Zeitung,* which was close to the Austrian high command, published a remarkable editorial which started out, "The hour has struck. War is inevitable." After recounting numerous grievances against Serbia, Russia, and Italy, it ended with: "Our blood throbs in our veins, we strain at the leash. Sire! Give us the signal!"[5] Aehrenthal himself toyed with far-reaching plans against

5. Luigi Albertini, *The Origins of the War of 1914* (London, 1952), I, 264.

the Serbs. But the pressures against it were strong. The Hungarian government was resolutely opposed to war and, as always, to annexing any more Slavic territories. The Heir Apparent, the Archduke Francis Ferdinand, was also opposed. The Emperor was extremely hesitant. Although at one point the agitation in Belgrade became so active that the Monarchy responded with plans for partial mobilization, Aehrenthal and his colleagues in the end agreed that war would be, for the moment, unnecessary and imprudent.

It was Austrian hesitancy, and that alone, which prevented war against Serbia. At first, nobody else did anything to stop it.

The news of the annexation had been initially received throughout Europe with astonishment and extreme irritation. Everyone thought Austria was behaving with impudence in violating the Treaty of Berlin. It is interesting to observe that nowhere was the response more exasperated than in Germany. The Emperor William, who like everybody else had been left unwarned of what was going to happen, was offended in his "deepest feelings as an Ally." Like Izvolsky, he felt he had been "duped, in a most unheard-of-fashion." He was particularly annoyed by the injury done to Turkey, whose friendship and support he had been sedulously cultivating as part of a large program of replacing British with German influence in Constantinople and establishing himself as the "Protector of the Moslem World." He was inclined to feel considerable sympathy for the Turks and even for the Russians.

But the German attitude changed, and so did that of everyone else except the Serbs and the Russians. In Italy, where there had been great annoyance, there developed a policy of trying to squeeze some compensating benefits out of Austria for the price of diplomatic support. In France, there was a good deal of sympathy for the Austrian position, a good deal of contempt for Izvolsky's folly, and a strong disinclination to get mixed up in the Balkan mess on behalf of an egregiously inept Russian politician. Everyone, including the English, felt that the Russians had brought their trouble on themselves. There developed, accordingly, a marked willingness to try to settle things.

Izvolsky's official response to the annexation had been to demand an international conference to discuss Austria's violation of her treaty obligations. This involved a great deal of discussion about terms and conditions, and had the advantage, from the Austrian point of view, of delaying any possible Russian response. After much equivocation, the Austrians and the Germans decided that they did not want a conference. Talk dragged on, the Serbs still agtiating furiously and the Russians still complaining.

By the middle of winter, however, certain things were clear. The most important was that Russia was not in a position to fight the Austrians. The second most important was that Russia's partners in the Triple Entente were not at all eager to go to war to support Russia. The time was ripe for a formula—and the Germans produced one. Let the Austrians negotiate a settlement with Turkey (which meant, in effect, let the Austrians bully the Turks into accepting the annexation) and then let the other Powers of Europe give their consent to the Austro-Turkish agreement as a form of revision of the Berlin Treaty. The legalities would be preserved, if only retroactively. A measure of face-saving for Russia would be provided.

The Russians demurred. It was then, on March 21, that Bülow produced his principle bludgeon. He threatened, among other things, that if Izvolsky did not accept the formula, and force the Serbs to do so as well, he (Bülow) would see to it that the Austrians published the ruinous secret correspondence between Izvolsky and Aehrenthal over the past two years. Izlovsky capitulated. The formula was agreed to. The Serbs were frightened into stating publicly that the annexation of Bosnia was of no concern to them and that they abandoned their claims to compensation. The crisis was over.

But a good deal had happened to inject new elements into the European situation. For one thing, the Russians were now able to present themselves as victims of German pressure. They had been given, they said, an ultimatum: Either surrender or face war. In fact, the German threat was not an ultimatum, and what was threatened was not war but mainly embarrassing revelations about Izvol-sky's conduct of affairs. But the threat was clear enough, and Russia's friends, particularly Sir Arthur Nicolson and the other Russophiles in the British diplomatic service, enthusiastically dis-seminated the theory that Germany had threatened offended Russia, and therefore the world, with war. This was extremely advanta-geous to the Russians and to the strength of the Entente. It was equally disadvantageous to Germany, which was made in the end to share the heaviest weight of blame for a crisis with whose coming it had had nothing whatever to do. The Austrians themselves recognized this. An Austrian diplomat happily wrote, even before the final German pressure had been applied on Russia: ". . . the strong indignation which, after the proclamation of the annexation, was directed against Austria-Hungary now turns in increased meas-ure against Berlin . . . the lion's share of the crisis itself is now laid at the door of the German Government."[6]

After the first World War, when the documents were published and the animosity against Germany in the allied countries had abated, there was a tendency to exculpate Germany by pointing out that its role had been more that of peacemaker than of warmonger. It is true that in some respects the Germans behaved as "honest brokers" in a situation not entirely different from that of 1878, and it is true that they never—contrary to Russian insistence—actually threatened military action. But it may be argued that such a threat was quite superfluous, given the degree of Russian impotence at the moment; and it may be definitely stated that the Germans were engaged in a policy of supporting Austria—to the bitterest of ends, if necessary—which made the question of the culpability a seman-tic one.

The fact was that, despite the initial reactions of William II, the German policy was evolving not only into unreserved support for Austria but of actual provocation. The policy was not unanimously, or even entirely consciously, planned. It was the product of inter-action among a determined and rather ferocious Secretary of State,

6. Berchtold; quoted in Albertini, I, 292–93.

Alfred von Kiderlen-Wächter; a military establishment nervous about the lack of precise planning for a war against Russia in support of Austria; the long preachments of Baron Holstein; the over-subtleties of Bülow, who was still acting in the belief that a strong line would split the Entente; the flamboyance of the Emperor (now rather muted as a result of the shocking political mess he had got embroiled in through *The Daily Telegraph* episode, which took place immediately after the Bosnian crisis broke); and a generally growing conviction in Berlin that Germany's only reliable ally must be shored up, no matter what the cost.

What this meant was the underwriting of Austria-Hungary as a Great Power, which meant in turn not merely the defense of its frontiers but the support of such aggressions as it might wish to take. It is remarkable how calmly, almost unreflectively, this was accepted as a policy in high places in Berlin. Already at the outset of the crisis, in October of 1908, it was observed that Russia was too weak to protect Serbia, should Austria care to use the occasion to attack the Serbs. Bülow explicitly told the German Ambassador at Vienna that Germany would not object to strong measures against the Serbs or to a partition of Serbia:

> The idea that . . . Serbia should be partitioned between Austria-Hungary and Bulgaria has no terrors for us. We should raise no objection if the merging of the existing Kingdom of Serbia in the Danubian Monarchy should bring the whole Serb people under the Habsburg sceptre. . . . The consideration of our alliance relationship imperatively demands that with Baron Aehrenthal we avoid all that might be capable of crossing him in this so vital question for Austria-Hungary.[7]

Aehrenthal, who had previously considered such a measure but had decided against it, was grateful for Bülow's support; if drastic measures were to be considered later, German support for them could be looked for.

But more than this was to be involved in German support for

7. *Die Grosse Politik der Europäischen Kabinette, 1871–1914* (hereinafter GP) III, 254; quoted in Albertini, I, 231.

Austria. Both countries realized that, in the event of a war, their military plans were insufficiently coordinated for comfort. It was necessary to make definite plans, and a minimal caution required planning for a maximal array of enemies. By January of 1909, conversations had begun between Conrad and Moltke, the Austrian and German chiefs of staff, and they envisaged simultaneous campaigns against Serbia, Russia, France, and Italy, whose loyalty to the Triple Alliance was now regarded as vestigial. In the course of the discussion, Moltke, like Bülow before him, emphasized the composure with which he would view an Austrian attack on Serbia: "It is to be foreseen that the time will come when the longanimity of the Monarchy in the face of Serb provocation will come to an end. Then nothing will remain but for her to enter Serbia."[8] And he proceeded to an equally calm appraisal of subsequent war with Russia. The support of Germany against Russia was taken as a matter of course.

There was no doubt that all this represented the culmination of a gradual change in the attitude of the Germans, which had once been one of caution in supporting Austrian ventures. The Near Eastern Question was now seen in Berlin as well worth the bones of the entire German Army. Nor was there any doubt that this abandonment of Bismarck's precept and dictum was the consequence of the evolving insecurity of the Habsburg Monarchy in the face of the "centrifugal" pressures of an aroused Slavdom and, at the same time, of Germany's encirclement.

This was one crucial consequence of the Bosnian crisis; it clarified and committed the Germany policy toward the Habsburg Monarchy, and set in course a military program for a war that might arise from an attack on Serbia. But it was not the only consequence. If the Germans, with more enthusiasm than was necessary, committed themselves to Austria, the Austrians were emboldened, spasmodically, to an even more positive policy against the Slav threat. They undertook to publicize the extent of the Serbian threats by forging a number of subversive documents

8. Franz Conrad von Hötzendorf, *Aus meiner Dienstzeit*, I, 379–84; quoted in Albertini, I, 270.

purporting to show the complicity of the Serbian government, and also of some Slav politicians within the Monarchy, in conspiracies to destroy it. They arrested and, through some high-handed judicial meddling, arranged the conviction of fifty-three Serbs within the Monarchy on charges of disseminating Yugoslav propaganda. Both measures were mistakes; the forgeries were revealed, and the case against the revolutionaries proved nothing except the pliability of the courts. Both measures discredited the government of the Habsburg Monarchy.

In Serbia and Russia there were effects scarcely less important. The Serbs, now violently and permanently inflamed and, also, painfully humiliated, organized still more nationalist societies, including one called "The People's Defense" (*Narodna Obrana*), which was to prove particularly energetic in provoking the Austrians. An even more dangerous organization appeared at the same time, the highly secret and conspiratorial group called *Union or Death* and known to its enemies as *The Black Hand*. It was led by a violent and slightly deranged colonel named Dragutin Dimitrievitch and a band of colleagues (including some of the regicides of 1903) of varying degrees of influence. Their ideas and their contacts were intertwined with many and powerful personages in Serbia. It is known that at times they were in touch with the King and the crown prince. Terrorism, propaganda, and conspiracy proliferated. Austria-Hungary was now universally regarded by Serbs as a deadly and implacable enemy. The government, itself expansionist, began to be violently attacked by the secret societies for being insufficiently so. And in Russia, the degree of animosity was scarcely less great. Izvolsky, although his reputation had been formally saved by conceding the German demands, still suffered from the disgrace of his surrender and his ineptitude. But the disgrace was felt to be a national one; and it was determined by many persons in high places that there must never again be such a surrender of Russian interests or such a betrayal of Russia's client Serbia. *The last chance of continuing the 1897 agreement, of reaching some adjustment of Russian-Austrian interests, was gone.*

THE LONG FUSE

A Sick Man Dies

The revolution of 1908 had promised, or threatened, a revivified Turkey. The threat miscarried. The Young Turks, being Turks and also being nationalists, found that their efforts to modernize the Empire annoyed the Christian populations and bred further trouble. They also found that the traditional routines of government—by cunning and corruption—were not easily changed, and that the traditional meddling of the Great Powers was not easily stopped. The Young Turks rapidly lost their illusions, their hopes, and their power.

The activities of the Balkan states, incessantly scheming for the liberation of their fellow nationals still languishing under the Turkish yoke, multiplied in the years that followed the Bosnian crisis. The best way to liberate the provinces remaining under the control of Ottoman Rule would be by cooperation among the interested governments: of Bulgaria, of Serbia, of Montenegro, and of Greece. But to this there were serious obstacles arising out of an almost total lack of agreement about what area pertained properly to which liberator. As usual, the core and the touchstone of the difficulty was Macedonia. There were, inextricably confused, Serb Macedonians, Bulgar Macedonians, Greek Macedonians, not to mention others, including a good many Turkish Macedonians, to whom nobody paid any attention. There were also strategic and economic considerations: Who, quite aside from nationality, should inherit the great port of Salonika? Who should inherit the great Turkish fortresses? To whom belonged the Adriatic sea coast, inhabited by a confusion of scattered groups, mainly tribal and Moslem, with its fortress towns of Scutari and Janina and its desirable harbors? There was also the problem of Thrace, which lay south of Bulgaria on the Aegean and whose population was so mixed as to defy computation; and there was the question of the great metropolis of Constantinople itself, which Greece, quite as passionately as Russia, and on grounds rather less speculative, regarded as its natural capital temporarily occupied by an alien regime for four and a half centuries. And there were other problems for the predators: Austria might reasonably be expected to oppose, and quite possibly to oppose by arms, the destruction of Turkey and the aggrandizement of its own natural enemies; Italy, with an increasing interest in Balkan affairs, might confidantly be expected to demand compensations—the Italians were developing an appetite, verging on the pathological, for Turkey's Adriatic port of Valona, which had once been Venetian—and there was, of course, Turkey itself. It was severely shaken and badly administered, but its army was still formidable and its population and resources vastly outweighed those of the Balkan states.

Encouragement to face and solve these problems came from Russia. Immediately after the Bosnian crisis, a new Russian minister had arrived in Belgrade. His appointment was intended to console the Serbs for their humiliation and injury and to restore confidence in Russia as a protector. He encouraged the nationalist operations of the Serbs and the secret societies. Of more immediate importance, he undertook to eliminate the obstacles to a quiet understanding among the Balkan states, looking toward the creation of an offensive alliance against Turkey. By the use of some diplomatic sleight of hand—in the form of a decision that, should Turkey be defeated, the allocation of the controversial liberated areas would be decided after the war—agreement was finally reached between Serbia and Bulgaria early in 1912. The Greeks and the Montenegrins, prudently approached, gave grounds for anticipating their participation in the attack on Turkey when the moment was ripe.

It ripened early, sooner than was expected. The opportunity came, rather strangely, as a result of the appearance in 1911 of a German battleship off the Moroccan port of Agadir. The background and aftermath of this incident are of no great interest in themselves: the Germans had sent the *Panther* as a strong-arm demonstration that French violations of the Algeciras Treaty would not be tolerated. The French had been expanding their influence and were now, at the request of the Sultan of Morocco, about to occupy the capital, Fez, on the ground that it was threatened by tribal invaders. But before the demonstration was made, Franco-German discussions of "compensation" for Germany had already been begun, and, after it, they followed their course without major complications, although to the accompaniment of angry outbursts from public opinion on both sides. Some rather uninviting territory in Central Africa was given to the Germans as compensation for the violations of the Algeciras Treaty, and the extension of French power in Morocco proceeded unhindered.

But the now open movement toward a French protectorate knocked down a Mediterranean domino. The Italians had for a generation been preparing for the acquisition of the two remaining Turkish provinces in North Africa: Cyrenaica and Tripolitania, known collectively as Libya, which lay across the Mediterranean from the Italian peninsula. These were mostly desert, largely uninhabited except by nomadic Arabs of great ferocity, and so far as anyone knew utterly without economic value. But the Italians had hankered after them ever since the French seizure of Tunisia, for reasons of strategic importance and (perhaps mainly) of prestige, although the government afterward claimed that large financial and commercial interests of Italian citizens were being imperiled by Turkish hostility and misrule. As early as 1887, in the negotiations for a renewal of the Triple Alliance, they had begun assuring themselves of German and Austrian approval of a Libyan venture. Great Britain had also given its approval, in return for Italian acceptance of the British occupation of Egypt. In 1900, the French had agreed to the project, in return for Italian support of the French venture in Morocco. In 1909, the Russians had agreed, in return for Italian promises to accept the opening of the Straits. Now, with the French cashing in in Morocco, the time had come for the Italians to seize Libya, and without either warning or pretext, an ultimatum was dispatched to Turkey in September, 1911, troops were landed, and Tripoli and Bengazi, the capitals, were occupied.

This small essay in colonialism might have passed over without incident had local resistance not been a good deal more vigorous than anyone expected. The war dragged on for more than a year.

The Turkish government forces were chased out of the towns, but the ferocious Arabs declined to accept the conquerors, and they waged a long and effective guerrilla operation. The Italians created a diversion by landing in Rhodes, a Turkish island in the eastern Mediterranean, and adjacent islands, but this in no way affected the power of the Turkish government or the Arab inhabitants in Libya. The Powers considered it likely (which was true) that the Italians intended to keep the island as well as Libya. There was a good deal of annoyance in the European capitals. In Vienna, among circles that regarded the Italians more as potential enemies than as allies, there was advocacy of a sudden attack, with the aim, as the more starry-eyed of the Austrians saw it, of recovering Lombardy and Venezia.

Less idiotic counsels prevailed. In the event, it was not embarrassed Italy but Turkey that was stabbed in the back. The Turks were heavily committed. In the summer of 1912 the occasion had been seized by various revolutionary groups to stage insurrections throughout Balkan Turkey, and in the capital itself, thus further weakening the government. The temptation was now very strong indeed; an arrangement between Greece and the Serb-Bulgar allies was hastily contrived, and in October of 1912 war was declared against the Turks by Montenegro, Serbia, Bulgaria, and Greece.

If the Italians had startled the world by the inadequacy of their war effort, the Balkan countries startled it even more by the extreme efficacy of theirs. The betting was, at the outset, rather strongly on the Turks. But there was a series of fantastic battles, in the first days of the war, and to the astonishment of everybody, including the victors, a single month's campaigning brought the Balkan armies to the gates of Constantinople, in full control of all Turkish territory in Europe except for the capital itself and the two major fortresses that still, besieged, held out; Scutari invested by the Montenegrins, and Janina by the Greeks, both in the mountains above the Adriatic.

The results were stunning as well as decisive. Not many campaigns in modern history against a major adversary had been so promptly, so completely, and so unexpectedly successful. In a month the whole balance of power in the Balkans and, therefore, in Europe, was changed. The Sick Man, whose painful malady had lasted for a hundred and fifty years, had suddenly been murdered. In Vienna there was, naturally, utter consternation; in Saint Petersburg there was a startled, and somewhat apprehensive, jubilation. Everywhere was the belief that a general war, so narrowly averted in 1909, would now take place. It seemed improbable that Austria-Hungary, which had been willing to precipitate a major crisis for the minor and gratuitous purpose of annexing Bosnia, should now hold back in the face of the loss of positions always previously described as vital; or that Russia, which would almost surely have been willing to fight in 1908 had its armies been strong enough, and had told the Serbs in that year that in eighteen months they would be fully prepared, would now abstain from the defense of interests always previously described as vital.

There were, in fact, both grounds and excuse for action by Austria-Hungary. The Serbs and their allies had, in violation of good manners and of legal obligations, been guilty of aggression. They were occupying, and clearly intended to retain, territories essential to Austria: the province of Novibazar, which had divided the Serb brothers in Serbia and Montenegro; the route to Salonika; the Albanian coast, so much coveted in Serbia. Drunk with triumph and more nationalistic than ever, they now would pose a military as well as a political threat to the Habsburg Monarchy. The entire defensive structure against Serb expansion had collapsed.

The crisis of 1908–09 was not, however, repeated. The Powers, including Russia and Austria-Hungary, all behaved in a manner that was, if not exactly calm, at least restrained. It seemed miraculous; in point of fact, it proved a catastrophe.

The reasons for the restraint of the Monarchy and of Russia lay in the personalities of the foreign ministers now in power. Aehrenthal had retired early in 1912 and died a few months later, to be succeeded by Count Leopold Berchtold. Izvolski had prudently exchanged his ministry for the Embassy at Paris, to be succeeded in 1910 by Sergei Sazonov. The contrast between the two sets of ministers was very great; instead of being ingenious, bold, and vain, as Aehrenthal and Izvolski had been, the new incumbents were tentative, vacillating, and conciliatory.

From the beginning, Russian policy in the year that followed the outbreak of the Balkan Wars was pacific, as well it might have been. Russia's battles were being fought and won by others, and all that was required was to guarantee the victories and to prevent, if at all possible, the intromission of outsiders, and particularly of Austria-Hungary, in a manner threatening or unfavorable to the victors. A Balkan coalition—leading perhaps toward a Balkan federation—was precisely what the Russians wanted most. When the alliance broke down six months after the victories, the Russians were distressed but not despondent. They were undertaking a policy of wooing the remaining Balkan power, Rumania, which had been uninvolved in the first Balkan War. They sent the Emperor Nicholas on a visit to Bucharest and produced a suitable Grand Duchess as a possible bride for the Rumanian Crown Prince. The Russians were leading from strength now and were emboldened to courtships. They were also able to appear as pacifiers and appeasers, and in the protracted negotiations among the Powers which were designed to bring peace, butter would not melt in Russian mouths.

The position of the Habsburg Monarchy was much less agreeable, and its policy was both less consistent and less effective. A good many people expected that the original attack on Turkey would produce a violent, perhaps armed, reaction, as a number of influential Austrians hoped. It might have, had the position of Vienna been slightly different. Aside from the presence of Berchtold, new to his job and indecisive, there was, secondly, the extreme rapidity of the (from the Austrian standpoint) disaster. There was also a curious and costly fact: Aehrenthal, for all his audacity and aggressiveness, had as part of the general Bosnian project abandoned the occupation of Novibazar. It is odd that he had not only offered this as a concession to Russia during the negotiations but, after the agreement with Russia had been abandoned, still insisted on the evacuation by Austrian troops. It was a loss of a real position, conceded without much cause, in exchange for the achievement of the purely formal transfer of sovereignty in Bosnia and Hercegovina. And now this oddity was a serious disadvantage; if Austria had been still in the province, it could have prevented the union of Serb and Montenegrin forces and exerted a powerful influence in the crucial regions west toward the Adriatic and south toward the Aegean. A wage and warranty had been thrown away, and it could not be recovered without invasion.

There were, moreover, important elements in the Austro-Hungarian governments strongly opposed to adventures. These included the Emperor, who was elderly and cautious, and who retained from his memory of military misfortunes in the 1860's a very lively distrust of gambling on battlefields. There was the Heir to the Throne, the Emperor's newphew, Archduke Francis Ferdinand, inclined to be sympathetic to the Slavs and strongly opposed to the Magyars; he therefore hoped for the conciliation of the Slavs within the Monarchy and possibly for a South Slav state to which the Serbs might one day be persuaded to adhere— a view that met of course with the cast-iron opposition of the Magyars. (Francis Ferdinand was realistic, if nothing else; he was prepared to face the need for subduing and dismembering the kingdom of Hungary by force.) Moreover, the prime ministers of both Austria and Hungary, when consulted, expressed extreme reluctance to consider an invasion of Serbia in support of Turkey. There was opposition to this inactivity, mainly now as always from the chief of staff, Conrad von Hötzendorf. But Conrad and the military circles that supported him were canceled out by more cautious voices and by Berchtold's own vacillation in the first few weeks; and by the end of those weeks, the situation of Turkey made it almost impossible to contemplate military action except of a punitive nature and on the largest scale.

Once the outcome of the war was clear, the Austro-Hungarian

position was both embarrassing and uncertain. One point the people in Vienna could agree upon, and, apparently, only one: that Serbia, having won its war, must under all circumstances be denied its outlet to the sea. It is difficult to see why, in view of the extent of the disaster, this bulked so large in Austrian minds. Commercially and strategically, a port on the Adriatic would not significantly have enhanced the power of a Serbia that was bound to be enormously inflated anyhow, especially in view of the outcome of the Pig War. Moreover, there was now some halfhearted disposition to try to lock the stable door, along the lines of Francis Ferdinand's precepts, by trying to conciliate the Serbs with the hope of luring the entire kingdom into the Monarchy in the future; and it was perfectly well known that the Serbs were as passionately desirous of securing their seaport as the Austrians were of withholding it, so that this insistence upon a token demand could only destroy what slight hopes a policy of reconciliation might hold out. It seems plausible to conclude that the Habsburg government, taken by surprise, intensely vexed, and badly defeated in its struggle to contain the Serbs, felt obliged to make one demand, however inconvenient and insignificant, and to make it stick. In the interminable international negotiations that followed, it was to this point that Austria-Hungary clung, and while this tenacity involved endless crises and difficulties it was, in the end, effective.

Meanwhile, the attitudes of the major allies of both Russia and Austria were developing in quite different ways. While the two empires most intimately concerned were inclined to policies pacific or at least dilatory, the Germans and the French were more bellicose.

Berchtold, after the Turkish defeat when he was confronted with charges of weakness and ineptitude at home, was inclined to put the blame for his failure on the Germans by suggesting that Berlin had warned him against an active policy. But this was disingenuous; the reverse was more nearly true, although German policy was unclear. Having been taken by surprise by the annexation of 1908, Berlin had warned against *faits accomplis* but was very free with advice as to what the Austrians ought to do, and most of this advice was in the direction of a strong stand, both before and after the Turkish defeat. At times William II was inclined to grandiose and quite unrealistic proposals for a Balkan federation to be presided over by the Habsburgs and to other even more chimerical notions, and the new Chancellor, Theobald von Bethmann-Hollweg, on one occasion dismally told the Austrians that a war against Serbia would probably lead to a general European war. But in general the inconsistent advice from Berlin favored some drastic measure against Serbia to "preserve the Monarchy as a Great Power." On several occasions the German messages to the government at Vienna were both categorical and extreme.

The attitude of Germany was not surprising; it represented no considerable change from the line that had been taken in 1909. More surprising was the attitude of the French toward their Russian ally. This was something new, and in a way it was a complement to the German policy toward Austria. Both Powers were now inclined to urge their allies to take strong and even warlike stands in the defense of their interests. The two alliances, both in theory and, in the past, in practice, purely defensive, were now being broadly interpreted to include promises of military support under all circumstances.

In 1908, the French had expressed great hesitation in supporting the Russians in their policy of hostility toward Austria. In 1912, they were actually egging the Russians on. The principal reason for change was a new administration in France, along with some domestic political disputes and a new diplomatic calculation. Raymond Poincaré became Prime Minister and Foreign Minister in 1912, after having occupied other posts in the Cabinet. He was a conservative and vigorous nationalist, a man of provincial rather than cosmopolitan outlook, a native son of Lorraine, the province partly lost to Germany in 1871. In contrast to most recent leaders, he was inclined to revive the dream of *revanche*, of a successful war against Germany to be followed by the recovery of Alsace and

Lorraine. French foreign policy in the past decade had been highly
successful, but as directed by the liberal-minded politicians who
controlled the government it had looked toward security rather than
revenge. Now, with Poincaré, an altered tone appeared in France.
Articles called things like "The Decisive Hour" appeared in the
rightist press, and militant demands for action to recover the lost
provinces were once again heard. The bellicosity mounted steadily.
A witness of the Paris scene in 1913 might well have found that
aggressiveness was expressing itself in ways quite as strident, widespread, and irresponsible as in Germany or Austria-Hungary.

   This was due to more than Poincaré's personal militancy, although he helped to translate it into policy by such appointments as
that of a new ambassador to Saint Petersburg, the very aggressive
Maurice Paléologue, who tried to make both the French and Russian governments take a more "positive" view of the Franco-Russian
alliance. It was also the product of a long-simmering inclination
to violent measures that after 1910 boiled over in France, as in so
many parts of Europe. There was fear of the growing power of
socialism, parts of it passionately revolutionary and anti-national,
which evoked corresponding ferocity on the nationalist Right. There
was the heritage of the Dreyfus Affair, which had at once frustrated
the Right and made it more extreme. There was a new interest in
Alsace-Lorraine, provoked by growing and rather gratuitous pro-
French agitation there which sought actively and successfully to
mobilize French opinion and was met with ill-judged harshness by
the German authorities. Most of all there was, in 1913, a passionate national controversy about a bill to extend the period of military
training from two to three years. This touched off an uproar, and
the "old" France, army officers, royalists, angry chauvinists of all
kinds, contrived a very new sort of demagoguery to galvanize the
country into action. A London newspaper observed in 1913 that the
"soul of France" was being reborn, and if the soul of France consisted of frenzied militarism this was perhaps true for a large part
of the nation. The rebirth emboldened the government to press
more active measures on Russia during and after the Balkan Wars.

   Turkey, having lost everything in Europe except the capital and the fortresses, agreed on December 3, 1912, to a cease-fire. The Powers, at the initiative of Great Britain, called a conference of ambassadors in London to assist in the arrangement of a peace. It was eventually signed in May, 1913, and was disrupted by a new war within the month.

The principal problem was Albania. The name was associated with no definite area, but it lay along the sea coast where the Serbs hoped to have their port. The Austrians, determined to thwart them, and the Italians, eager to expand their influence with an eye to Valona (Vlonë), demanded an independent Albania, and this was in principle early agreed upon. But its boundaries remained difficult to determine in view of Serbian obstinacy and of Greek claims to the south. In Scutari (in the north of what Austria regarded as Albania and the west of what Serbia regarded as Serbia) the Turks were still holding out. When it fell to the Serbs and the Montenegrins, it looked as if Serbia would have its way and establish a corridor to the sea. Then they could not be ousted without a war. The Austrians, now facing the surrender on their final line of diplomatic defense, would be obliged to choose between a disastrous humiliation and a general war. But this time they were rescued by the Russians. Sazonov, fully understanding the gravity of the situation, intervened to restrain the victorious Serbs and Montenegrins. They reluctantly agreed to evacuate the area, their thirst further whetted but once again unslaked.

But the whole question was soon reopened, and a new chapter of embarrassments awaited Austria-Hungary after the peace was signed. Even while the war had been at its most violent phase, the Bulgars were deep in disputes with both the Greeks and the Serbs. They were voracious in their appetite for territory; so, almost equally, were their allies, and since no delineation of boundaries had been agreed in advance, tensions among the victors were very acute. The Austrians encouraged them, believing that a friendly Bulgaria would help offset an inimical Serbia. And now the Bulgars were much put out by the terms of peace they were obliged by the Powers to accept on May 30. For a month they brooded and then, at the end of June, attacked the Serbs without warning. In Vienna there was rejoicing, and hopes that the Serb triumphs might now be annulled at no cost to Austria-Hungary. Once again, as in their hopes the previous year for a Turkish victory, they were rapidly and decisively disappointed. The Montenegrins and the Greeks, the latter eager for the territories that Bulgaria had just sullenly acquired, joined the Serbs. So did the Rumanians, who had ambitions of their own in northeastern Bulgaria. So, not surprisingly, did the Turks, who recovered to the extent of threatening the recently lost fortress of Andrianople, which covered approaches to the capital. Bulgaria was promptly defeated.

It is probable that Berchtold would have liked this time to go to the aid of the Bulgars, whom he may have encouraged in their original attack on Serbia. This time his allies restrained him; it was clear to the Germans and the Italians that the moment was inopportune and the cause—support for an imprudent and barefaced aggressor—poor. In any case, as in the previous autumn, the campaigns were too promptly decisive to give Austria-Hungary much time to engage in the ponderous process of making up its dual mind. Things were back to the point they had been before, except that Austria's position was even worse, the Serbs stronger and more brash. The negotiations in London resumed, and dragged on painfully, to the boredom and alarm of everybody.

The Serbs, confronted with interminable discussions by foreigners about just how much of the territory they had conquered they should be allowed to keep, now ran out of patience. In October, they flatly refused to end their occupation of the most tender of all the numerous areas in dispute: northern Albania, with its inviting view of the Adriatic coast. The conference in London had drawn up boundaries for a state of Albania and had supplied it with a prince acceptable to the Austrians, an impoverished German nobleman named William of Wied. But the Serbs pointed out, with some reason, that the boundaries were purely theoretical, since nobody knew anything about the nature of the terrain, and said that they would just remain in occupation of the new principality until surveys had been made upon the spot.

The Serbs having run out of patience, the Austrians now at last lost their tempers. For once, opinion in Vienna was united; even the Hungarians were disposed to feel that something must now be done in the way of taking a strong stand. The Serbs had put themselves in the wrong with the Powers; and at this juncture a strong stand would raise none of the long-range problems about an "ultimate solution" of the South Slav problem which had prevented any previous agreement on what steps to take. An ultimatum was dispatched to Belgrade; Belgrade, once again cheated, humiliated, and abandoned by its patron Russia, gave in. Albania was evacuated. A second peace treaty was signed.

Everyone was thoroughly discontent. The Turks had recovered Adrianople (now called Edirne) but little else. The Bulgars ended up with net gains of territory, including an outlet to the Thracian coast, but far, far less than they wanted, and far less than they had gotten by the first treaty. The Greeks had done extremely well—they had acquired western Thrace and Salonika, which was their main objective—but they had been frustrated in eastern Thrace, and in southern Albania, which they called Epirus and regarded as Greek. The Serbs were in a rage; victorious, they were thwarted in their main objective. The Russians were also battered in their egos; once again, as in 1909, they had been obliged to desert their small Serb friend. They promised not to do it again. Sazonov was constrained to raise Serbian morale by writing the fatal words, "Serbia's promised land lies in the territory of present-day Hungary."[9] The words were designed, at the moment, to distract the Serbs from expanding in other directions, but they constituted a program and even a proposal. And they were accompanied, on other occasions, by solemn promises of support for future aspirations.

And Austria-Hungary, above all, was in a state of tension, anger, and disarray. Berchtold, violently criticized for his ineptitude, had in effect sworn to himself, his colleagues, and his German ally that he would permit no further surrenders. It was clear to almost everyone now that Serbia, having become an irreconcilable enemy,

9. Quoted in Albertini, I, 486.

was also an extremely dangerous one. In Vienna, there was a general tendency to consider frantically what could be done to save the Monarchy from the small jackal venemously nipping at its Achilles heel. Almost nobody questioned the wisdom of doing something rapidly and drastically, at the first opportunity. The only strong and consistent opponent of measures against the Serbs was the Heir to the Throne, the Archduke Francis Ferdinand.

The action taken in 1908 had been imprudent and inadequate; it had infuriated South Slavs both within and without the Empire and outraged the Russians, without conferring any durable advantage on the Habsburg Monarchy. The inaction of 1912 and 1913 was equally regrettable in its effects. The difficulty of taking any adequate steps to maintain the Monarchy and its prestige had been thoroughly illuminated. This difficulty arose, it was clear, from the very situation that made such steps necessary.

The Second Sick Man Sinking

And so, after the end of the second Balkan War, the Habsburg statesmen felt that something had to be done—the statement was endlessly repeated. Berchtold had come near to discrediting himself through his weakness and his inaction. The one success had been the withholding of the seaport from Serbia. This solved nothing; it merely aggravated the Serbs. And the aggravation was reflected in a growing Serb nationalist movement, which rapidly extended its activities in the Monarchy.

It is difficult to appraise the gravity of the situation among the South Slavs. There is no question that a desire for change was spreading. There were already Serb nationalist parties, respectable, open, and more or less devoted to legal methods, in Bosnia and Hercegovina, and there were nationalist Croat and Slovene parties in the legislative bodies at Zagreb (the capital of Croatia) and at Vienna. The South Slav *idea*—the notion that the related nationalities of Slovenes, Croats, and Serbs ought someday all to be brought together from their various sovereignties into one political unit—

was growing. It was, however, an idea that had supporters among very respectable and loyal people in Vienna, who wanted them all united under the Habsburg crown. It was not in itself subversive, although almost *any* proposal for any change of any sort within the structure of the Monarchy tended to shake it and to breed violent enmities, no matter how loyal its sponsors.

What mattered most urgently, from the point of view of the authorities in Vienna and Budapest, was the spread of specifically Serb nationalist activities aimed at destroying the Monarchy and attaching its southwestern provinces to Serbia, and these were also growing after 1908. In that year, as noted above, there had been founded something called *Narodna Obrana*. It was publicly organized and included a number of high officials of the Serbian government, and it was ostensibly devoted to encouraging cultural and national activities within the kingdom. In point of fact, however, it also encouraged para-military activities, and devoted a good deal of its efforts to building up communications with like-minded groups in Bosnia and Hercegovina. Activists were smuggled back and forth, propaganda disseminated, training groups organized.

Naturally, there was violence. A boy named Zerayich, from Hercegovina, who had been trained in revolver practice by a Serbian Army officer, tried in 1910 to shoot the Bosnian governor and, after failing, committed suicide. He was acclaimed openly in Belgrade, as a hero and a martyr, and the Serbian press made no secret of its complete sympathy with his effort to wipe out the agent of Habsburg rule. Bosnian youths of the nationalist persuasion were given to laying wreaths on his tomb.

Wreath-laying proved insufficiently stimulating, however, for the bolder spirits of *Narodna Obrana;* increasingly the attractive and important outfit was the highly secret group of ex-assassins called Union or Death, or The Black Hand. It was growing more powerful, more active, and more ramified every day, although its existence was unknown to the Austro-Hungarian authorities, an illuminating comment on the huge but inefficient intelligence system they maintained. Union or Death combined the more unattractive features of the anarchist cells of earlier years—which had been responsible for quite a number of assassinations in Europe and whose methods had had a good deal of influence via the writings of Russian anarchists upon Serbian youth—and of the Ku Klux Klan. There were gory rituals and oaths of loyalty, there were murders of backsliding members, there was identification of members by number, there were distributions of guns and bombs. And there was a steady traffic between Bosnia and Serbia. Men and arms and ideas passed the border secretly but in copious flow, and the feverish excitement of the terrorists communicated itself to a number of Bosnian youths, most of them frustrated, poor, dreary, and maladjusted.

Mounting agitation was met first with repression when in 1912 the Habsburg authorities imposed on Bosnia a series of strenuous repressive laws, and then, a year later, with conciliation, when the laws were suspended and civil liberties restored. It was uncertain, in fact, how the situation could have best been handled, and it was equally uncertain how serious it was. Nobody doubted, what was true, that highly placed Serbian personages were associated with *Narodna Obrana*. Nobody doubted that the movement was spreading and that it was potentially a serious threat to Austria-Hungary. But the threat was not immediate; terrorism, even when widespread, does not cause successful revolutions, and in fact there was no reason to suppose that anything but a small percentage of the population—and that consisting mostly of juvenile delinquents—was involved in the terrorist activities. If the kingdom of Serbia had not existed to protect the terrorists, the threat would have been negligible. But Serbia did exist, and enjoyed the friendly support of Russia; so the threat could not be dismissed as negligible.

The result was extravagance and annoyance in Vienna. The reaction almost certainly exceeded the cause for alarm, but there was now some basis for supposing that the whole vast structure of the Monarchy was about to blow up.

The representations of General Conrad von Hötzendorf were

more strident and more apposite than ever: the South Slav problem must be "solved," which for him meant invasion. The German Emperor and some of the German statesmen were making clear their belief that the interests of both powers also demanded a solution. The mind of William II was fertile with vast and puerile projects, the most rational of which, proposed in October of 1913, was that the Serbian government should be bribed into biddable amity by money payments and the promise of large commercial advantages.

The most practical proposal, and one that commanded large support in Vienna, was to set about strengthening Bulgaria and converting it into an ally. A strong and allied Bulgaria would create a new balance of power in the Balkans; Serbian activities could be constrained by the threat of Bulgarian action. The King of Bulgaria, Ferdinand, was accessible to such proposals. His own position had been badly affected by the imprudence of June, 1912, which had been partly his personal scheme. But there were grave obstacles. For one thing, Bulgaria was unfortunately a democracy, and elections were held in December in which the left, which was equally hostile to Austria and to Russia, won strikingly. The new government was not very accessible to proposals to convert itself into a Habsburg pawn, although common prudence, and the influence of the King, kept the possibility of negotiations with Austria open. The second obstacle was Rumania.

Rumania was becoming a problem for Austria-Hungary and for reasons that singularly illuminate the difficulties that the government faced in conducting its foreign affairs. One part of the problem was purely international: Rumania, which had joined in the war against Bulgaria the previous summer and picked up some coveted territory in the Danube delta, was an ally of Austria-Hungary; while it remained one, Bulgaria was likely to be cool to an Austrian alliance. But beyond this diplomatic fact, which patience and tact might in time have overcome, was a deeper and much more intractable tissue of facts. There were Rumanians within the Monarchy—some three and a quarter million of them

—and their future was of very immediate concern to Rumanian public opinion and to some Rumanian politicians. The resulting situation was never as acute as the comparable situation with the Serbs owing partly to the sympathetic attitude of the Rumanian King. Still, it was growing worse, and the ability of King Carol I to maintain the link with Austria-Hungary was underminded by several facts. First, the alliance was secret, which meant that the public and the politicians supposed Rumania had a free hand and would have been angered if they had found out differently; second, the Russians were busily and effectually courting Rumania and making covert promises to support Rumanian claims on Transylvania, where most of the languishing brothers resided; and third, the Hungarians, in whose kingdom Transylvania lay, were treating the languishing brothers with an increasing degree of severity and repression. Count Ottokar Czernin, one of the most clear-headed of Austrian diplomats, was sent to Bucharest to try to overcome the obstacles. He immediately perceived that they were insuperable, at least as long as the Hungarian government continued to maltreat its Rumanian subjects. He told his government that Rumania could not be counted upon as an ally; the prospect of a future coalition of Russia, Rumania, Serbia, and Montenegro united to destroy the Monarchy was beginning to open up before the dazed spectators in Vienna. The sense of urgency, naturally, mounted.

These and other matters occupied the winter and spring of 1914. There was trouble, too, in newly created Albania, where tribal factions imprisoned the unfortunate William of Wied in his capital. The Montenegrins and the Serbians were openly discussing the possibility of uniting their countries in a federation. In response to this harrowing prospect, William II proposed in April to Vienna the confiscation of the Montenegrin sea coast, to be given as a present to Albania. This, he said, would force the Serbians to turn to Austria-Hungary. The Austrians considered the project, but it was found that Italy, which had its own eye on Albania, would not permit a common frontier between that principality and the

Habsburg Monarchy. At least, the Italians said, they would have to be given the Austrian province of Trent, largely inhabited by Italians, in compensation.

The proposal was wholly unrealistic in any event, but the response of the Italians was, like the position of the Rumanians, illuminating. The Monarchy's diplomatic initiative was everywhere frustrated by neighbors (at least *some* of whom had to be conciliated), who wanted portions of its territory inhabited by their co-nationals. The fact was quite sufficient to explain the climaxing desperation in Vienna.

The situation grew worse in every area. Serbian activities in Bosnia and Hercegovina were more noticeable and more ominous. In early June of 1914, the Emperor and Empress of Russia paid a state visit to Rumania and at the seaside resort of Constanta were informed by King Carol, who doubtless made the promise reluctantly, that Rumania could not look on with indifference at an Austrian attempt to weaken Serbia. The visit was cordial enough for the Austrian minister at Bucharest to write to Berchtold, on June 22, that the Rumanian alliance was now a dead letter: "Rumania's swing over to the Triple Entente, which had been expected for a year, took place before the public eye today at Constanta."[10]

By summer, agonizing reappraisals of the dangerous and humiliating position were in course in high places. The German Emperor paid a state visit to Austria. He had talks with the Heir to the Throne, Francis Ferdinand, at the latter's castle at Konopischt on June 12 through 14. They felt that Bulgaria must be written off and everything possible done to save the Rumanian connection. Francis Ferdinand expressed the gravest doubts about Italy's loyalty. William II, who had great confidence in the power of monarchs, reassured him; the kings of both Rumania and Italy, he said, were entirely loyal to their Habsburg ally. Francis Ferdinand, who loathed the Magyars, agreed that strong pressures must be applied to dissuade the Hungarian government from its oppression of the local Rumanians.

10. Quoted in Albertini, I, 531.

On June 24, the Foreign Office at Vienna undertook the preparation of a long, morose memorandum dealing with the Balkan situation and the proper direction of the Monarchy's foreign policy. Some of the same themes were stressed: reconciliation with Rumania, the negation of Russian influence there, must be a major goal. Through the Rumanians, it was hoped, some better relations might be patched up with Serbia. Count Berchtold read the memorandum and crossed out the part about Serbia. It was, he thought, unrealistic. But he accepted without question the statement that the Russians were now driving for a union of the Balkan states and promising as lures the prospect of territory to be seized from the Habsburg Monarchy. Should this venture succeed, it would involve war against the Triple Alliance under conditions unfavorable to it. The only possible counter to the program, he thought (in contrast to Francis Ferdinand and William II), was to try again to make an alliance with Bulgaria and, most vital, to draw even closer to Germany.

At the same time Conrad von Hötzendorf was composing a dismal survey. He had a genius for facing certain kinds of realities. Now, he said, the prospects were daily growing greater for an encirclement of the Monarchy by openly aggressive enemies, Russia, Rumania, Serbia, and Montenegro, and by a treacherous ally, Italy. Its only friend, Germany, was itself encircled by Russia, France, and perhaps England. The situation was very serious and getting worse.

While these reappraisals were being completed, the Heir to the Throne, Archduke Francis Ferdinand, went to take part in army maneuvers in Bosnia. At the end of them, on Sunday, the twenty-eighth of June, which happened to be the Serbs' national holiday, he and his wife paid a state visit to the capital of the province, a city called Sarajevo. They reviewed the troops and were received by the mayor, and at eleven-thirty that morning they were both shot to death by a member of one of the Serb nationalist societies.

CHAPTER SIX

THE THIRD MAN FALLS SICK

TURKEY, the Sick Man of Europe, had expired. Austria-Hungary, in the judgment of its leaders and its ally, was in serious danger of following him to the grave. And then in July, 1914, the whole of Europe fell into a mortal illness.

War was expected. It had been expected by many, with a mounting sense of urgency, for several years. Against the prospect, those who believed that it would be a catastrophe had been doing what they could. The international Socialist movement had attempted to rally its forces to forestall a general war, and some of its leaders hoped that it might be able to take effective and united action when a crisis came. In Great Britain, despite the growing antipathy to the Germans and their policies, an important and influential school of thought, led by people who had taken up the anti-imperialist position in the Boer War, fought to prevent Britain's entanglement in the Continental war when it came. And many, perhaps most, people in Great Britain thought that British participation was unthinkable: war was something indulged in by irresponsible foreigners.

But whether fearing it or not, many believed it was likely. There was warrant for this, in the arms race, in the growing solidity of the Franco-Russian alignment, in the tense and tortured events since Bosnia; and the warrant of likelihood slid into the conjecture of inevitability. Once influential people were convinced that war was inevitable, then prudence demanded that suitable preparations be made and that a propitious moment be chosen. This state of mind afflicted not only soldiers and statesmen but public opinion as well. "We are going," people said to one another, "to have to fight someday. Perhaps it would be better to fight now."

In view of what happened, the statement suggests moral bankruptcy. But it must be seen against the background of a time when war was not so grim an eventuality as it later appeared. Perspective may distort as well as clarify. The words of the German Emperor, reported by the Austrian diplomat to whom they were spoken in December of 1913, seem today stupefyingly frivolous: "The final decision in the South-east of Europe may, we know, sooner or later, call for a serious passage of arms and we Germans will then stand with you and behind you." The Emperor is reported to have said, "It was hoped that the advantage of the racial struggle [within the Monarchy] would fall back into second place when it was a question of assuring the supreme future interests of the Monarchy and in particular of attracting the Serbs into their natural sphere of influence."[1] Not a word, not an idea, in this is based on realities, or upon the complex risks and portents for the future that were evoked. It seems incredible that a head of state could talk—not for public consumption but for the purposes of private diplomatic negotiation—about a "natural sphere of influence" for the Serbs within the Monarchy. He need only have asked any Serb to have the assumption blown to bits.

But the words are read now from a mid-twentieth-century perspective, with the background of a social science that embeds generalities in data, and so cloaks error. Grandiloquence might be more *baldly* wrong than are thirty-page intelligence reports, but it was not necessarily more wrong in substance. And the words are read now also through the screen of subsequent events. It must

1. Quoted in Albertini, *The Origins of the War of 1914*, I, 490.

be borne in mind constantly that "war" did not mean for William II what we know to be the nature of twentieth-century war, but campaigns of a month or six weeks, fought as *part* of intricate chess games. The world-shaking, revolutionary wars of the Napoleonic era were forgotten; they had remade European society, but in 1914, peace, not war, seemed to some people at the time a more probable source of social change or social revolution. Statesmen sometimes contemplated war, in fact, as a means of preventing revolution; and if the war they contemplated had turned out to be a six weeks' war, their calculations might today have been deemed correct. The error was a failure to understand the depths of emotion that nationalism and democracy were capable of producing, and, equally disastrously but perhaps more justifiably, a failure to foresee the coincidence of technologies that would bring great armies into deadlock and to overlook insoluble problems that would be opened up, like old wounds, once war began.

The tendency of many of the leaders to anticipate a short war was of the highest importance, and it raises a semantic issue also important. The word "war" is singularly imprecise, and when it was said after 1918 that such-and-such or so-and-so helped to cause the war, we must remember that the word meant something entirely different from what it had meant before 1914. John Hay, later to be the United States Secretary of State, could speak of the Spanish-American War as "a splendid little war"; the phrase might, at the time, have suggested a certain frivolity, but it carried no implication of criminal and bloodcurdling irresponsibility in a day when automatic arms had not yet quite submerged the ancient tradition of warrior virtues. The nearest thing one can get, perhaps, to a definition is to say that war is a relationship between two organized political authorities usually conducted with organized armed forces and with violence, and involving a set of laws and customs different from those of other political relationships. So reduced, the word is meaningless, but it must be so reduced to include, say, the Punic Wars, the Hundred Years War, the Balkan War of 1912, and the first World War.

There were many people in 1914 who thought that a war might

be a good thing. Most of these people thought so for one of several reasons: a war might strengthen the domestic social fabric; a war would disperse mortal and endemic threats from neighbors; a war would assure one's nation its "proper place in the world"; a war was in any case inevitable and should be undertaken at the moment when the terms looked most favorable. There were many leaders in all countries—including, by some interpretations, Winston Churchill in Great Britain—who believed one or more of these rubrics. They were not necessarily incorrect: they merely failed to see what a war, once started, would turn into.

So—it cannot be too strongly emphasized—the war that was anticipated in 1914 was not the first World War. It was widely believed that the trend of modern technology would make wars shorter rather than longer. The reasons for the assumption were partly economic: modern arms and mobilizations were so *expensive,* it was thought, that nations would rapidly run out of money while ingenious armaments were forcing a quick decision in the field. The authors of this cockeyed reasoning incredibly underrated the productivity of industrial societies, the flexibility of modern government, the tensile strength of populations, the artificial and formal nature of budgets and currencies.

There was no general agreement on what war would mean. A few, like Sir Edward Grey and Moltke, guessed that it might be long, costly, and drastic in its effects. Others imagined that it might be fought mainly at sea. Many assumed—and this was important—that it would be fought to a conclusion with the armaments in being at its outset; remarkably little thought was given to the possibility of replacement of equipment or the mobilization of nations' economies. The assumption contributed to what was widely described as the "arms race." It helped explain, for example, the insistence of the Germans on their new military laws in the years before the war, on the grandiose Russian plans for expanding their army, on the French Army's preoccupation with the three-year term of service in 1913.

The arms race was itself of great importance, though in a subtle way. Arms races do not themselves cause wars; but a particular aspect of this one was a contributory cause of the outbreak of war in 1914. French, and particularly Russian, military plans were of a sort that appeared threatening to a Germany preoccupied with encirclement by those countries. It was the calculation of many Germans, particularly in the army, that the balance of military power was going to begin to move against them. They were confident, in 1914, that they could defeat France and Russia, but they were less certain of victory if war were delayed by a few years. This calculation operated in the crisis in two ways: first, it predisposed the Germans at least to run risks, and to think of a possible general war as a "preventive war"; second, because of the peculiar structure of the German government, the thinking of the military permeated the court and the civilian officials as well. The arms race, or rather a particular view of it grafted onto German policy, vitally affected German attitudes toward Austria-Hungary and its policies.

The German theory would not have been so deplorable in its results if it had been shared by others. But neither the French nor the Russians believed that the moment was as unfavorable for them as the Germans thought it was, and unlike the Germans they thought Britain would enter the war on their side. It is possible to construe German actions in the crisis as an attempt to push the Russians and the French into war: but in fact they were willing to be pushed. Indeed, they were eager. In the end, it turned out that all parties were wrong; the moment was favorable for nobody. And this was because they mistook the nature of the war that was to come.

Another aspect of the mistake was the belief that war might be helpful as a means of quelling internal problems. Europe was in a state of ebullience in 1914; conservatives might imagine that the calling forth of patriotism would help to solidify the social structure, and their opponents might believe that it would help to destroy it. Both were in the event, at different times and in different ways, proved right.

Such hopes and convictions appear repeatedly and explicitly in the documents from Russia and Austria: an international success, diplomatic or military, could be counted on to strengthen the regime. Diplomatic failure might jeopardize it. In other countries, where the regime was less noticeably in need of strengthening, the motive appears less openly. But it appears nonetheless, entwined with attitudes toward the developing domestic unrest and social demands. Everywhere, there were signs that regimes were ultimately endangered. The Labor Party was making modest but portentous gains in England, accompanied by serious strikes and the appearance of extremist movements. The Socialists in France, recently united, were advancing, also to the accompaniment of strikes, and of sabotage and syndicalism. The German Social Democrats had in 1912 won a plurality of seats in the Reichstag. And in Italy, for the first time anywhere, Socialists were occupying cabinet posts. The Socialists were, or claimed to be, anti-militarist and in some cases pacifist. Wars, they said, benefited no one except the capitalists. Quite aside from the dangers of their domestic programs, their international attitudes struck at what was, for conservatives and moderates, the root of all stability, the security of the state and the power of the armed forces. A weakening of defenses would lead to invasion, anarchy, and massacre.

Violence was in the air, and it did not emanate from the arms race alone. Other winds were cold over Europe. Syndicalism, a new form of socialism, preached the destruction not only of property and armies but of the state itself, and it preached that this destruction was to be—and morally ought to be—achieved by violence. The syndicalist influences in labor and politics were strong and growing stronger in the Latin countries and in Great Britain as well. They were not yet taken very seriously, but the gratuitous accent on violence was interesting.

Not only syndicalists believed in violence as a desirable form of self-expression, a necessary gesture to dispel the dowdy shibboleths of the nineteenth century. There were also the anarchists who for a generation had been assassinating heads of state as a matter of principle. And there were conservatives, too; some professional militarists, the Conrad von Hötzendorfs, who thought of war as a natural and commendable way of solving problems, cleaner than politics. There were frantic rightists like the French Royalist Youth who threw bricks and rioted against civil liberties and the separation of Church and State. It was something new for monarchists and conservatives to throw bricks. The response of conservativism to the advancing democracy of the day, and the rising socialism, was to go into the streets.

Violence was resorted to on an increasing scale. In London, women obsessively preoccupied with securing the vote were throwing themselves under the horses of the King's carriage and—what was still more alarming because it suggested the fragility of a civilization that depended on reliable communications—putting jam in the post boxes. The British Army had recently threatened mutiny when faced with the prospect of being ordered to shoot down loyalists who opposed the creation of a self-governing Ireland. In the constitutional debates that accompanied the passage of the Parliament Act of 1911, the Tories who resisted limiting the powers of the House to Lords had, some of them, ranted in ways that indicated readiness to abandon legal methods for securing political ends.

Strange and unsettling ideas were circulating in every sphere; for twenty years before 1914 they had been growing more strident, and more alarming to cautious people. Painters were painting pictures that were not intended to represent objects the way ordinary eyes saw them. Writers were dealing with subjects like sex and poverty in ways and words that no respectable publisher a generation earlier would have dared to print. Poets who cheerfully described themselves as decadent were declaring that morality was no criterion of beauty. Women, hitherto bound by law and custom to their husbands, were not only demanding the vote, and achieving it, by 1914, in scattered cities and in classless Norway; they were also demanding and sometimes getting the right to their own property, to employment, and to equal wages with men. The Protestant churches, shaken by Darwin and the higher criticism a half-century earlier, were losing their influence to purely secular leaders, if not to outright atheists. In Vienna, Dr. Sigmund Freud was undermining the great intellectual heritage of the Renaissance and the eighteenth century by demonstrating that men's motives were not, and never could be, the product of reason. Everywhere, certitudes were being shaken, and respectable people were taking alarm.

It would be a mistake to suppose that there had ever been an age, in modern times anyway, when certitudes were clear and universal, or one that did not regard itself as witnessing the decay of admirable values that had commanded acceptance a generation earlier. The world, seen by the middle-aged, is always in the process of disintegration: taste and morality were always sounder thirty years ago. But it is true that the middle years of the nineteenth century had bred, for very many people in Europe, a singular confidence in peaceful progress to a new and better age, and that the tokens of that age were tangible and visible on every hand. Stability, even though only relative stability, had bred in turn an Hegelian antithesis. It was the harvest of stability against which Nietzsche had so unnervingly revolted. Cubism was exciting, and so was syndicalism. There was a need for exhilaration, a need that imperialism had earlier helped to meet, and which now was leading to a willingness to accept the prospect of violent actions.

The first World War undoubtedly took place at a time when some Europeans were being driven to extreme attitudes by threats to the social order and others were anxious for the excitement of change; some of them, even such genteel and bookish reformers as Beatrice and Sidney Webb, the leaders of the British Fabian Society, exulted in the prospect of drastic change that they thought the war promised; others, perhaps more numerous and certainly more powerful, saw in it a hope for preventing just such change. Both were proved right; the cathartic effects were very great. When France declared war, the most conservative of the Deputies, the monarchist Albert de Mun, crossed the floor of the Chamber to shake hands with Jules Guesde, the fire-eating orator of revolutionary socialism. The two had never spoken before.

In Germany, the atmosphere of impending violence, the conviction that war was inevitable—some years earlier, men like Gustav Krupp, the arms manufacturers, had been prophecying an ineluctable showdown between Slavdom and Germandom for the control of Europe—was coupled with a flaming confidence in the rising star of Germany. Germany was unquestionably rising, and had been rising fast; and as the Chancellor, Bethmann-Hollweg, was later to remark, its spectacular growth had blinded Germans to the realities of power in the rest of the world.[2] There was undoubtedly a kind of dreaminess about Germans' views of world affairs. It is strikingly illuminated by the incredible confidence they had in the prospects of confounding their enemies through the sponsorship of a Moslem uprising against the British Empire, and revolutions in South Africa, India, and Russian Poland; and, most remarkable of all, in Moltke's belief that the United States might be brought into the war on the German side by promising it Canada as a prize for victory.

Illusions, ambitions, and dispositions to violence are only in the vaguest sense causes. There were more who thought that war would be a tragedy than an opportunity or an adventure. None of the conflicts that might have become causes for war seemed to be urgent that summer, and some of them seemed to be in the process of appeasement. But violence now seemed necessary and acceptable to many people. War seemed to offer a chance for achieving varied ends. A short, decisive war seemed likely, and sometimes inviting.

The European Powers Before Sarajevo

For Great Britain, the great issues in foreign policy in the early twentieth century were importantly determined by relations with the German Empire. The fact has imprinted itself, along with many and some misleading implications, upon the histories that are most often read by English-speaking people. There has been a strong tendency to view the Great War, as it was usually known in Great Britain, as an Anglo-German duel, which among other things it

2. Fischer, *Griff Nach der Weltmacht,* p. 99.

did become, once it started, and to treat its causes with heavy emphasis upon Anglo-German tensions.

Those tensions formed the background for Britain's participation in the war on the Entente side, but they had only an indirect—indeed, a paradoxical—bearing on the outbreak of hostilities, and this fact is sometimes lost sight of in the natural inclination to view events from national standpoints. Britain's declaration of war was not produced by the long background of animosity to Germany, its government and its policies. The fact was, despite the mounting antagonism in Britain, relations with Germany before Sarajevo were slightly but definitely better than they had been for some time. It is of interest to consider briefly the recent background of that antagonism and of the small improvement.

The most powerful causes of the deterioration of relations between Berlin and London in the decade before 1914 were the existence of the Triple Entente and the naval question. It will be recalled that the development of the *Dreadnought* had raised for its builders the peculiar threat of negating their existing naval supremacy. Conversations aimed at securing an agreement on rates of navy-building had taken place on several occasions, most lately in 1912. A new navy-building law was to be introduced that spring to the German parliament, and both British and German quarters hoped to secure some modification of it. The initiative came, in fact, from the Germans. There were some preliminary diplomatic negotiations, indicating an area open for discussion, and in February the British Secretary of War, Lord Haldane, had arrived in Berlin.

The negotiations failed. Haldane was told privately by the Germans that the only way to secure agreement on naval matters was to preface it with a politcal agreement—which meant, in effect, the detachment of Britain from the Triple Entente and the understandings with France. The demand was not, on the face of it, unreasonable, but it was precisely the thing that the Foreign Minister, Sir Edward Grey and the other "anti-Germans" in the Cabinet, notably Churchill and Lloyd-George, were resolutely determined not to consider. The fact was that both parties regarded a naval agreement as an unnecessary restriction on their freedom and perhaps security. On the German side was the impulse to world power, which produced many random provocations. On the British side was the understanding with France.

The fructifying effect of Algeciras on Franco-British cordiality had been immediately followed by a still more favorable development: a change in government in Britain, which brought to office the Liberal Party, several of whose leaders were strongly Teutonophobe and Francophile. The new Secretary of State for Foreign Affairs, Sir Edward Grey, shared these views. He was an odd and contradictory personality, lovable but secretive, highly conscientious but indolent, intelligent but sometimes indecisive. He rather disliked his job; he much preferred bird-watching on his country estate, and he spent a good deal of time at it. More, perhaps, than with any of his predecessors, his policy was shaped by his subordinates and other civil servants or military experts.

With the approval of Grey, conversations between the defense authorities of the two countries, already planned, were now continued with greater willingness on the part of the British. There was nothing in the nature of an alliance or a British commitment, although the French pressed uninterruptedly for something of the sort. But the making of plans for the cooperation of the two armies and navies in the event that both countries should find themselves at war with Germany continued. The British Cabinet was not informed for several years of the military obligations.

The dispositions of both the British and the French navies were henceforth made on the assumption that they might be fighting together in the same war. The British Army, in the process of extensive reorganization, made its plans with an eye to the need for placing an army in France as promptly as possible after the outbreak of hostilities. Britain promised that in the event of war, whether they were involved or not, their navy would cover the French Channel ports.

The British authorities involved were acutely conscious of the danger of forming moral and strategic commitments. Winston

Churchill, as First Lord of the Admiralty, remarked in 1912:

> Freedom will be sensibly impaired if the French can say that they had denuded their Atlantic seaboard and concentrated in the Mediterranean on the faith of naval engagements made with us. . . . Consider how tremendous would be the weapon which France would possess to compel our intervention [in a war] if she could say, "On the advise of and by arrangement with your naval authorities we left our nothern coasts defenseless."[3]

And even Grey was prudent, to the point of annoying the French mightily, in refusing military commitments.

The reason for this caution lay in political and constitutional subtleties and in the hesitancy of public opinion. Grey was diplomatically fastidious; he refused to give even personal pledges so long as they could not carry constitutional authority. The Liberal Party, traditionally conciliatory and pacific in its international outlook, contained influential leaders, including several ministers, who would certainly have balked at a formal commitment to France, and might well have broken up the government on the issue. And even if the Cabinet had been agreed, a commitment would have required parliamentary discussion and approval. It was clear that Parliament, still less the public, was not prepared to accept an alliance. And the reopened question of Irish Home Rule was already cleaving public opinion and weakening the position of the Liberal government.

At the time of Sarajevo, the British government had no commitment, and no inclination, to enter a European war unless Great Britain's own vital interests were in jeopardy. A German attack on France *might* threaten them. A German attack on Belgium was bound to do so.

Although no one knew it, the Germans had long considered Belgium as a necessary route to France. The position of Belgium was a peculiar one. It was a small country, with a population of seven and a half million. Its independent existence dated only from

3. Quoted in S. B. Fay, *Origins of the World War* (1928), I, 321.

1830. But it was a rich country; its seaport, Antwerp, was one of the most important in Europe; and its coastline faced the narrows between Great Britain and the Continent and offered bases from which British control of the passage between the North Sea and the Channel might be threatened. As a consequence of its location, its legal position was also peculiar. It was bound by treaty to neutrality. The Powers had promised to respect Belgian neutrality; in return, the Belgians had agreed to maintain it, to prevent by force if necessary the use of their territory for military purposes by foreigners. The Belgians had given up their diplomatic freedom of action—they could not make alliances or take sides. They had made it clear on many occasions that they were prepared to fight to prevent violation of their neutrality. In the nature of things, however, their military effort could scarcely amount to more than a token of good intentions.

The German position with regard to a possible war against France was also peculiar. There was a long Franco-German frontier, of course, but most of it lay in extremely hilly country, and on both sides of the border there had been erected formidable and, it turned out, effective fortifications, centering on the French side around the huge fortress system of Verdun. An invasion of France could not be carried out through these obstacles with any hope for quick success. On the other hand, to the north the terrain was much more favorable to rapid advances: the French fortifications facing the Belgian border were negligible and the Belgian forts themselves were not taken very seriously by the Germans. If a quick invasion of France was to be achieved, it must—for purely military reasons—be by way of Belgium.

Invasion of France was a necessary and basic part of the German plans, should a European war break out, although this fact implied no aggressive intention but simply a fact of geography. Once it became clear, after the Franco-Russian Treaty was signed, that Germany might have to fight on two fronts if it ever fought at all, elementary prudence required that it make preparations to do so. It was believed that German resources could not possibly suffice to win on either front if the armies were equally divided. It was also highly likely that the size of Russia, and its armies, would mean a prolonged campaign to achieve victory. The Russian armies, however, were notoriously slow to get ready; it was confidently expected in Germany that there would thus be several weeks of inaction in the east; and this expectation in turn immediately suggested that the respite be used to achieve a decision in France. If victory could be rapidly won in the west and the armies then transported east, the German advantage of interior lines would come into play and the chief military disadvantages of encirclement would be annulled. A very quick and overwhelming advance into France was required, and this meant the use of the route through Belgium. And the Germans were persuaded that Belgium, confronted by the crushing power of the German Army, would not fight. It seems not to have occurred to them at all that an invasion of Belgium would imperil Britain's vital national interests; but the prospect of Belgian resistance seemed so remote that the question was not regarded as urgent.

These crude reckonings were the basis for exceedingly thorough war plans. Their chief architect was General Alfred von Schlieffen, the German chief of staff from 1891 to 1905. He left as his legacy a detailed memorandum that became the basis for German strategy, a holding operation in the east and a rapid march through Belgium into northern France. Six weeks and seven eighths of the army were to be devoted to the initial campaign in Belgium and France. The goal was to be a "decisive engagement," which meant inflicting upon the French a defeat so nearly total as to make a continuation of the war impossible. The notion of a "decision" was based upon experiences of the Austro-French War of 1860, the Austro-Prussian War of 1866, the Franco-Prussian War of 1870, not upon the precedent of the American Civil War, which proved, in the event, to be the true one.

As its authoritative historian, Gerhard Ritter, has observed, the Schlieffen Plan was intrinsically, if not intentionally, aggressive, since it required an attack on two neighbors. Ritter believes, with every warrant, that neither Schlieffen nor the Emperor and his civilian advisors, ever envisaged a "preventive war" against France. But the *form* of defense that was laid down undoubtedly encouraged those in Germany who thought that France, with its ineradicable hostility and its yearnings for Alsace-Lorraine, constituted a "problem" that must some day be "solved."

Once the strategic principles were accepted, there followed planning that involved an amount of detail so vast that made it impossible to alter the principles quickly; and this meant, in practice, that they could not be altered at all, since Germany might have to fight at a moment's notice. It is striking that Schlieffen's successor, Moltke, had very grave doubts about both the wisdom and the feasibility of the plan.[4] But it was too late to change. The Schlieffen Plan remained in all its major outlines, including the transit through Belgium, unchanged after 1906. And this was a crucial fact, far more crucial than the naval or commercial rivalry with Britain, in deciding the future. The first World War and Britain's part in it was the product of the Schlieffen Plan, which was a means for dealing with Germany's difficult strategic position; and that was the product of the breakdown of the connection with Russia in the eighties, which was in its turn the product of Austro-Russian rivalries.

British neutrality was expected by the Germans, should war break out. And there was something to lend credibility to the expectation. Relations were improving in the summer of 1914. The improvement arose from the successful negotiation of the problems raised by German railway-building activities in Turkey which had been, along with the naval question, the most troublesome of the tangible issues between the two countries. It had begun in 1902 when the Turkish government requested the Germans to build a railway from the existing railhead in Anatolia to Bagdad and on to the Perisan Gulf. The German government was

---

4. Gerhard Ritter, "Der Anteil der Militars auf der Kriegskatastrophe von 1914," *Historische Zeitschrift,* 193 (August, 1961), 72–91.

already beginning its patronage of the Turks, hoping to replace Britain as the traditional protector (and beneficiary) of the government at Constantinople. The railroad looked to the foreign powers like political penetration, and its terminus was alarmingly close to India. The British press and public were deeply, and rather hysterically, suspicious, and the attitude of the government was on the whole hostile. The situation long remained unsettled and unsettling, but in the end an accommodation was reached. In July of 1914 a treaty was signed transferring the southern part of the railway to British responsibility, and it was welcomed by parties as a signal contribution to an Anglo-German *détente,* which, translated from diplomatic jargon, meant a reduction of tension.

There were other signs of *détente* as well. A friendly visit by the British Fleet to the naval base at Kiel was also planned for the end of July, and some important colonial issues had recently been adjusted. There seemed, in the month that followed the assassination of Francis Ferdinand, less reason to fear a war between Germany and Britain than there had been six months earlier—or for some years past. As Winston Churchill wrote, "The spring and summer of 1914 were marked in Europe by an exceptional tranquility. Ever since Agadir the policy of Germany toward Great Britain had not only been correct but considerate. Some at least of those who were accustomed to utter warnings began to feel the need of revising their judgment."[5]

The improvement in Anglo-German relations had an ironic effect. For some time it had been Bethmann's principal purpose to secure a political agreement with the British that would detach them from the Triple Entente and assure their neutrality in case of war. The attempt had failed at the time of the Haldane Mission; now the colonial and Berlin-Bagdad Railway accords suggested that it was attainable, and upon this assumption much of German policy in the crisis seems to have been built. The extreme optimism with which the government assayed the prospects of British neutrality, an optimism unwittingly encouraged by Grey's extreme

5. *The World Crisis* (1928), I, 178–79.

cautiousness, undoubtedly affected German judgments of the balance of risk, should "complications" develop out of Austria's attempt to discipline Serbia. The lightheartedness with which the possibility of complications was faced was thus in some measure a consequence of what seemed on the face of it a development likely to diminish the chances of war.

There were slight indications of *détente* in other spheres as well. From some points of view the penultimate crisis of prewar Europe may be so regarded. This imbroglio, the Liman von Sanders affair, did nothing at all to help German-Russian relations, and it may, by contributing to the "crisis" atmosphere, have edged other fingers nearer the trigger as well. But it showed that certain kinds of diplomatic tensions, however acute, were negotiable, and that governments were still perfectly capable of making reasonable concessions.

General Otto Liman von Sanders was a German officer who was called upon to assist in a much-needed reconstruction of the Turkish Army after the 1912 catastrophe. In most respects this mission was perfectly routine; governments of underdeveloped states habitually called on more developed ones to provide "military missions" to train or reorganize their armies. There had been German military missions in Constantinople before. But General Liman's position was to be different from the previous visiting officers'. He was to take active command of Turkish troops, not to behave as a semi-diplomatic adviser. Such a position, which seemed to infringe upon the independence of Turkey and even to suggest the beginnings of a German overlordship, would have been a subject for controversy at any time; it was all the more so in view of the prevailing tensions and of the deep suspicions with which German activities in Turkey were in any case being regarded by the Entente Powers. As the Russian Foreign Minister put it, the move could not help provoking "violent irritation in Russian public opinion, and would certainly be interpreted as an act manifestly hostile to us."[6] The intentions in Berlin in acceding to the Turkish

6. Quoted in Fay, I, 500.

request do not, as a matter of fact, seem to have been very sinister; apparently the German military were sensitive about their reputation after the cataclysmic defeats of an army previously coached by another German general, Colmar von der Goltz,[7] although there was also the thought that the Turks could hardly enter into combinations hostile to Germany if their army was under German control.

The eruption in Saint Petersburg when the details were announced was, however, violent. There was a corresponding reaction, though more sympathetic than violent, in Paris and London. In a general way it may be said that the Russian motives were at least as sinister as the German; if the Germans wanted to use General Liman to ensure a cooperative Turkey, Russia wanted to exclude him from his command because they hoped to keep Turkey weak against the time, which might come soon, when they could acquire Constantinople for themselves. There was some discussion, in Saint Petersburg, of going to war against Germany if that country did not withdraw its general.

It was the Germans who produced the formula. They were not prepared to back down, but they were willing to reach a settlement. It was simply done; Liman von Sanders was promoted to a rank equivalent to that of field marshal. At that rank he could not take personal command of troops, and his presence in Constantinople would cease to be provocative. The Powers agreed.

The atmosphere of crisis persisted. By midsummer of 1914, war was being prophesied in many quarters of Europe, including London. The feelings of the British might be perceptibly less bellicose toward Germany than they had been. British attention might be distracted by extremely severe labor troubles and the threat of a first-rate crisis in Ireland, where Protestants were still strenuously resisting, with the support of much English opinion, the government's plan for Irish Home Rule. But there persisted some sense of an approaching show-down. Franco-German relations were bad. There was the oratorical display of patriotic fireworks pro-

7. Albertini, 1, 541.

duced by the military service question. There was Poincaré's energetic support of Russia in its Balkan concerns. There was the reviving interest in Alsace-Lorraine. After a period of relative quiescence around the turn of the century, rising anti-German feelings and action had culminated in a major disturbance, in November, 1913, in the town of Saverne. Provocative actions by the German army had produced even more provocative actions by the local populace, which in turn led to the arrest of civilians by army officers. The affair was taken (both in France and among German liberals) as a sign of the ineffable and uncontrollable arrogance of the officers' corps. The Lost Provinces were again much in the headlines and in Frenchmen's minds, and talk of Revenge was again widely heard.

There was everywhere a sort of autonomous hysteria, a sense of inevitably approaching doom. It is said that the German Emperor was himself a victim of it, that he was kept awake at night by fears of an approaching holocaust. In this sense, an emergency did exist throughout Europe. But it must not be exaggerated. Most people went about their work as usual, and so far as tangible facts or politics went, there was no urgent problem outside the Balkans; the emergency existed only in Austria-Hungary.

Crisis: The Austrians Contemplate a Solution to the South Slav Problem

The Heir to the Throne of Austria-Hungary had been murdered by a young man named Gavrilo Princip, who was at the time nineteen years old. He was a Bosnian by birth; he had some years earlier become involved with Serb nationalist activities; he had been in Belgrade, where he and two other Bosnian youths had been selected by the Black Hand leader, Voya Tanksovich, for the performance of violent deeds, had received suitable equipment and instruction, and had been sent back to Sarajevo on June 3 to perform them. On June 28, 1914, violent deeds were done. One of the three had lost his nerve. The second, whose name was Chabrinovich, had thrown a bomb at the Archduke's car but had missed the occupants—it injured an aide and several bystanders. Princip, who happened to be waiting on the sidewalk at the moment when the Archduke's chauffeur had made a wrong turn and stopped to back up, succeeded in killing him.

There is now no doubt at all that the conspiracy was organized in Belgrade by "Union or Death" and with the connivance of a number of Serbs of position: army officers and some government officials, including frontier authorities. The Austro-Hungarian government, and practically everybody else, suspected this much at the time and the Austrian authorities found evidence to prove most of it, although they were not aware of the existence of the Black Hand and mistakenly blamed the plot on the guiltless and relatively respectable *Narodna Obrana*. Most of the rest of the background of the agitation and the conspiracy remained unclear, however; some of it still does today. The evidence, while voluminous, was by its nature difficult to uncover. But in 1966 a scholar of Yugoslav origins, working at Oxford, produced a book that clarified most of the remaining mysteries and dispelled most of the remaining doubts. Vladimir Dedijer, working with Serbian sources, gave what now appears to be a complete, authentic, and probably definitive account of the conspiracy. He has elaborated in great detail the organization and personnel of "Union or Death" and the role of its leader, Colonel Dragutin Dimitrievitch, who was known in the organization as "Colonel Apis."

In 1914, and at the trials that followed the assassination, the Austrians failed to demonstrate, although they openly suspected, the complicity of the Serbian government. Piecemeal revelations followed long after the event. The most sensational of them came from a Serbian politician, Ljuba Jovanovich, who had been Minister of Education in the Serbian Cabinet. In an article published in 1925 he rather casually mentioned that the Cabinet had known of the plot and discussed it in May or early June, and he gave accurate details of its organization. The soundness of his memory was strenuously challenged, but the systematic denials of his colleagues remained unsupported, and his story was accepted by many people as correct.

Dedijer has shown that some of the cabinet members who knew what was afoot and discussed it. They tried, not very efficiently, to stop it, as, indeed, at the last minute, did Colonel Apiso. But the ministers' hands were tied, so far as official action went. They could not reveal what they knew without inculpating large numbers of high-ranking Serbs, and bringing on charges of compassing national disgrace. The cabinet certainly did not sponsor the plot, or approve of it. They were themselves the victims of terrorism and of unleashed national anger and ambition. The terrorists had long been organizing opposition to the Pasitch government—for almost as long, in fact, as they had been organizing opposition to Austrian rule in Bosnia—and the very ferocity and fanaticism of the leaders made it difficult for ordinary politicians to oppose them.

But until very recently, these facts were not established. The passive collusion of the Serbian government was for a long time ardently denied by Serbian sympathizers throughout the world. In England, where pan-Serbism had powerful friends, it was even suggested at one time that the Austrian government itself had arranged the assassination in order to get rid of the Archduke, who was disliked in Vienna, and to provide a pretext for invading Serbia. The theory was always untenable, but it indicates the extent to which strong opinions could be formed and disseminated in the absence of reliable information. And there is a real question about why Francis Ferdinand was chosen as a victim. So far as the assassins themselves went, the choice was probably unimportant. They had been taking lessons in Marksmanship in Belgrade some time before the Bosnian visit was planned. For ardent and neurotic youths, a gratuitous act of violence was more important than a rational motive.

Dedijer's most important single contribution has been to explain in great detail the interaction of the callow activists in Bosnia, bored, poetic, desperate youths, with the unseemly jobbery of Serbian politics under the House of Karageorgevitch, and the megalomaniac ambitions of Colonel Apis.

The act of violence was an imperative; it was intended as a demonstration, and its authors certainly did not expect to start a war. But for Colonel Apis the selection of Francis Ferdinand was probably no accident. He may well have died because of his sympathies for the South Slavs. He was known to be a violent antagonist of the Magyars and a supporter of trialism—of the creation of a third state within the Monarchy, the equal of Austria and Hungary, for the Slav populations. There were formidable obstacles, but the power of the Habsburg Emperor was also formidable, and the obstacles might have been overcome if Francis Ferdinand had ascended the throne. Then the grievances of the Bosnians, and of the Croats and the Slovenes, might have been alleviated; the pan-Serb dream would have been wrecked if the Yugoslavs within the Monarchy had had their nationalist ambitions satisfied, and the existence, as well as the ambitions, of the Serbian kingdom might have been jeopardized. For rabid nationalists, Francis Ferdinand was a dangerous man.

In any case, his Bosnian visit provided an ideal target. Even if the only purpose of the plot was a spectacular demonstration of pan-Serb terrorism, the plotters must have counted upon the eminence of the victim to assure it. If they did, they were right.

The fact that they were right reduces somewhat the importance of the discussion about how the conspiracy developed and who was responsible for it. Proof of the complicity of the Serbian government might conceivably have deterred the Russians from acting to protect their client, but it was extremely unlikely that real proof could possibly have been made available on short notice. And as it turned out, the damaging evidence that the Austrians *did* acquire was not used. The learned and interminable investigations of the plot that have since taken place have high interest, but it is the interest of a tragic drama or a detective story. The real facts did not at the time matter much; what mattered was the ignorance of them and the suspicions that replaced them, and what the Habsburg Monarchy would decide to do.

What it decided was, forseeably, the product of debate among people who had entirely different points of view about the nature and future of Austria-Hungary. The same paralysis, so much deplored, that had seized Vienna in 1912 was now again evident.

But this time there were differences. The lamentable consequences of inaction on the earlier occasion were on everyone's mind, and they bred determination to avoid its repetition. While strong action, any action, seemed to be imperative "if Austria-Hungary were to survive as a Great Power."—as Dedijer says, the real importance of the murders was to strengthen the war party. And this time, too, the Germans were determined that their decaying ally should act.

Another difference was the absence of Francis Ferdinand. In 1912 he had been, in general, a moderating influence, and he had represented a relatively clearheaded and sympathetic attitude toward the Yugoslav problem. Now his moderation and his clearheadedness were absent. It is often overlooked in discussing the aftermath of the Archduke's assassination that its most salient consequence had been his death.

There was, moreover, the element of shock. The murders everywhere called forth horror, anger, and outrage. In Vienna, where the shock was naturally greatest, it had a double effect; it was apprehended by some that the moment for action was now more favorable than it was likely to be again; and action was otherwise elicited by the circumstance of genuine horror and grief. The latter was not, to be sure, universal. The Archduke's odd personality, his odder political views, his marriage to a lady of lower rank— which had shocked the court—had made many enemies. The Emperor himself took the dreadful news with remarkable calm, and some of the officials behaved scandalously. There was public criticism of the funeral, which had obviously been arranged by inimical elements. It was hasty and unceremonious, and less than honor was done the remains of the unroyal consort.

It was the conduct of the obsequies that produced in England the singular theory that the murders had been the work of the Austrian government. To support the theory, there was also the evidence of extremely casual security arrangements in Sarajevo (they undoubtedly were inadequate, but this was the result of inefficiency, not scheming), and the assertion that the Serbian government had warned Austria against the dangers of allowing Francis

Ferdinand to visit Bosnia, and that the warning had been deliberately suppressed. As a matter of fact, the Belgrade Cabinet *had* sent a warning to its minister in Vienna. The original form was vague, since the Serbian government could scarcely reveal that it knew of the plot, and it became much vaguer in the transmission through the minister. The authority to whom he delivered it, the Austro-Hungarian Minister of Finance, thought that it could scarcely refer to the visit that was actually planned (it seemed to refer rather to the danger of being struck by a bullet from soldiers on Serbian territory if the Archduke strayed too near the frontier, where he had no intention of going) and he never bothered to mention it to anyone.

His lapse was less strange than it sounds. One of the striking and unattractive facts about the Habsburg Monarchy was the atmosphere of fear and suspicion in high places. Francis Ferdinand had long had reason to apprehend personal dangers from many quarters, as had many other personages in Vienna. The court, for all its elegant and formal façade, was alive with scheming and threats. People were so accustomed to threats, indeed, that they tended to discount them; for years, everybody had been warning everybody else about the hazards that beset the Heir to the Throne.

Despite the oversight of the Minister of Finance, despite the disgraceful conduct of the funeral, despite the lack of sorrow among highly placed officials, there was no doubt that the impact of the assassination in Vienna was immense. There were moving manifestations of grief in the press and among the public. In Sarajevo there was anti-Serb rioting and looting by loyal subjects, who seemed to be in a large majority. And abroad there was also shock. The Russians, at least at the beginning, expressed conventional distress, and Nicholas II ordered a memorial service to be held and the court and government to attend it. In Berlin, there was real horror and anger. In London, where one sensational paper had the headline, TO HELL WITH SERVIA, even the respectable press, not anticipating that Europe might face a serious crisis, reprobated the irresponsible and murderous Serbs. Nobody had forgotten 1903. Nobody seemed to doubt that organized pan-Serbism was reprehensibly behind what had happened, or to believe the rather uncertain Serbian publicity about demented boys acting on their own responsibility.

Even in Saint Petersburg, pan-Serbism was regarded as a nuisance. Nor did subsequent behavior in Belgrade do much to mitigate this impression. The Serbian press, in the days following the murders, widely transgressed the limits not only of minimal decorum but of elementary prudence. The murders were openly applauded, the Habsburg Monarchy vituperatively denounced. The Serbian election campaign then in course perhaps contributed to the aggravation of feelings. Undoubtedly it made it difficult for the government, accused of being insufficiently anti-Austrian, to adopt a more conciliatory policy toward the bereaved authorities in Vienna. Its public statements were to the effect that the conspiracy had been none of its business and that it had no power to control the press. Understandably, the Austrian press replied in kind, and alarming denunciations of Serbia daily appeared. The unseemly polemics grew more fervid; and they affected the outlook of people who mattered in the days that followed.

Among the people who mattered was the Austro-Hungarian Foreign Minister, Court Berchtold. In the cumbersome machinery of the Dual government his position as Joint Foreign Minister was decisive. Berchtold was a slothful and vacillating man whose dilatory attitudes in 1912 had left Austria-Hungary with no policy except the futile and fatuous insistence that Serbia must be excluded from the Adriatic littoral. He was aware that this deplorable performance must not be repeated, that his personal reputation and professional future depended upon a more resolute defense of the interests of his state and his sovereign.

There was at hand, as there had been in 1912, a party with a consistent and closely reasoned argument and a clear program for action, and this time the views of that party prevailed, although not quickly or completely. The leader, Conrad von Hötzendorf, was supported by many others, including some of the higher officials in Berchtold's foreign ministry—in particular his chief adviser Count A. Hoyos—and the influential and determined German

Ambassador Heinrich von Tschirschky. These people wanted to make war on Serbia; they had wanted to do so for a long time, and they knew that with every delay the Monarchy would grow weaker, its prestige would sink, its enemies, notably Russia, would grow bolder and stronger. Their reasoning was forceful and cogent; and the reaction of the war party to the news from Sarajevo had been instant and unequivocal. "The hour has struck for the Monarchy," Conrad felt, and he hurried to convert the opposition.

Berchtold was converted. It is not clear by what steps this was accomplished, but his urgent need for a strong policy must have made him singularly responsive to the one that Conrad suggested, and had been suggesting for years. It is not clear, either, how consistent or convinced the convert was; there were signs later that he wavered. But Conrad's representations were undoubtedly effective; *his* hour, if not the Habsburgs', had indeed struck.

Another essential figure in the formation of policy was the Emperor Francis Joseph. Again, there is debate over his views. It is said by some that he was both pacific and somewhat senile—he was eighty-four and he was certainly declining in vigor. On the other hand, there is some warrant for believing that his views and influence by now coincided with those of Conrad and the war party—and it is certain that he feared and disliked the Serbs.

Further, and most important, there were the Hungarians. The Hungarian government was led by an imposing and independent-minded man, Count Stephen Tisza, whose approval in any decision was constitutionally and politically necessary. (So, of course, was that of the Austrian Prime Minister, Count Karl von Stürgkh, but he raised no difficulties.) The Hungarians were less nervous about the future than were their partners in Vienna, and also less persuaded of the expediency of drastic demonstrations of power. Tisza was a stern and extremely rigid man, a devout Calvinist, and he had a deep aversion to war. He perceived with clarity the dangers presented by Serbia and pan-Serbism, but he thought in terms of a carefully prepared and long-run solution. Immediately before the assassination he had prepared a long memorandum on future policy which had won the support in principle of Berchtold and the Austrians: in it he had recommended an alliance with Bulgaria, looking toward the formation of a Bulgarian-Rumanian-Greek-Albanian front against Serbia and possibly, in the end, an armed attack by those neighbors and the division of Serbian territory among them.

The program was reasonable, although speculative, and its end coincided precisely with the familiar, unchanged doctrine of the Magyars: *No More Slavs in the Monarchy.* The slogan advanced by Andrassy in 1878 was still unswervingly adhered to in Budapest, and along with his own aversion to force, it consolidated Tisza's dislike of the war policy. For if Serbia were attacked by Austria-Hungary and not, as he hoped, by its small Balkan neighbors, the question would arise of what to do with it afterward. He suspected the Austrians of wanting to annex it, and perhaps of flirting with trialism, of envisaging a third, Yugoslav, state that would include Serbia and Montenegro within the Monarchy. Nothing could have been more repulsive, from the Hungarian standpoint.

There were other matters that had to be settled before a policy could be agreed on. Conrad had wished, on the receipt of the news from Sarajevo, to mobilize the army against Serbia instantly. But this was not feasible. Berchtold's inclination was always to equivocate, and he found ample reason for doing so. Public opinion, he felt, must be prepared for strong measures. Evidence must be provided to demonstrate the guilty complicity of Serbia. The German ally must be solicited; nothing whatever could be risked without positive and unconditional guarantees that, whatever action Austria-Hungary might take and whatever its consequences, German support was certain. Finally—and here a new and peculiar consideration entered the situation, perhaps urged by Tisza—it was thought imprudent to do anything that might precipitate a European crisis until the evening of July 23.

On that date the President and the Prime Minister of the French Republic, Raymond Poincaré and René Viviani, would end the state visit to Russia which they were planning. They were to arrive in Saint Petersburg on July 20, and it was thought extremely undesirable to precipitate matters until they were once again safely on the high seas homeward bound. Poincaré was known to be a bad influence on the Russians; he tended to egg them on by assuring French support of Russian policy in the Balkans, and it was sure that zest for the Franco-Russian Alliance would be at a peak during the visit and that French influence might be exerted on the conciliatory Nicholas II. On the other hand, the allies would be embarrassed if the French leaders were afloat when a crisis broke.

The Germans Are Consulted

The first thing was to consult the Germans.

The atmosphere in Berlin on the morrow of the assassination was one of distress and excitement. The Emperor was summoned home from the sea by the news of his friend's death, and a number of other high officials (though not the chief of staff, Moltke, who was taking the waters, or the Secretary for Foreign Affairs, Gottlieb von Jagow, who was on a trip) assembled to discuss the matter. The Emperor's reactions were very strong indeed; he had been close to Francis Ferdinand, and he had been conferring with him only a few weeks earlier about the difficulties of Austria-Hungary's position. In response to Sarajevo, he was inflamed and inflammatory. Tschirschky reported from Vienna, two days after the murder, that he was urging calm and moderation on the Austrian government. William commented, in his own hand, on the dispatch: "Now or never! Who authorized him to act that way? That is very stupid. It's none of his business, as it is solely the affair of Austria what she plans to do in this case. . . . The Serbs must be disposed of, and that right soon."[8]

William's reaction is clear, but its implications are not. Here he seemed to be saying merely that Austria must not be prevented from solving its own problems in its own ways, however drastic. This attitude might be irresponsible, but it would not put William

8. Karl Kautsky (ed.), *Outbreak of the World War* (1924), Document No. 7. (Hereinafter, KD.)

in the role of a principal in subsequent developments. Other evidence supports such a view; but there is more evidence to suggest that William, and most of his advisers, presently began to urge Austria to take strenuous action and even to contemplate, at this early date, the likelihood of general war. On July 4, Victor Naumann, a publicist who had on previous occasions acted as a private messenger for the German Foreign Office, was sent to Vienna to assure the Austrians that if "complications" followed an Austrian war against Serbia, Germany would be prepared to take on both France and Russia.[9] The Germans, he is said to have told the Austrians, were worried about the growing military strength of the two hostile powers; moreover, they believed that an agreement might be reached with Great Britain and its neutrality procured.

Questions of interpretation remain. Fischer suggests that this and other evidence may show that the Germans were themselves using the assassination as a pretext for launching a preventive war and that, far from being mainly concerned about the future of Austria-Hungary, they were now exploiting their ally as an excuse for starting it. But this is not a necessary or final interpretation of the material he uses, and the history of previous German policy argues against so simple a construction of events. Furthermore, a recent, careful study has shown that the German General Staff had made virtually no plans for a coordinated Austro-German strategy in the event of war, a fact that suggests rather strongly that the German military, much given to careful planning, did not expect, let alone contrive, to use an Austro-Serbian dispute as the occasion for a war intended to destroy France and Russia and satisfy their own ambitions for world power.[10]

What the evidence does prove is not a long-run plan of aggression but a fairly accurate, if emotional, appraisal of the general

9. Fischer, p. 59.
10. Gordon Craig, "The World War I Alliance of the Central Powers in Retrospect," *Journal of Modern History*, XXXVII, no. 3, Sept. 1965, pp. 127-143.

situation: Germany and Austria encircled, Austria threatened by Serbia, Germany threatened by France and Russia. The moment, it might have been argued, had come when something had to be done, and the moment was seen to be (wrongly, as it turned out) favorable. To such an interpretation, both previous and subsequent developments lend weight.

In any event, Naumann's trip to Vienna, where he talked to Hoyos, was followed by Hoyos' trip to Berlin. The head of the Austrian Foreign Office arrived on July 5.

The Hoyos Mission has been the subject of endless controversy. Written minutes of the conversations do not exist, and the reports that the various participants wrote afterward vary somewhat and are open to different interpretations. In the first place, it is not absolutely certain what Count Hoyos and his colleague the Austrian Ambassador at Berlin, Count L. de Szögyény, told the Germans. Professor Fay has insisted that they merely asked for promises of support (and got them) in any venture the Monarchy might decide to undertake against the Serbians, without specifying what they had in mind. In support of this interpretation is the fact that the subsequent German dispatches and memoranda summarizing the conversations nowhere indicate definitely what Hoyos and Szögyény *did* say, and, since, Tisza had not yet been converted to the war plan, the Austrians may have been unable to present a definite project. It has also been suggested that Berchtold was beginning to have cold feet, and rather hoped that the Germans would decide the issue in the Austro-Hungarian government by vetoing the project of the war party.

Whether this last suggestion is correct or not, there is every indication, if not quite final proof, that the Germans positively urged an attack on Serbia. The Emperor said, clearly and consistently, that he could not presume to advise another state on the conduct of its own affairs and that the decision was up to the Austrians. It is clear that he repeated and unconditionally promised that they would support the Austrians in whatever they decided, and Professor Fay interpreted this to mean that the Austrians were given "a blank check." The "blank check theory"[11] became a center of violent controversy.

But it is now tolerably clear that the check was not blank and that the Germans had a clear idea of what was being discussed, approved it, and urged Vienna to quick and decisive action.

The various reports available concerning the Potsdam Conversations of July 5 and 6 seem to indicate that some Germans not only recommended the use of force against Serbia but were worried lest it be delayed or abandoned. The Austrians had brought with them the long memorandum, prepared by Tisza and edited by Berchtold before the assassination, proposing a policy of surrounding Serbia by an alliance with Bulgaria. To this was appended a brief note about the changed conditions after Sarajevo which suggested, although it did not say, that more immediate and direct measures were planned. They also brought a long letter from Francis Joseph. Both documents suggested, at least, the possibility that war was being planned. According to Count Szögyény's report, the Emperor William, while sympathetic and while promising loyal support, felt that he could make no definite commitments until Bethmann-Hollweg had been consulted. He discussed the possibility of Russian intervention and urged speed.

After seeing William, the Austrians spoke to the Chancellor and to other officials, and William consulted those of his advisers who were available, including the Prussian War Minister, Erich von Falkenhayn. The possibility of a general war was freely discussed, and William, in his grandiloquent way, asked if his armies were ready. Falkenhayn assured him that they were, and went home to write an account of the interview to Moltke, who was taking the waters at Carlsbad. He said that it was not yet decided in Vienna what steps were to be taken. It seemed likely, he thought, that diplomatic representation against Serbia, and nothing more spirited, might be intended. This he deplored. Familiar with past vacillations in Vienna, he feared that the Austrians might now relapse

11. The phrase was apparently first used, in a dispatch from the British Embassy in Berlin, to summarize the *chargé d'affaires'* guess about the German policy.

into passivity. Bethmann-Hollweg, reporting to Tschirschky on *his* conversations, observed that the Emperor William had assured Austria of full support in any venture but had added that the selection of ventures must be up to Austria.

It seems likely that the Austrians had told the truth: Berchtold and Conrad thought an attack on Serbia was necessary, but others were opposed, and in any case it could not be made ready for some time. They may also have mentioned that a list of stiff demands was being considered. In return, it seems certain that the Germans not only promised unconditional support but tried to stiffen the Austrian backs. On both July 5 and 6, and in the days that followed, there is ample evidence that the Germans constantly reiterated these themes: Austria *must* act if its position as a Great Power was to be preserved; it must act decisively and quickly; Germany would support it unconditionally; it was hoped and expected that no general European complications would follow, but if they did, Germany was prepared to face them; the military position of Germany was stronger, in relation to France and Russia, than it would ever be again, in view of French and Russian military expansion; and it was very likely that Great Britain would remain neutral.

After the Hoyos Mission, the conduct of the German leaders was strikingly, indeed suspiciously, relaxed. Moltke remained at Carlsbad with his mineral waters. The Navy Minister, Tirpitz, was at another spa, similarly sipping. Jagow, the Secretary of State for Foreign Affairs, was still away. And now the Chancellor left for his vacation and the Emperor went for a cruise on his yacht. After July 6, the conduct of affairs in Berlin was left to the Undersecretary, Zimmerman, who was presumably well briefed on German policy. There is evidence that this wholesale holiday-making was a ruse to conceal the approaching crisis, and it is clear from the documents that the Emperor decided that his trip must not be canceled if speculation and nervousness were to be avoided. In any case, ruse or not, the dispersal of the German leaders made it impossible for Germany to take any effective action during the course of the next week or so.

In Vienna, when the encouraging dispatches from Szögyény and the no doubt encouraging report of Count Hoyos were received, the formulation of plans got under way. There was no great urgency, since they had decided to wait until July 23 in any case. The Emperor Francis Joseph was informed of the German assurances and advice. Tisza and other members of the Ministerial Council were also informed of the unconditional German promises, and probably of German eagerness for prompt and decisive action. At this Council, Tisza still opposed action that might lead to war. But strong forces were working against him. Count Stürgkh, the Austrian Prime Minister, warned that if the Monarchy failed to act this time, it would lose the confidence of its German ally. And Berchtold wrote to the Hungarian Prime Minister on July 8, "Tschirschky has just left me, who told me that he had received a telegram from Berlin, by which his Imperial Master instructs him to declare emphatically that in Berlin an action of the Monarchy against Serbia is fully expected and that Germany would not understand why we should neglect this opportunity of dealing a blow."[12] The exact nature of the blow envisaged is not indicated, and it has sometimes been argued that this telegram was entirely mythical, an invention to Berchtold to bring pressure to bear on Tisza. But while its text does not appear in the documents, there is a good deal of circumstantial evidence to support its authenticity. And its tenor was perfectly consistent with what the German Emperor and people like Falkenhayn were saying immediately after the Hoyos Mission.

It might be argued that the views of the Germans were only slightly relevant as long as they promised their support. What mattered was what could be agreed on in Vienna. But German encouragement, whatever its intention, was translated by Conrad and Berchtold into an instrument of pressure, and it proved effective. Tisza had already accepted in principle the idea of some stern representations to Serbia, including such demands as punishment of the guilty conspirators and restraint of the Serbian press,

---

12. *Austrian Red Book* (1920), Vol. I, Document No. 10. (Hereinafter, ARB.)

but he required that they be of a sort that the Serbians could reasonably be expected to accept. The war party wanted demands, too, but unacceptable ones.

Berchtold now played his strongest card: he agreed to promise that under no circumstances would any Serbian territory be annexed to the Monarchy, aside from "frontier rectifications" and— it was later added—possible permanent occupation of bridgeheads. He also promised that Austria-Hungary would not mobilize its armies unless and until the demands were rejected.

The exact nature of the demands was settled piecemeal, and it is not clear at exactly what point Tisza acquiesced in their being framed in terms so far-reaching as to be quite possibly unacceptable. For one thing, he had wanted to avoid setting a time limit on the Serbian reply; a time limit suggested an "ultimatum," a definite and sinister term in diplomatic usage implying the expectation of categorical acceptance or the use of force. Eventually he accepted a time limit, but it was to be made clear that the demands constituted not an "ultimatum," but rather a "timed note." He also agreed to far-reaching demands. But he insisted that the text be submitted for approval to another Ministerial Council, and it is possible that he, and even Berchtold and Francis Joseph, thought there was a serious chance that they might be accepted.

Judging by the documents, it seems likely that the terms of the note to Serbia were shaped by four considerations: the general conviction that something drastic had to be done to force Serbia to amend its behavior; the urgings of the Germans; the unwillingness of certain parties, almost certainly Tisza and possibly Berchtold himself, to proceed in ways designed to make an invasion of Serbia absolutely unavoidable; and the demands of others that the note should be merely a pretext for invasion. The first consideration was unanimously accepted; the terms agreed on were probably a compromise designed to realize it, and they were probably a compromise of the last two considerations, strongly influenced by the second.

By July 14, Tisza's acquiescence was substantially complete, and Berchtold hastened to summon Tschirschky to tell him that "to his great pleasure, a *general* agreement on the *tenor* of the note to be transmitted *to Serbia* had been arrived at."[13]

Tisza had been influenced partly by Berchtold's promise to foreswear territorial acquisitions—the slogan, *No More Slavs in the Monarchy*, would thus be satisfied. The reported attitude of Germany no doubt had an important part in his decision. So, perhaps, did the unconscionable misbehavior of the Belgrade press, with its dramatic demonstration that the Serbs had no regrets and would make no promises. In any case, he, too, was prepared to echo the refrain that direct, drastic measures, possibly ending in the use of force, were necessary to preserve Austria-Hungary as a Great Power.

Matters now proceeded in a leisurely way. In accordance with Tisza's demand, there were no serious military preparations, much to Conrad's alarm, but the drawing up of the note continued. Everything possible was done to assure secrecy, in striking contrast to Berchtold's earlier conviction that "public opinion must be prepared." The terms were discussed in the Ministerial Council on July 19 and, after some debate, approved. They were also approved by the Emperor, and arrangements were made for handing the note to the Serbs in the late afternoon of July 23. The French were to leave Russia at eleven that night; word of the note would not have time to reach them before they embarked. In the meantime, nobody, not even the Germans, were told what the text was.

The Germans, however, were impatient. It is arguable how much they knew about the contents of the note; Fischer argues that the main points, at least, were known on July 12; but the evidence is not final.[14] Urgent inquiries were made in Vienna, and on July 22 the Germans were shown the text. Zimmerman in Berlin remarked that it was "too sharp," but Zimmerman was always the most cautious of the German officials, and he had no authority to suggest their revision. There was, moreover, little time to do so. In any case, no objection to its harshness was expressed to Vienna.

13. KD, Doc. No. 50.
14. Fischer, pp. 64–65.

THE THIRD MAN FALLS SICK

Europe in the Dark

Despite Berchtold's efforts, rumors were spreading. As early as July 16, the British Ambassador at Vienna (who had excellent sources of information) reported that "a kind of indictment is being prepared against the Servian Government for alleged complicity in the conspiracy . . . [the] Austro-Hungarian Government are in no mood to parley with Servia, but will insist on immediate unconditional compliance, failing which force will be used."[15] This news evoked remarkably mild responses in London, where all attention was focused upon the desperately serious situation in Ireland. Grey was strikingly *dégagé*. Earlier, he had told the German Ambassador, Prince Lichnowsky, that he hoped any demand that might be made would be of a moderate nature. Now, he rather placidly suggested to the British Ambassador at Saint Petersburg, Sir George Buchanan, that perhaps it would be a good idea for the Russians to talk things over with the Austrians, and expressed the hope that whatever they intended doing in Vienna would be suitably supported with documentary evidence. There was no sign that Grey regarded the situation as particularly threatening or that he thought the Austrians imprudent in contemplating the use of force.

In Saint Petersburg, however, opinion was agitated. Since the Liman von Sanders business the Russians had been very sensitive, the nationalists very raucous. There was a counterpart to Austria's war party, a trend of opinion not exactly in favor of aggression but quite as anti-Austrian as Conrad was anti-Serb. Bosnia still rankled; Russia then had been damaged and insulted, and pious Russians, on hearing the news from Sarajevo, were inclined to see in the Archduke's death an expiation for Habsburg sins in 1908. It was with reluctance that many court officials attended the memorial service that the Emperor Nicholas decreed.

15. *British Documents on the Origins of the War* (1926), Vol. XI, Document No. 50. (Hereinafter, BD.)

Alarming rumors had begun to circulate. There was a general conviction that war was possible; the lapse of time since the assassination apparently was having just the effect that William II feared; shock was wearing off and normal diplomatic wariness and sensitivity replaced it. Nothing definite was known, by July 20, about Austrian plans. The very mystery had an upsetting effect, although the Austro-Hungarian Ambassador was issuing soothing reassurances on every occasion.

The mystery, in Saint Petersburg and elsewhere, was deepened by an odd coincidence in Belgrade. On July 10, the shrewd and influential Russian Minister to Serbia had dropped dead. He had been one of the architects of pan-Serbism, and had ardently supported it in the name of his government, but his reactions to the crisis, if he had lived, might have served to alleviate its consequences. Russia was deprived of the benefits of direct information from Serbia (there was a minor official in charge of the legation), and the Serbs of the advice of the one foreign diplomat they were likely to listen to.

When the French arrived, both mystery and alarm mounted. On July 21, Sazonov told the German Ambassador, Count Pourtalès, that "Russia *would not be able to permit* Austria-Hungary to make any threat against Serbia, or to take any military measures." The Germans were not much alarmed by this; William II wrote in the margin a skeptical, *"qui vivra verra."*[16] Sazonov was both dilatory and fickle, and there was some reason for the Germans to suppose that neither he nor the sporadically pacific Emperor, if left alone, would take a strong line.

They were not, however, left alone. The French presence unquestionably excited some Russians. No records have been found of the private conversations that the Frenchmen had with the Russian leaders. But the atmosphere was ebullient. The French breathed unconditional enthusiasm for the alliance. Innumerable toasts were drunk to Franco-Russian solidarity. Indiscreet grand duchesses at state banquets gossiped with their French dinner partners about the joyous prospect of liquidating the Habsburg Mon-

16. KD, Doc. No. 120.

archy and redeeming Alsace-Lorraine. These frivolities need not be taken very seriously, but the flush of solidarity and self-confidence was strong in Saint Petersburg, and it is certain that Sazonov was, for the moment anyway, in no mood to be docile about Serbia.

Meanwhile, back in Vienna, the text of the note had been decided on. Three days of inaction ensued while the merrymaking proceeded at Petersburg. The chief concern was to discourage discussion. In view of Berchtold's earlier concern about "preparing public opinion," this was surprising and it was almost certainly injudicious. Almost everybody was still saying that, if Serbian guilt could be demonstrated, it would be hard to object to the Austrians' taking strong measures. No effort, however, was made to demonstrate Serbian guilt. A hasty judicial investigation had been made, and on July 13 the investigator's report had been handed to the government at Vienna. It was not as conclusive as might have been wished, since it contained no evidence of connivance or even foreknowledge by the Serbian Cabinet. But it showed beyond doubt that the conspiracy had been made in Belgrade and that some Serbian officials had been involved. In view of what was being planned, the earliest and widest dissemination of even conjectural evidence against Serbs would have seemed expedient. The report was not made public and no statement was distributed to the European capitals before—or for some days after—the presentation of the timed note to Serbia. Europe knew of no legal justification for it.

This was folly. The Germans realized that the most important weapon for disarming critics of the Vienna policy was a public indictment of Serbia and a promise that no annexation of Serbian territory was intended. They were themselves trying to prepare the way by informing their own embassies abroad of an appropriate line to take with foreign governments once Vienna had acted: the ambassadors were to explain the grave condition of Austria-Hungary, the imminence of its collapse as a Great Power if no action were taken against Serbia, and the extreme desirability of preventing the dispute from leading to "European complications." It may be that this position was designed to conceal the fact that Germany was planning to use the occasion for a preventive war if "complications" arose. It may also be argued that the Germans were at this time trying their best to conceal that they knew what the Austrians were intending, so that they might, when the time came, appear to be as surprised as anybody else. But this again is conjectural; and there is not much reason to suppose that the explanation offered in advance to the embassies was not fairly true to fact.

Whether it was or not, the behavior of the Austrians did nothing to ease the position of the Germans. It seemed that they were determined to carry out their private vendetta and to let nothing and nobody interfere with it. Now that agreement had been, with so much trouble, finally reached, and now that German encouragement had been given, there was apparently enormous reluctance on the part of the Austro-Hungarian government to do anything that would reopen discussion. The Austrians were being almost incredibly cavalier.

One explanation for this was the smug complacency that Germany would deal with any complications. Another can be found in the long story of provocation and alarm since 1903. Austrian attention had become so narrowly focused on the South Slav problem that all other objects in their field of vision were seriously blurred. And the focus was further narrowed, during those first weeks of July, by the difficulty of securing agreement on a policy, any policy, for dealing with the desperate problem.

The reason for the difficulty was partly constitutional. For major policy decisions a complicated process of negotiation and compromise was necessary; it had rarely if ever been achieved in recent years. Now that it was, publicity meant jeopardy. The reason was also in part national. The diversity of nations in the Monarchy involved not only dangers but basic disagreements about foreign policy. To submit a decision once made to public discussion imperiled not only the decision but the state. It was this vulnerability that cloaked Austrian policy in these days with the quality of mystery that was so poor a preparation for the steps that were contemplated.

CHAPTER SEVEN

THE BREAKDOWN OF EUROPE

The Ultimatum Rejected

THE timed note was duly delivered to the Serbian government by the Austrian Minister at Belgrade at six o'clock on the afternoon of July 23, 1914. For its time it was a formidable document, perhaps, as Grey was to say of it, the most formidable document ever presented by one independent state to another.

The note began with a long preamble recalling the obligations the Serbs had assumed, in the humbling aftermath of Bosnia, to refrain from provoking Austria-Hungary, and proceeded to assert that, far from honoring this promise, they had encouraged the growth of a subversive movement aimed at "detaching a part of the territories of Austria-Hungary from the Monarchy." The "culpable tolerance" of the Serbian government had permitted, the preamble continued, "all manifestations of a nature to incite the Serbian population to hatred of the Monarchy and contempt of its institutions," as well as the making of the conspiracy against the Heir to the Throne on Serbian territory. The results of the plot were to impose upon the government of the Monarchy "the duty of putting to an end the intrigues which form a perpetual menace to the tranquility of the Monarchy."

All this was true enough, although by the standards of diplomatic usage it was stated with staggering baldness. What followed was much balder. There were ten demands, starkly but not precisely phrased. The imprecision may have been intentional, or it may have represented the difficulties of securing agreement on the purpose of the note. The first three required the immediate cessation of anti-Austrian publications, the dissolution of anti-Austrian societies (the relatively harmless *Narodna Obrana* was mentioned by name, but not the guilty Black Hand, of whose existence the Austro-Hungarian government was ignorant), and the elimination of anti-Austrian books and instruction from Serbian schools. The fourth required the removal from office of anti-Austrian civil servants and army officers whose "names and deeds" the Monarchy "reserved the right of communicating" to the Serbian government —a demand that at least suggested that the Serbian government must fire anybody the Monarchy wanted fired.

But this was only the beginning. The fifth demand required "the collaboration of representatives" of Austria-Hungary for the suppression of the subversive movement directed against the territorial integrity of the Monarchy; the sixth required the participation of delegates of Austria-Hungary in an investigation leading to trial of the conspirators and their accessories. The seventh required the arrest of Tanksovich and Ciganovich, the two leading conspirators in Serbian territory. The eighth required effective measures to prevent illegal frontier traffic, and punishment of conniving frontier officials. The ninth demanded explanations of "unjustifiable utterances of high Serbian officials," apparently but not certainly in connection with the assassination; and the last required that the Austro-Hungarian government be notified without delay of the measures taken to execute the previous demands. Unconditional acceptance with forty-eight hours was required. On the early morning of July 24, the news of the ultimatum began to filter into foreign capitals. And Europe began to erupt.

The first and most violent of the volcanic reactions was of course in Saint Petersburg. There, the Foreign Minister, exhausted by the festivities in honor of the departing French, was wakened by a terrible alarm: the text of the ultimatum, received by wire from Belgrade at seven that morning. Sazonov, dilatory but volatile, was furious: "This means a European war," he prophetically cried, and berated the Austro-Hungarian Ambassador with charges of criminal bellicosity. In more diplomatic language, the Ambassador wired to Vienna, "The minister . . . was noncompliant and hostile."[1] The Emperor Nicholas II, never quick to grasp implications, professed himself disturbed.

The flames of Sazonov's fury were fed at the luncheon given that day for him—and the British Ambassador—by the French Ambassador. Paléologue, instead of trying to soothe him, encouraged him in his rage with advocacy of a firm policy and renewed assurances of French support. But these affirmations were scarcely needed. Sazonov, like most of the important people in Russia, had been convinced by a hasty reading of the ultimatum that war was possible and might be imminent, and, in his anger, he was already anxious to take military measures.

The reasons for the violence of this reaction, like the reasons for the demands that provoked it, were cumulative. Sazonov, whose personality was in some ways similar to Berchtold's, was in a rather similar position. He was inclined to indecision and superficiality. His record, since he had succeeded Izvolsky, had been far from brilliant. Like Berchtold, he had been criticized for insufficient resolution. Berchtold's humiliations in 1912 had been succeeded by Sazonov's in the Liman von Sanders affair. But unlike Berchtold he was given to passions, and now he was in the middle of one.

The personality of the Foreign Minister was not the only thing that directed Russian policy toward ferocity after the delivery of the Austrian ultimatum, although it was the most important. Sazonov was only one of many influential people who had been developing a morbid distrust of the Central Powers, as Germany and Austria-

1. ARB, II, 19.

Hungary were called. The army, and in particular, Grand Duke Nicholas, the commander-in-chief, were belligerently anti-German. Liman von Sanders had confirmed well-founded suspicions, long growing, that the Germans were themselves working toward domination of Turkey. The German patronage of the Turks, the Berlin-Bagdad Railway, the general aura of German chauvinism, confirmed the statements of German publicists that German destinies lay "in the East." The Russian preoccupation with Constantinople made them view the *Drang nach Osten*—the German "Drive to the East" —as a matter vital to Russian national interest and national honor. Since Constantinople did not belong to Russia (and never could, without a major war), it was difficult for them to complain about the merely suspected threats of Germany to it. But almost everything that had happened since the embarrassment of 1908 had been interpreted in the light of a sinister plot to secure something that the Russians wanted for themselves. The only socially acceptable counter to this plot was to insist on the rights of the Balkan peoples to develop free from "Germanic" interference (by which was meant interference from either Austria-Hungary or Germany). Russia therefore had presented itself, from time to time, as the protector of the independence and the aspirations of the Balkan peoples. But this altruistic concern veiled a dog in the manger, whose existence was perfectly, though tacitly, apprehended everywhere.

It was therefore natural that the Russians should see in the ultimatum a German plot to occupy the Balkans, and a form of indirect aggression against Russia. Many other people thought so, too. For this reason the Austrian failure to prepare the ground by suitable advance explanations was doubly ill judged; and for this reason Sazonov had gone off half-cocked on Friday, July 24. Purple with rage, he told the German Ambassador to his face that Austria was planning to gobble the Balkans piecemeal and that Germany was conniving in the project. On Friday evening, at seven o'clock, he had a talk with the Serbian Minister, Spalaikovich, at Saint Petersburg, in which he apparently said that Russia would support Serbia and may have urged that the Austrian demands should not be accepted. And he proposed that the Russian Army should be mobilized against Austria as a form of deterrent.

All of this was ill considered; the mobilization proposal was proof of it. It put Russia in the position of being the first Power to consider military measures. Moreover, it violated the very carefully laid mobilization plans that had been developed on the assumption that Austria-Hungary and Germany would fight together; mobilization against Austria alone would throw out all the intricate planning, and would mean the reallocation of reserves. But the general fury was so strong that the rash project was accepted in principle. At a Council of Ministers on Saturday, July 25, it was agreed that measures preliminary to mobilization—called the Period Preparatory to War—should be decreed, and that, if Austrian forces entered Serbia, Russian mobilization against Austria would be proclaimed.

In less than forty-eight hours after the delivery of the timed note, then, the Russian Army was alerted for "mobilization." The term, now obsolete, deserves comment. Mobilization was a recognized act and condition; it meant not merely, as the word suggests, making the armies mobile, but also calling up reserves, cancelling leaves, transferring troops to battle stations, imposing martial law in frontier areas, manning fortresses, taking over rail transport, and a thousand other measures that transformed the standing army into a much larger national force ready for action. It involved very careful and detailed plans in advance which, like all military plans, were practically impossible to alter, and difficult to arrest, once they began to be carried out. It was sometimes stated before 1914 that "mobilization means war." This was not in any literal sense true, but there *were* implications in mobilization even more serious than the mere difficulty of halting it once started. One was the matter of timing, already noted as a crucial consideration in the making of the Schlieffen Plan. Once one neighbor started to mobilize, another neighbor was practically obliged to do so if he were not to be left defenseless in the face of an enemy poised for attack. The fact that

Russia—because of huge areas, poor transport, and general bureau-cratic lethargy—required much longer for mobilization than any other Power undoubtedly played a role in Russian calculations on Friday and Saturday, July 24 and 25. The clumsiness of Russian military arrangements required early decision, but once the decision had been taken it meant a threat to Austria-Hungary and Germany.

Sazonov, in his impulsiveness, had conceived the foolish scheme of mobilization against Austria merely as a form of pressure, a political action. But the dangers of trying to improvise an unplanned partial mobilization were fully understood by Russian generals, and it was because of them that mobilization was, in the Council on Saturday, delayed pending actual invasion of Serbia. The Period Preparatory to War, however, was quite ominous enough to drive home the danger of the situation. The hair-trigger reaction of the volatile Sazonov had already transformed a Balkan into a world crisis. The decisive step had been delayed, and Sazonov's temper began to cool; there followed a brief period when he and his colleagues showed a greater willingness to try to reach a diplomatic settlement.

Reactions elsewhere to the ultimatum were strong but not violent. In Rome, the government contented itself with pointing out that if war resulted from the Austrian ultimatum, Italy would not be obliged, under the terms of the Triple Alliance, to take part in it, since it would not be the result of an aggressive action against Austria or Germany. In Paris, Bienvenu-Martin, the Minister of Justice, was in charge of the government—the President and the Prime Minister (who was also Foreign Minister), being afloat in the Baltic, could be communicated with only via radio from Stockholm. The reactions of the Justice Minister were on the whole mild; in conversation with the Austrian Ambassador he expressed a friendly understanding of the Austrian problem in connection with Serbia. The reaction of the seaborne dignitaries was confined to urging, by radio, that Serbia request an extension of the time limit.

In London, reactions were mildest of all. The government was deeply involved in the Irish problem, and a Cabinet meeting devoted to it occupied a good deal of the day on Friday, July 24, and, no doubt, much of the attention of Sir Edward Grey. On Saturday the ministers dispersed for weekends in the country, in accordance with the pleasant British custom. Sir Edward remained in town for the night, but although he grasped the formidable nature of the Austrian demands and was concerned to prevent complications, his attitude was curiously detached. Britain, he said, could take no direct part in a Balkan crisis, and added that British opinion would never support a war on behalf of Serbia. He realized that Russian reaction was bound to be strong, and he actually approved and encouraged the Russian program for partial mobilization as a legitimate form of political pressure. He hoped that the time limit on the ultimatum might be extended. In conversation with French Ambassador Jules Cambon, he suggested that the four Great Powers less immediately concerned in the affair, Britain, France, Germany, and Italy, ought to mediate.

Mediation was a recognized form of diplomatic activity, a somewhat less formal and precise version of arbitration. Its applicability to the present situation was, however, questionable. The problem was what was to be mediated, and between whom. Cambon suggested mediation by the four Powers of the dispute between Austria and Serbia, and this Grey proposed at once to the German Ambassador, Prince Lichnowsky, on the late afternoon of Friday, July 24. The proposal was badly received. Austria and Serbia were not equals; for Austria to accept mediation would be to compromise its dignity. But as between Austria and Russia, if trouble arose, mediation by the other Powers would be possible. The suggestion was sent to Berlin, with Lichnowsky's backing. Tardily, and in a way that gives every reason to doubt their good faith, the German authorities told Lichnowsky that they would accept the British proposal should the occasion arise. They also said that they had forwarded Grey's simultaneous suggestion for an extension of the time limit to Vienna, but this they delayed doing until after the time limit had expired.

Sir Edward was already being urged by his own officials to do

something more positive than this. It was pointed out to him that
Great Britain, not committed by alliance, was in a position to bring
strong pressure to bear. This could be done by threatening Germany
with British participation in any European war on the side of the
Entente Powers. But this Grey refused to do. With his diplomatic
scruples, and perhaps because he did not fully grasp the dangers of
the situation, he thought it would be improper to do privately what
he could not dare do publicly; it would have been constitutionally
dubious and politically perilous. Opinion would not support him,
in either the country or the Cabinet; there was a powerful, articulate,
perhaps predominant, school of thought, well represented among
the ministers, strongly opposed to any steps likely to lead to British
participation in a war that seemed likely to benefit no nation so
much as autocratic Russia. Moreover, Grey believed that Britain,
standing aloof and invoking the good offices of Germany and France
and Italy, and the good sense, if any, of Russia and Austria, could
perform its most useful service. Now convinced, apparently, that
he had done so—and having delayed for a day his customary weekend in the interests of saving the world from war—he departed for
a well-earned rest at his cottage in the country.

It is impossible to say that a more positive British policy would
have had any effect on the course of action. It is uncertain that even
in the absence of the Irish crisis a more positive policy would have
been possible. It is an undoubted fact that the Cabinet and the
public viewed the Serbian situation as remote from British interests,
and were recalcitrantly reluctant to envisage a British commitment
to engage in hostilities, which limited Grey's ability to make very
effective threats. But Ireland had its effect: the Germans were count-
ing on Ireland to distract British attention, and they believed it was
doing so.

The reactions to the ultimatum in Berlin are less clear. Many of
the German leaders, including the Emperor, were still on their
holidays. The Chancellor and the Foreign Secretary, however, were
back in Berlin, resolute in their support for Austria-Hungary—
nowhere is there any documented echo on their part of Zimmer-

man's reaction to the text of the ultimatum that it was "too sharp." As will be seen presently, it seems probable that Bethmann-Hollweg and Jagow were urging Vienna to act, and to act fast. The line they took with other governments was to express hopes that the Austro-Serbian dispute should be "localized." This word, much used by German ambassadors abroad in their discussions with agitated foreign ministers, sounded well. It suggested a due concern for European peace. But the notion was either naïve or disingenuous; to localize the Austro-Serb dispute meant, simply, letting Austria have its way and preventing anybody's interfering with its projected crushing of the Serbs. And this meant preventing the Russians from interfering.

It will be observed that, while the Germans thought Russia must and could be prevented from interfering, the Russians thought that Austria must be persuaded or threatened into abandoning its project. The two notions were precisely incompatible.

In Belgrade, after the delivery of the Austro-Hungarian demands, there was at first confusion. The Prime Minister was on a campaign trip in southern Serbia, and did not get back to the capital until Friday morning. What happened when he did is not certain. Many historians assumed (in the absence of any reliable documentary evidence from the Serbian archives) that the Serbian ministers, from their first glance, found the demands unacceptable. This is to some extent borne out by the reported first reaction of Ljuba Jovanovich, "Well, there is nothing to do but die fighting";[2] and by the spirited tone of defiance the Serbian Foreign Office sounded in its notes to foreign governments. But the most authoritative writer, Luigi Albertini, has been at pains to prove that this was not the case. The government, he says, was acutely aware of the military inadequacy and political weakness of Serbia; they knew, of course, that it did not stand a chance against Austria. The Serbian ministers abroad, and especially in Saint Petersburg, were asking for foreign aid and support; unless it was forthcoming, Albertini believes, the

2. Quoted in Fay, *The Origins of the World War*, II, 337; variously quoted in other authorities, and in any case based on secondhand evidence.

ministers were prepared to consider accepting the Austrian demands
—unconditionally or with reservations. He produces much sug-
gestive information to support the theory, which seems on the face
of it plausible; in such circumstances, differences of opinion were to
be expected. And it is also plausible to accept the statement of another Italian scholar that the Serbian chief of staff urged, and the
Cabinet agreed, that no decision be reached until Russian advice had
been solicited.

Russian advice was presently available. Sazonov, it will be re-
membered, had a talk with the Serbian Minister at Saint Petersburg at seven on the evening of Friday the twenty-fourth. Published
accounts of this conversation indicate that Sazonov urged on the
Serbs a calm and conciliatory attitude, but the documents are
unreliable in this case and from what is known of the Russian
Foreign Minister's mood that day, it seems unlikely that he did so.
It is at least probable that he told Spalaikovich that Russia would
support Serbia and that he was trying to secure approval for partial
Russian mobilization; there is circumstantial evidence to suggest
that this was indeed the tenor of the conversation. In any case, the
news of the Russian military measures, along with Spalaikovich's
dispatch, did reach Belgrade at noon on Saturday, six hours before
the expiry of the time limit. In those six hours the Serbian response
to the ultimatum took a definite, and determined, form.

At three o'clock Saturday afternoon, the Serbs ordered the mobilization of the army. They made plans, the execution of which began
immediately, to transfer the government from Belgrade, dangerously exposed to Austrian guns across the Danube, to southern
Serbia. And they drew up their answer to the ultimatum. The translation of the text was completed barely in time to be delivered to
the Austro-Hungarian Legation at the moment the time limit expired.

The Serbian reply was a masterpiece of diplomatic language,
especially considering the speed with which it was composed. The
Serbs had been advised by everybody to be conciliatory, and they
were; butter remained visibly unmelted in their mouths. Five of

the ten demands were accepted outright; four others with reservations or reasonable requests for clarification. Only the sixth, the somewhat anomalous demand that Austro-Hungarian agents collaborate in investigations relating to the bringing to trial of accessories to the plot, was rejected. The appearance of the reply was so conciliatory, even sycophantic, as to be seriously embarrassing to the Austrians, who felt obliged before passing it to their representatives abroad to append a long essay pointing out in precisely what ways it was evasively and cunningly contrived to negate the reality of the demands.

The Serbs had done the best they could, which was from one point of view the best imaginable. The Austrians were correct; the reply, if carefully analyzed, was very far from acceptance, although it made a telling propaganda point and served the Serbian cause well. But as far as the Austrians went, the subtleties of the text were of no importance. The Austrian Minister, Baron Giesl, was already under orders to reject any reply that was not a complete and unconditional acceptance. The text was handed him at six o'clock on Saturday evening. He immediately signed and sent off a previously prepared note announcing to the Serbs the breaking off of diplomatic relations; then he burned the code books and managed to catch the six-thirty train from the Belgrade station, where he noted crowds of soldiers already answering the proclamation of mobilization issued three hours earlier. By six-forty that evening, the train had crossed the Danube bridge and Giesl was on Habsburg territory. By six-forty-five, he was on the telephone to Tisza, in Budapest, from the Hungarian frontier town; all that was needed, in reply to Tisza's anxious question, was a single word to inform him that the reply had been unsatisfactory and that relations had been broken.

Austria Goes to War

The reaction in Austria-Hungary to the Serbian rejection of the ultimatum (everybody was calling it that now, forgetting the minute distinction of a "timed note") was varied, reflecting the deep differences that had accompanied its drafting. Public opinion in Vienna was jubilant; when the news broke, there were parades and singing in the streets and what the British Ambassador referred to as "a frenzy of delight."[3] The delight, if not the frenzy, was presumably shared by the war party and its leader, General Conrad, who now at last received permission to mobilize against Serbia. It was not shared by the Emperor, who wearily observed on receiving the news of the diplomatic break that it did not necessarily mean war; or by Tisza, who still hoped for a diplomatic settlement. And it is not certain that it was shared by Count Berchtold, who seems to have regarded acceptance as a serious possibility and who had written on July 21 (before the ultimatum was sent, but after its terms were decided) to the Austrian Ambassador at Rome indicating that he hoped for a peaceful solution.

Mobilization, *against Serbia alone, not general mobilization,* was authorized. Conrad decided to take preliminary steps on Monday (it being now late Saturday night) and to proclaim it publicly on Tuesday, July 28. But no decision to declare war was made. Conrad, asked for the date when he could conveniently commence hostilities, replied that August 12 would be suitable. It would take some time to complete mobilization. There did not appear to be much sense of urgency in Vienna.

Reactions differed elsewhere. In the country for his abbreviated weekend, Sir Edward Grey received on Sunday morning the alarming news of the break in relations, along with a suggestion from the head of the Foreign Office, Sir Arthur Nicolson, that it might be well to renew in a different form the proposal for Four-Power discussions of the problem. What Nicolson suggested specifically, and what was then proposed to the governments concerned, was an ambassadors' conference along the lines of that which had been successful in ending the Balkan Wars of 1912 and 1913. The precedent was a happy one, but now the circumstances were different, for it was a question, not of a conference of Great Powers to deal with a small war among the Balkan countries, but rather of one to settle a dispute between one Balkan country and one of their

3. BD, XI, 676.

own number. Nonetheless, it seemed to be the best thing the British could propose, given the fact that Sir Edward thought circumstances precluded him from exerting pressure on either his friend, Russia, or his opponent, Germany.

The proposal was duly made. In Rome and Paris it was accepted, although the Italians said that they did not feel it would be proper to bring any pressure to bear on their allies, Austria and Germany. In Paris, with Poincaré and Viviani still absent at sea, a good deal of confusion was produced by the Acting Premier's inexperience and uncertainty. He was trying to reassure the Germans about his peaceful intentions—reassurances that gave rise to quite misleading impressions about French policy in Berlin. The British proposal was in time referred to the absent leaders, who immediately accepted it.

But in Russia, Grey's proposal met with an odd fate. Sazonov's attitude had changed during the course of the past day. For one thing, he had gotten over his temper. For another, he was surprised and relieved to learn, on Sunday morning, that the Austro-Serbian break had not been accompanied, as he had feared, by an immediate invasion. He was inclined now to think that a solution might be found and that the Serbian reply might serve as the basis for negotiations. This more cooperative frame of mind was greatly enhanced by an interview that took place that morning with the German Ambassador, Count Pourtalès, when they happened to meet on the platform of a suburban railroad station. The tactful Pourtalès took advantage of the Foreign Minister's more equable mood; in response to assurances about Russia's eagerness to avoid trouble, he urged the desirability of friendly conversation with Austria-Hungary. Sazonov was willing. That evening a remarkably friendly discussion did indeed take place between him and the Austro-Hungarian Ambassador, Count Szápáry. Szápáry did not know exactly what was happening at home; otherwise, he might not have gotten on so well. As it was, he explained in great detail that Austria's purpose was purely one of self-preservation and that nobody in the Monarchy had the slightest desire to damage Russia's interests.

Sazonov visibly melted. He was much assuaged by the assurance that Austria-Hungary would under no circumstance annex any Serbian territory. He told Szápáry how exasperating the Russians themselves had been finding the Serbs, with their terrorism and their ambitions, and he suggested that the Serbian reply be used as a basis for negotiation and that perhaps the whole question might be submitted for mediation to the King of England. Szápáry was not authorized to make, or accept, any definite proposals, but the meeting was so encouraging that Sazonov told London that he thought that the proposal for a conference should be postponed while Russia continued direct conversations with Austria-Hungary.

In Berlin, a less favorable reaction was encountered by the British. The British Ambassador was told on Monday that the suggested conference would involve summoning Austria-Hungary before "a European court of justice," and that this could not be permitted. Renewed hopes of "localization" were expressed. And hope, too, was placed in the "direct conversations" between Russia and Austria, which had now been reported by Pourtalès.

The situation in Berlin, where anti-Russian and anti-Serbian street demonstrations were beginning, was complicated by the absence of the top men. The Emperor did not return from his yachting trip until Monday afternoon. Of the military and naval authorities, Moltke reached the capital from his spa Sunday night and Tirpitz Monday noon. Meanwhile, the conduct of affairs continued in the hands of Chancellor Bethmann-Hollweg and Secretary of Foreign Affairs Jagow.

Their policy seems to have been a consistent application of principles laid down in early July. Most historians have thought they were consistently backing strong Austrian measures, and many think that they were urging Austria to invade Serbia as soon as a Serbian rejection of the ultimatum was received. There is documentary evidence for this: on Saturday, before the time limit had expired or the Serbian reply been made, the Austro-Hungarian Ambassador in Berlin, Szögyény, had wired his government: "Here every delay in the beginning of war operations is regarded as signifying the danger that foreign powers might interfere. We are urgently advised to proceed without delay and to place before the world a *fait accompli.*"[4]

Szögyény's telegram is definite; and it is not only perfectly harmonious with what is known of German attitudes at the beginning of July but it is confirmed by telegrams to and from Tschirschky, the German Ambassador at Vienna. This German attitude of urging a speedy *fait accompli* is further confirmed by the extreme casualness with which the text of the Serbian reply was treated; it was available from the Serbian Legation, but nobody apparently bothered to read it for several days—apparently the Germans were not interested in knowing anything except that it was "negative" and had led to the breaking of diplomatic relations. It is further confirmed by the perfunctory reception of Grey's proposals for Four-Power mediation and, later, Four-Power ambassadors' conference, as well as mild British suggestions that a moderating influence should be exerted by the Germans at Vienna. These were hastily dismissed by Bethmann-Hollweg and Jagow, and while Berchtold was informed of the second proposal, it was not suggested by the Germans that he ought to consider accepting it.

The presiding authorities no doubt thought that they were taking a line previously agreed. It is known, too, that they were also beguiled by misjudgments. The Italians were refusing suggestions from London that they exert influence on Austria and Germany. The French, represented by an Acting Prime Minister nervously equivocating and muttering soothing words to the German Ambassador at Paris about the peaceful intentions of France, were quite erroneously viewed as unwilling to become involved on behalf of their angry ally, Russia. Things were not to change in this respect until Wednesday, when Poincaré and Viviani finally got home. And as regards London, serious misunderstandings persisted. The Ambassador, Prince Lichnowsky, was stern in his reports about the chances of Britain's remaining neutral in case of war. But his telegrams of warning were disregarded. He was suspected of Anglophilia and was discounted as a Cassandra: as early as July 18 he had told his government that "localization" lay in "the realm of pious

4. ARB, II, 34.

wishes. There were, moreover, conflicting and encouraging reports from other quarters. A conversation on July 24 between Winston Churchill and the influential German shipping magnate, Albert Ballin, left the latter with the impression that Britain would fight only if Germany tried to "swallow up" France.[5] Later the King of Great Britain, on Sunday afternoon, had a conversation with his cousin Prince Henry of Prussia, the Emperor William's brother, who happened to be visiting England, which left the Prussian Prince with a similar impression: the King was understood to have said he hoped that England would remain neutral if a Continental war broke out.

It is probable that Ballin misunderstood Churchill, and it is certain that nothing King George might say would have any importance in the making of British policy, but the two statements had the effect in Berlin of contradicting Lichnowsky's gloomy warnings, consolidating the impression caused by the recent improvement in British-German relations, and emphasizing Grey's steadfast refusal to say anything that might hint in any way, shape, or form at Britain's future policy.

The result of these misjudgments was to fortify the "pious wish" that Russia would be left unsupported if it tried to make trouble and that the diplomatic situation was favorable for Austria. Whether or not there was a firm policy of urging the Austrians to quick military action, the confused impression that obtained in Berlin suggested that prudence demanded speedy and decisive action.

It must be kept in mind—what is obvious but easy to overlook—that nobody in Berlin knew what was going to happen. The mistaken optimism about Italy, France, and England enveloped them; and the situation in Vienna was still unclarified. As far as the men in Berlin knew anything about it, they believed that hostilities were being scheduled by the Austrians for August 12, the date officially determined in Vienna on Saturday, July 25, a delay that understandably seemed dangerous to them. Moltke, reaching Berlin Sunday night, wrote on Monday, "The situation continues to be extremely

5. Quoted in Albertini, *The Origins of the War of 1914,* II, 412.

obscure . . . It will be about another fortnight before anything definite can be known or said."[6]

The Emperor reached Berlin on Monday afternoon, having interrupted his yachting trip against the advice of Bethmann-Hollweg. He arrived in a characteristic rage. Everything that had happened in the past couple of days had been exasperating. Bethmann-Hollweg had been giving him advice—not to return from his cruise, not to order the navy back to its bases—which the Monarch regarded as both impertinent and unwise. He had been, he thought, insufficiently supplied with information. Bethmann-Hollweg was trying to keep him calm and prevent him from interfering. By the time he got back, most of the important decisions had been taken.

The most important of all was taken in Vienna. Instead of delaying a declaration of war until August 12, when they would be able to begin fighting, the Austrians suddenly decided to issue it on Tuesday, July 28, and so informed the Germans late Monday afternoon, when William II was trying to catch up on accumulated papers. He did not, for example, read the text of the Serbian reply until Tuesday, nor was he, apparently, informed of the latest proposal for mediation from Sir Edward Grey.

The reasons for the change of mind in Vienna have been the subject for much debate. There are two principal theories: One, that Berchtold and Conrad were alarmed by the reactions of Europe, and especially Russia, and began to fear pressure from other quarters that would oblige them to negotiate instead of carrying out their private war. Second, that they were persuaded by Bethmann-Hollweg and Jagow (before the Emperor returned) that Austria must present the world with a *fait accompli*. There is not much direct evidence for the first theory, and as noted above there is a good deal for the second. It is also quite likely, though there is no real evidence, that Bethmann-Hollweg and Jagow were deliberately trying to keep the Emperor William ignorant of what they were doing, both before and immediately after his return to Berlin. It is plausible enough; anyone trying to pursue a consistent policy would

6. Moltke's *Memoirs*; quoted in Albertini, II, 437.

certainly have wished to prevent his meddling; he was maddeningly fickle and trivial. There is good reason to believe that the Emperor had told them that it would be impolitic to disregard or decline further proposals from Great Britain for mediation and that they *pretended* both to their own sovereign and to the German Ambassador in London that they were willing to cooperate with Sir Edward while simultaneously and furtively urging the Austrians to declare war as soon as possible.

By that afternoon, Sir Edward had read the Serbian reply and felt that it met all reasonable demands the Austrians might have. He therefore insisted to Lichnowsky that England must now take an active interest in the matter, and pressed a new proposal for intervention. Lichnowsky so informed Berlin, adding his own exhortation in favor of accepting Sir Edward's suggestion. Bethmann-Hollweg replied that Germany *did* accept.

Upon the terms with which this latest English proposal on the evening of Monday, July 27, was forwarded to Vienna, hinges the controversy about Jagow's and Bethman-Hollweg's sinister behavior. The chief evidence for their wickedness and duplicity is again a telegram from Ambassador Szögyény in Berlin to his own government in Vienna which was sent at nine-fifteen Monday night. In it he said that Jagow had emphatically disassociated himself from the English proposals and had passed them on merely to avoid irritating Sir Edward Grey. Jagow, Szögyény said, could not himself support the English proposals, "because the conflict with Servia was a question of *prestige* for the Austro-Hungarian Monarchy, which Germany shares to some extent."[7] Jagow was reported as not in the slightest degree favoring consideration being given to Sir Edward's proposal; but he thought it very important that England should not side with Russia. There is supporting evidence from other sources that this was a true reflection of the line that Jagow was taking.

The principal defense for Jagow and Bethmann-Hollweg in this connection rests upon the assertion that Szögyény misunderstood. He was, to be sure, an old man, whose retirement had already been

7. ARB, II, 68.

ordered. Jagow himself later claimed that he often thought Szögyény was unclear in his understanding. But there is no real evidence of confusion in this case. And the conversation as he reported it was, in many ways, natural enough. Bethmann-Hollweg and Jagow had for some days been executing a policy aimed at a *fait accompli* by Austria-Hungary. It coincided with previous German policy, defined in early July, to the effect that (a) strong measures were necessary to preserve the Habsburg Monarchy; (b) the quicker such measures were taken, the better; (c) the Austrians were notoriously given to backing down at the last moment, and needed stiffening. To these had been added, during the period when the Emperor was on his yacht and the military chiefs occupied with their mineral waters, the additional considerations (d) once the ultimatum had been presented and diplomatic relations broken, Austrian inaction became more and more a sign of weakness and an invitation to meddling by Europe, and (e) the moment seemed opportune for frustrating Russian intervention by the reluctance of the rest of Europe to start a general war for which, in any case, Germany was well prepared.

But the theory that they resolutely and deceitfully egged the Austrians on does not—and so far as the telegram about Grey's proposals goes, cannot—mean that they were responsible for the change of date for the declaration of war. *The decision had been taken earlier.* If German influence was decisive, it was influence exerted before Szögyény's telegram arrived. On Sunday, Berchtold had summoned Conrad (according to the latter's memoirs) and told him that, regardless of when military operations could actually begin, an immediate declaration of war was expedient, and by Monday afternoon the necessary arrangements had been made. The telegram giving notice of the decision reached Berlin a little after 4:30 P.M., some five hours before Szögyény's was sent.

The influence of Bethmann and Jagow, previously exerted, may have been important. But other influences had been at work in Vienna. Berchtold was himself receiving reassuring reports from Szápáry, who was telling him all about his friendly interview with

Sazonov. At the same time they were hearing rumors about the Period Preparatory to War—on Monday they had told Tschirschky that they found them worrisome, and may have wanted to get started on Serbia before the threat of complications led anybody to put pressure on them. It probably did not require the Germans' disclaimers to convince people in Vienna that Grey's proposals, however embarrassing to reject, would lead to endless complications if accepted. Both the Austrians and the Germans presumably apprehended the danger that European negotiations of any sort would bog down in the kind of compromise that would leave the authority of the Habsburg Monarchy seriously damaged without any compensating alleviation of the Serbian threat. That had happened before; it could not be allowed to happen again. If the Germans had not bothered to read the Serbian reply, the Austrians had, and they knew that they were up against the danger that Europe might believe the Serbs truly anxious to please. In fact, Sir Edward Grey's reaction to the reply demonstrated precisely this; and an even more stunning demonstration of it was to be forthcoming after William II had had time to peruse the text. One might hazard the suggestion that the cleverness of the Serbs, as well as the pressure of the Germans and the threat of the Russians, was responsible for the speed-up of the plans. As the Austrians began to understand what its effect would be, the need for a *fait accompli* became urgent. And Berchtold in Vienna, and Bethmann-Hollweg and Jagow in Berlin, now had reason to hope that "localization" was feasible. In any case, the decision to advance the date for war was taken.

In accordance with the plan agreed to on Monday, the Serbian government was notified at noon on Tuesday, by telegram to Nish, whither it had been removed, that a state of war existed between Austria-Hungary and Serbia. It was stated in the telegram that Serbian troops had attacked Austro-Hungarian forces at the border town of Temes-Kubin. This was the legal pretext for the declaration, and it may have been used as a means of persuading the Emperor Francis Joseph to agree to it. There *had* been a rather anomalous incident at Temes-Kubin, involving a boatload of Serbian troops on the river, late Monday night, but it had nothing to do with the decision to declare war, which, as far as Conrad and Berchtold went, had been reached some hours before it took place.

The Powers Mobilize

From the standpoint of the realities of power, the Austrian declaration of war on Tuesday, July 28, changed nothing. The troops of the Habsburg Monarchy were no more nearly ready to march than they had been the day before. The interests of the Powers remained what they had been. But in law and in attitudes the effect was revolutionary. For the first time in a generation a Great Power was at war against another European state; making peace before hostilities actually began would be extremely difficult, although not everybody regarded it as impossible; and Russia and its friends and allies were powerfully confirmed in their conviction that Austria-Hungary and Germany were bent upon a course of invasion and chastisement regardless of consequences. Whatever they might do now, the Germans could not escape the odium for having done nothing earlier to restrain their ally; and the failure to do something seemed to many so grossly apparent and so appallingly irresponsible as to suggest that it must have resulted not from misunderstanding of the consequences but from ulterior motives to set Europe on fire.

There was no intention deliberately to set Europe on fire in Berlin, at least among the civilians who were still making decisions, or on the part of the Emperor. The events that followed the Austrian declaration of war demonstrated it. But these events could not be made publicly known. Germany was committed to support Austria-Hungary and was perfectly willing to risk a general war, even though many Germans were now alarmed by what was happening. They could not, they thought, openly admit either their mistakes or their willingness to run risks; they were, therefore, obliged to keep their misgivings secret and, in the end, to accept a general war that they had expected to avoid.

The Emperor William II read the text of the Serbian reply on the morning of Tuesday, July 28, before the declaration of war had been dispatched and apparently before he had been told it had been decided on. The effect on him of the Serbs' masterpiece was precisely what it had been on Sir Edward Grey when he had read it forty-eight hours earlier. In the margin William wrote in longhand a famous note: "This is more than one could have expected! A great moral success for Vienna; but with it every reason for war drops away, and Giesl might have remained quietly in Belgrade! On the strength of this *I* should never have ordered mobilization."[8] He wrote at once in the same tenor to Jagow, saying that he thought the Austrians ought to be congratulated on a brilliant success, that no more cause for war existed, that the most the Austrians should do would be to occupy Belgrade or other territory as a pledge for execution of the Serb promises, and that he himself would mediate for peace on this basis.

It is possible that the Emperor, having come upon the scene without the background of Bethmann-Hollweg's and Jagow's optimistic appraisal of the European situation, had a clearer understanding of what Lichnowsky's admonitory reports from London meant, what the French position really was, and what Italy's noncommittal attitude toward its allies signified. As well as sharing, he certainly understood the impact that the Serbian reply was having throughout Europe. It is possible that if Bethmann-Hollweg had troubled to read it he, too, would have felt it prudent to try to restrain, rather than to urge on, the Austrians.

It is striking that Sir Edward Grey, on the same or the next day, also devised a proposal almost identical to that of William II: that the Austrians should occupy Belgrade as a pledge for the execution of Serbian promises but should themselves agree to no further military action. Moreover, the Italian government had just made a similar suggestion, and it is conceivable that if the proposals had come *before* Austria-Hungary declared war, they might have provided a basis for negotiation. But the Emperor's proposal did not leave Berlin until late on Tuesday, after the dispatch of the telegram to Nish.

From the moment he read the Serbian reply, the German Emperor was anxious to settle the Austro-Serb dispute peacefully. His

8. KD, Doc. No. 271.

motives are open to doubt—they may have been composed of cowardice, of genuine concern about a general war, or of an understanding that, as things were shaping up, Germany was going to appear in a very unfavorable light before world opinion if one took place. But no serious student any longer thinks that William II was at this point anything but anxious to arrange a settlement, as long as the basic requirements of Austria-Hungary's security and prestige could be safeguarded. About Bethmann-Hollweg's and Jagow's aggressiveness on the other hand, there is almost equally general agreement. Apparently, they had anticipated that William might weaken, and were prepared to outmaneuver him. Albertini believes that they were still, on the Tuesday and Wednesday, pursuing their duplicitous policy of unconditional backing for Austrian aggression behind the Emperor's back. Fay is convinced that they were becoming extremely annoyed with Vienna for keeping them in the dark. Irritation is well documented—"This duplicity of Austria's is intolerable,"[9] Bethmann had written several days earlier—but it is not necessarily a disproof of Albertini's theory that the Chancellor and Jagow were still conspiring to secure a *fait accompli*. For that there is an unexplained delay between the early morning on Tuesday, when the Emperor William ordered Bethmann-Hollweg to propose his pledge plan in Vienna, and the time when the telegram was actually sent—ten-fifteen in the evening—after war had been declared and the fact made known in Berlin.

Bethmann-Hollweg approved, if he did not initiate, the next effort by his sovereign to prevent trouble. Late on Tuesday night, a telegram was drafted from William II to the Emperor Nicholas of Russia (signed: "Your very sincere and devoted friend and cousin, Willy") saying, among other protestations of friendship and eagerness for peace, "I am exerting my utmost influence to induce the Austrians to deal honestly and to arrive at a satisfactory understanding with you."[10] The wire was sent at one forty-five Wednesday morning.

By an odd coincidence, the mind of Nicholas II had turned in

9. KD, Doc. No. 301.
10. KD, Doc. No. 335

similar directions. Three quarters of an hour earlier there had left Saint Petersburg a telegram addressed to William II (signed: Nicky) expressing outrage at the *"ignoble* war declared on a weak country" and asking Willy "in the name of our old friendship . . . to *stop* your *allies* from *going too far."*[11]

The Willy-Nicky telegrams—there were others to follow—had little effect on the course of events, but they throw light on the generalization, still heard among popular writers, that it was "the autocratic monarchies of the East" who made the war, and that dynasts are inherently bellicose. It was weakness, not autocracy, that made the eastern empires bellicose, and it is clear that the dynasts in Berlin and Saint Petersburg—and in Vienna, too, where Francis Joseph had almost certainly balked at approving the declaration of war—were less lighthearted about war in the final crisis than many of their ministers and generals.

The declaration of war and the reactions to it in other parts of Europe at last made Bethmann-Hollweg and Jagow perceive the difficulties of their position as clearly as the Emperor did. Whatever they may have been doing before, now—when it was too late and *because of the event that made it too late*—they saw not only that European "complications" were almost certain but that if they took place the image of Germany was going to be very seriously tarnished. The curious sense of leisure, hastening a *fait accompli* and trying to prevent things from happening elsewhere, that had characterized statecraft in Berlin up to the Emperor's return, disappeared by Tuesday evening. By then Bethmann-Hollweg was learning from the German Ambassador in London that the Austrian Embassy there was freely saying that the ultimatum had been intended to be unacceptable and that no amount of accommodation by Serbia would have prevented war.[12] The effect was apparently to bring to a head Bethmann's accumulating irritation with the Austrian government. It may have been the fact that Vienna was not keeping him informed of its intentions; it may have been fears for the German image; it may have been concern for his personal position or orders from his sovereign. Whatever the motives, he

11. KD, Doc. No. 332.
12. KD, Doc. No. 301.

dispatched to Tschirschky in Vienna the famous Telegram Number 323, sent from Berlin at ten-fifteen on Tuesday evening. It represented a dramatic evolution of attitude toward Austria-Hungary. In it, William II's pledge plan—that the Austro-Hungarian forces should occupy Belgrade as a pledge for fulfillment of Serbian promises—was conveyed:

> . . . the Austro-Hungarian Government has left us in the dark concerning its intentions, despite repeated interrogations. The reply of the Serbian Government to the Austrian ultimatum, which has now been received, makes it clear that Serbia agreed to the Austrian demands to so great an extent that, in the case of a completely uncompromising attitude on the part of the Austro-Hungarian Government, it will be necessary to reckon upon the gradual defection from its cause of public opinion all over Europe. . . . The Imperial [German] Government in consequence is placed in the extraordinarily difficult position of finding itself exposed to proposals for mediation and conferences from the other Cabinets, and, if it persists in its previous reserve toward such proposals, the odium of having caused a world war will fall on it even in the eyes of the German people.

And he then proceeded to argue that Russia must be placed in the position of blame for a possible widening of the conflict; the prevention of war—and the placing of blame for it, should it break out, on Russia— could best be achieved by the pledge plan, coupled with renewed assurances that Austria-Hungary would abstain from the annexation of Serbian territory.[13]

Both the accusers and the defenders of Germany have found solace in Number 323. Clearly, it proves a belated effort to curb Austrian impetuosity; also clearly, it proves that Bethmann-Hollweg was much less worried about preventing war than about ascribing blame for it to Russia. But these considerations are beside the point; the Germans were faced with a real possibility of war now, and Bethmann-Hollweg was reacting with perplexity, exasperation, anxiety, and the perception of expediencies that he was—as it were —being paid to perceive. He believed, apparently, that assurances

13. KD, Doc. No. 323.

to Russia about Austria's territorial "disinterestedness" (the diplomatic phrase was *désintéressement;* the French word is slightly more categorical in suggestion) would suffice to deter Russia. If they did not, if the pledge plan did not, if the first Willy telegram did not, and if more plausible conduct by Austria did not—then the alternative to war was a humiliating retreat by Austria. And that, as he had earlier remarked, was impossible "unless it is willing to make the final sacrifice as a Great Power."[14] The policy was perfectly consistent with Germany's real needs.

To say this is in no way to suggest that Bethmann-Hollweg and Jagow were men either of integrity or of skill. They were almost certainly duplicitous beyond the common requirements of diplomacy or even expediency; and they were singularly inept in many of their judgments. They seemed to have failed to understand that the preservation of their only ally, Austria-Hungary, undoubtedly necessary to German policy, was being pursued in foolish ways *likely* to oblige Germany to fight most of Europe. This was not driven home until, on Wednesday, they received from London a warning clearly saying that Great Britain might not remain neutral in case of war. It was foolish to gamble on the belief that Russia might abstain from action; that Italy might, despite all indications, prove loyal to its allies; that France might prove disloyal to its ally; or that British neutrality could be counted on. But these were errors in judgment; they were not associated with a plot to start a war. As has been seen, and will soon be seen more clearly still, irresponsibility was general throughout Europe. So general that the word demands a restricted definition; it *must* be used to mean that irresponsibility was a failure to imagine that a general war would develop into a sort of historical phenomenon entirely unknown in previous history. It was known, of course, that the war would be general; but if it had been quick, as it was in 1870, then the actions of Bethmann-Hollweg and Jagow would seem perfectly orthodox, although not very wise.

By Wednesday, July 29, when the warning from London came, there was consternation in Berlin. The dream of Europe's allowing

14. KD, Doc. No. 307.

Austria-Hungary to chastise Serbia in peace was dispelled. Complications were burgeoning on every side. As early as Sunday, rumors of the Russian military plans had begun to reach Berlin; their effect had been allayed by Pourtalès' accounts of his affable chats with Sazonov, but after the declaration of war they emphasized the gravity of the situation. On Monday, Conrad was urging on Berchtold the need to ask for German mobilization if the rumors from Russia were substantiated, and Berchtold had reported this, in rather guarded terms, to Tschirschky, and asked that the Germans warn the Russians against military steps that might threaten Austria-Hungary. When he learned of the declaration of war, German Chief of Staff Moltke observed that an Austrian invasion of Serbia would almost certainly lead to Russian military measures; that this prospect meant that the Austrian intention of mobilizing only against Serbia would be folly, since it would leave Austria exposed to Russian attack; that the mobilization of both Austria and Russia would inevitably lead to conflict between them; that conflict between Austria and Russia would force Germany, under terms of its alliance, to mobilize in Austria's defense; that since this was inevitable, it had better be done before the Russians stole a march. Q.E.D.: Germany ought to mobilize at once.[15]

The German Emperor, Chancellor, and Foreign Secretary were by no means ready for such a drastic step. But Moltke's views illustrate the ways in which military considerations, and military leaders, began to bear upon policy, now that military steps had been taken by Russia. The exigencies of defense, only indirectly influential earlier, now were pressing considerations. Bethmann-Hollweg was sufficiently impressed to send off rather threatening telegrams to Russia and France, the former saying that "further continuation of Russian mobilization measures would force us to mobilize, and in that case a European war could scarcely be prevented."[16] A sealed envelope within a sealed envelope was sent to the German Legation at Brussels by messenger. It contained an ultimatum, drawn up three days earlier by the aggressive Moltke, demanding that German

15. Moltke, *Memoirs*, p. 381; quoted in Albertini, II, 488.
16. KD, Doc. No. 342.

troops be permitted to pass through Belgium. The German Minister was to open it only on receipt of subsequent orders.

On Wednesday afternoon and evening there was a series of meetings at Potsdam between the Emperor and his advisers. There was as yet no serious consideration of mobilizing; instead, a second Willy telegram was sent to Nicholas II, friendly in language but observing, "Of course, military measures on the part of Russia which would be looked on by Austria as threatening would precipitate a calamity we both wish to avoid."[17] Bethmann-Hollweg called in the British Ambassador and told him that he hoped that Britain would remain neutral in case of war, and in return promised that Germany would seek no acquisitions of French, Belgian, or Dutch territory in Europe (overseas holdings were pointedly omitted from the guarantee). This inept (and characteristic) offer made the British more suspicious than ever. Grey called it infamous. It was typical of the whole history of German diplomacy to seek peace through threats and promises that revealed a voracious appetite. But Bethmann-Hollweg also continued to work for peace in Vienna by securing Austrian agreement to the pledge plan. The telegrams to Vienna became more urgent, and by midnight Tschirschky was being instructed to convey the British warning to Austria and, indeed virtually to *order* the Austro-Hungarian government to accept the pledge plan. The Germans were now—as Bethmann wired—"clutching at every straw."[18]

The following morning, Thursday, with still no reply to the pledge plan received from Vienna (where Berchtold was saying the whole thing would have to be considered by Francis Joseph and Tisza) Bethmann telephoned to Tschirschky to apply still more pressure, and William II wired Francis Joseph asking for an immediate decision. At nine o'clock Thursday night, Bethmann sent a final telegram, which read:

17. KD, Doc. No. 359.
18. *Documents diplomatiques français 1871–1914* (1929), II, 365. (Hereinafter, DDF.)

If England's efforts succeed, while Vienna declines everything, Vienna will be giving documentary evidence that it absolutely wants a war, into which we shall be drawn, while Russia remains free of responsibility. That would place us, in the eyes of our own people, in an untenable position. Thus we can only urgently advise that Austria accept the Grey proposal, which preserves her status for her in every way. Your excellency will at once express yourself most emphatically on this matter to Count Berchtold, perhaps also to Count Tisza.[19]

Two and a half hours later, Bethmann issued instructions to Tschirschky to disregard it; Moltke, convinced by now that war was certain and mobilization esstential, had persuaded him that things had gone too far for a pledge plan to be safe. Moltke distrusted the Schlieffen Plan, which required war against France and the occupation of Belgium; but if Russia were to be fought, he had no choice but to obey its imperatives. The requirements of defense demanded that he insist on preparing for it. The time, he thought, had passed when he dared postpone military measures.

He was right. While the Germans were growing more and more agitated during Wednesday and Thursday, and while Moltke was pressing on the civilians (and on the Austrians) the inexorable logic of the law of mobilizations, things had been happening in Saint Petersburg that made diplomacy irrelevant.

It will be recalled that the first reactions of Sazonov to the Austrian ultimatum had been of fury and frustration and that he had sponsored the plan of partial mobilization against the Austrians, apparently partly in an effort to frighten or blackmail them. The program had been strenuously opposed by the military on technical grounds; but it had been provisionally adopted, to go into effect when and if Austria-Hungary invaded Serbia. Pending that, there was to be a Period Preparatory to War. Once these measures had been decided, Sazonov's anger had cooled, and the failure of the Austrians to take any action following the Serbian rejection led

19. KD, Doc. No. 441.

him to a more hopeful mood. He had chatted affably with both the German and the Austrian ambassadors and had been prepared to enter into direct "negotiations" with Vienna, although what the subject of these negotiations might be had not been discussed.

The Austrian declaration of war—the timing of which may have been in part the consequence of the Russian military measures—revived in even more violent form his earlier agitation. He was apparently convinced that both the Austrians and the Germans had been deliberately misleading him with their amiable talk while pursuing deep-laid plans for aggression; his state bordered on the psychopathic. In any case, he decided that the time had come to undertake partial mobilization, and as soon as he heard of the declaration he informed the Russian embassies abroad that it would be ordered. But here again the Russian generals intervened. The arguments that had been advanced earlier about the extreme danger of trying by improvisation to mobilize on one part of the frontier and not the other were renewed. It was repeated by the chief of staff, General Janushkevich, and the chief of mobilization, General Dobrorolski, that the mobilization of a few districts would jeopardize the success of a later general mobilization, should one become necessary, as they (like Moltke) thought it would. These arguments were presented to Sazonov and then to Nicholas II.

They prevailed. Sazonov was already convinced that the Germans were themselves prepared to fight. And it was—as it almost always is—difficult for civilian leaders to resist the urgent advice of the military, upon whose judgment must depend the safety of the nation. On Wednesday morning, less than twenty-four hours after the declaration of war on Serbia, the Russian Emperor reluctantly agreed that general mobilization might be necessary; *two* mobilization decrees were signed, one for partial and one for general mobilization, to be used as circumstances might dictate.

Meanwhile, Sazonov was hearing from the Austrian Ambassador that the Habsburg Monarchy had turned down the proposal for direct negotiations. He had already heard from the French Ambassador (acting on his own authority and possibly even in violation of instructions) that France was eager to support its ally. From Pourtalès he was hearing Bethmann-Hollweg's threat that, unless Russian military measures were called off, Germany would be obliged to mobilize. And he was hearing the first news from the front—of an Austrian bombardment of Belgrade. The news came when Sazonov was conferring with the Austrian Ambassador; the latter drily reported that from Sazonov's manner he judged further negotiations would be fruitless.[20]

The combined effects of these developments was to convince Sazonov of the necessity of general mobilization in the face of what he now deemed to be a certain European war. But while his resolution was being thus fortified, his sovereign tergiversated: Nicholas at first approved and then, a few hours later, revoked an order for general mobilization. It may have been the second Willy telegram that produced this shilly-shallying, or merely the natural tendency of Nicholas toward vacillation and a pacific solution. In any event, at nine-thirty Wednesday night, when Bethmann-Hollweg was busy trying to bring pressure to bear on Vienna to desist from its secretive and provocative policies and to accept the pledge plan, Nicholas II told his frantic generals to cancel the general mobilization and order partial mobilization instead.

There was thus a possibility, late Wednesday night, that German and Russian restraint might work. Partial mobilization was thought by most people in Berlin to be compatible with a peaceful solution —that is, it did not actually require German mobilization in reply. If Austria-Hungary were to accept the pledge plan, then the British would bring pressure to bear upon Russia to accept it too. Pourtalès worked mightily to convert Sazonov. He reiterated the Austrian promise that there would be no annexation of Serbian territory, and he reported—what was not true—that Germany was putting pressure on Vienna to accept the pledge plan. But Sazonov remained unconverted; he wanted absolute promises that Serbian sovereignty as well as Serbian territory would be respected. On Thursday morning, he told the German Ambassador that the only basis on

20. ARB, III, 74.

which peace could be secured was the elimination from the Austrian demands on Serbia of those points that were incompatible with its sovereignty. On the other hand, he did not actually insist that Austria refrain from all hostilities against Serbia. There seemed to Pourtalès a bare chance that the pledge plan might work.

But Sazonov was deceiving Pourtalès about the chances of negotiation. Russian policy was no longer in his hands. It had passed to the military, once agreement had been reached that some kind of military measures should be taken. Just as Moltke in Berlin was freely telling his own government and Austria's what the military requirements were, so the Russian generals now, on Thursday morning, determinedly renewed their campaign to prevent partial mobilization and to assure general mobilization, which they and everyone else knew would mean war with Germany. Sazonov was convinced; with his support, Janushkevich telephoned the Emperor at his suburban palace begging him to abandon partial mobilization. The Emperor refused. But he agreed to have a conference to discuss the matter with Sazonov, and this took place at two o'clock on the afternoon of Thursday, July 30. The Emperor was worried about his moral responsibility for "the thousands and thousands of men who will be sent to their deaths" (Russian casualties in the war were to be about ten million men, including some two million dead). Sazonov was speaking now for the generals: Partial mobilization meant endangering the defense of the Empire. He presented their argument; it was essential "to do everything necessary to meet war fully armed and under conditions most favorable for us. Therefore it is better without fear to call forth a war by our preparations for it, and to continue these preparations carefully, rather than out of fear to give an inducement of war and to be taken unawares."[21]

The Russian generals were probably right: consider the massive effort necesary to mobilize; consider the dangers of uncovering part of their frontier by mobilizing against Austria alone; consider the long background of fear and suspicion and the undoubted evidence of Austria-Hungary's determination to reduce Serbia; con-

21. Schilling's *Diary*, p. 65; quoted in Fay, III, 472.

sider Germany's granite support of its ally; then their conclusions seem plausible and persuasive. They appear to have misled Nicholas into thinking that Austria was already mobilizing against Russia, which was not true; but it does not change the fact that from a purely military standpoint their reasoning was sound. And so, for all his instability, was Sazonov's basic political reasoning: Austria-Hungary intended to destroy the independence of Serbia; this would seriously affect Russia's interests, and it could be stopped only by war. In any case, the Emperor Nicholas II was persuaded. Late on Thursday afternoon, Sazonov triumphantly telephoned the chief of staff with the news. "Now you can smash your telephone. Give your orders, General," he said. At five in the afternoon, the orders were given to the telegraph operators. In the early hours of Friday, July 31, the red posters proclaiming general mobilization were going up on the walls of every town in Russia. Nicholas II wrote in his diary: "After lunch I received Sazonov and Tatischev. I went for a walk by myself. The weather was hot . . . had a delightful bathe in the sea."[22]

In Austria-Hungary, too, final decisions were being made that Thursday. The Habsburg Monarchy had embarked, with German support and advice, upon the course of a *fait accompli*. Now they intransigeantly declined to turn back. They had given Russia the promise of "territorial disinterestedness," but they would not go further. They were at last decided, and they were determined not to negotiate, as all the other Powers including Germany believed they could and should, on the basis of the Serbian reply. They declined the proposals of "direction conversations" with Russia, although they pretended a readiness to renew them. They declined to listen to the German proposals for the pledge plan—which they may well have thought were motivated mainly by a desire to keep the British quiet. When Tschirschky delivered the substance of Telegram Number 323, with its admonitions and its support for the plan, they merely observed that they would have to think the whole thing over.

22. *Journal of Nicholas II*; quoted in Albertini, II, 569.

There was little time to do so. By Wednesday night, Vienna had been officially informed of the Russian intention to begin partial mobilization. They at once informed the Germans that, if this intention was carried out, Austria-Hungary would be compelled to supersede its own mobilization measures, so far directed only against Serbia and not involving the eastern frontier, with general mobilization. This was logical enough; they now had little choice. They acted before it was absolutely necessary—that is, before they knew that the Russians actually carried out their intention. This may have been the consequence of nerves in Austria-Hungary; it would not be surprising. Or it may have been that they were alarmed by signs of a drastic change in German attitudes—Bethmann's frantic telegrams were beginning to arrive in Vienna on Thursday morning—and wished to act before the Germans could withdraw their guarantee of support. In this they may have been aided by Tschirschky, who seemed to have been halfhearted in executing his government's new policy. In any case, Austria-Hungary now acted to present a *fait accompli* not to its opponents but to its ally. Conrad wrote to Moltke asking him to urge that the Germans, too, mobilize as soon as possible. And on Thursday afternoon, at exactly the moment when Sazonov was convincing the Emperor of Russia that the fatal order *must* be given, Berchtold and Conrad were convincing the Emperor of Austria that the corresponding order was necessary. Agreement was in both cases procured; in Austria, there was further characteristic delay and confusion; Tisza's agreement also had to be procured. But when news of the Russians' general mobilization came through on Friday, the Austrians at once proclaimed theirs.

In France and England, the military were also beginning to appear on the scene. On Wednesday, Poincaré and Viviani at last reached Paris after their long sea voyage. The situation was ebullient. There were patriotic demonstrations in the streets, and cries of *"A Berlin,"* The chief of staff, General Joseph Jacques Joffre, had already urged on Russia the need to be in a position to attack quickly should war break out; now it was decided to give Russia further assurances of French support, to seek a commitment of British support for the Entente, and to take precautionary defense measures. At the Cabinet meeting Thursday morning, the Minister of War urged the necessity to begin at least inconspicuous military preparations, the manning of the frontier defenses or *couverture* (blanketing), as it was called. The French were extremely cautious about anything that might appear provocative, probably because they wished to be quite sure that the British should see them as an innocent victim when the worst took place. Informed of Russian military measures, they urged similar caution upon their ally, although Paléologue, who was apparently deliberately deceiving his own government, was simultaneously failing to deliver Viviani's cautious advice to the Russians. They avoided the calling up of reservists for the present, and they ostentatiously announced that troops were to be moved back six miles from the German border to avoid incident. But at the insistence of Joffre the *couverture* began at once.

In London, as usual throughout the crisis, refined and high-minded confusion prevailed. But the First Lord of the Admiralty, Winston Churchill, the most resolute of the ministers, had given orders that the fleet should not be dispersed following its summer maneuvers. Then, on Tuesday afternoon, after word of the declaration of war reached London, Churchill gave further orders: the fleet was to proceed to its battle bases and be prepared for action.

The naval measure was important, for it meant that Great Britain would be in a position to fulfill its one definite commitment: to cover the Channel ports of France against German naval action in the case of war. But no one was as yet prepared to go beyond that commitment, and Grey's diplomatic efforts were still directed at a general conciliation. He was still of the opinion that by "working with Germany"—that notion in one form or another appeared in many of his dispatches and conversations—it would be possible to provide a satisfactory basis for negotiation. But he was now prepared, after the declaration of war, to issue a muted warning to Germany, and this he did to Ambassador Lichnowsky on the morning of Wednesday, January 29. With diplomatic obliquity, Grey told the Ambassador: ". . . if we failed in our efforts to keep the peace . . . I did not want to be open to any reproach from him that the friendly tone of all our conversations had misled him or his Government into supposing that we should not take action."[23]

The warning had its effect in Germany, though not the one intended: "England reveals herself in her true colors at a moment when she thinks we are caught in the toils and . . . disposed of," William II remarked. "That common crew of shopkeepers has tried to trick us."[24] But it was not enough to arrest the gigantic forces already working toward mobilization in Europe. Nor was it intended to be; Grey still believed that any stronger stand on behalf of the Entente would meet with violent opposition in Cabinet and Parliament and might cause the collapse of the ministry. Sir Arthur Nicolson and Sir Eyre Crowe, the ranking members of the Foreign Office, were urging a definite stand; from the beginning, they had shown a clearer grasp of realities than had any other European statesmen. But they were civil servants and not politicians, and the Foreign Minister was acutely aware of the extreme reluctance of most of Britain to participate in an Eastern European dispute.

There was one point of real concern, however, on which most people in Great Britain would unite, and that was the integrity of Belgium. On Friday, Grey accordingly asked both the Germans and the French for assurances that they would, whatever happened, respect the neutrality of Belgium. The French immediately responded in a satisfactory way; the Germans declined to commit themselves on the grounds that a definite guarantee would reveal their military plans. Sir Edward now reached the conclusion that general war was certain, that the Germans were probably designing the violation of Belgium, and that Britain would be obliged to go to war. But the Cabinet was still deeply divided; not until after Belgian territory had been invaded, and not until after several members of the Cabinet had resigned, was there to be the possibility of agreement on a foreign policy for Great Britain.

While these distressing uncertainties were driving British statesmen up the wall, events were moving rapidly in Central Europe. By

23. BD, XI, 286.
24. KD, Doc. No. 368.

Friday morning, reports of the Russian general mobilization were reaching Berlin. Moltke, now as desperate as Janushkevich had been the day before, was frenziedly urging military action before the Russian preparations could proceed further, and on his own responsibility was telling Conrad that it was indispensable that Austria commence general mobilization to prepare for a defense against Russian attack. He sent a telegram to this effect to Vienna early Friday morning. There, read in conjunction with Bethmann's messages urging caution, it gave rise to confusion about who was directing German policy and what that policy was. It has since become a showpiece for those who believe that Moltke was the chief villain of the drama. But it is certain that his admonitions reached Vienna when general mobilization was already under consideration and almost certainly after the decision had already been made. The Emperor William and the Chancellor declined to take action until there was official confirmation of the Russian proclamation, and it is possible that their refusal was what incited Moltke to take the initiative.

Official news reached Berlin, about noon on Friday, from Pourtalès. By now Serbia, Austria, Russia, France, and even Great Britain had begun military measures of one sort or another; Germany alone among the Powers concerned had not yet done so. Time was pressing; at noon the Germans proclaimed a State of Danger of War, a measure rather similar to that the Russians had undertaken six days before. At three-thirty in the afternoon was dispatched what has been called the Double Ultimatum. Russia was told, "Mobilization must follow . . . in case Russia does not suspend every war measure against Austria-Hungary and ourselves within twelve hours and make us a distinct declaration to that effect."[25] To the German Ambassador at Paris went a more complicated ultimatum: within eighteen hours, the French were to say whether or not they intended to remain neutral in a German-Russian war. It was secretly added that if the French said they were, then pledges of good behavior were to be demanded in the form of

25. KD, Doc. No. 490.

German occupation of French frontier fortresses. The occasion for making this demand never arose; but since there was not the slightest possibility of its being accepted, it may be taken as final evidence that the Germans were determined, if they fought at all, to fight both France and Russia. Their strategic situation made the existence of a powerful and temporarily neutral France intolerable; their strategic planning absolutely required a war on both fronts.

The time limit on the ultimatum to Russia expired on the afternoon of Saturday, August 1. No answers had been received from either Paris or Saint Petersburg, and at five o'clock the order went out for German mobilization. At six, Pourtalès saw Sazonov; he asked three times if the German demands could not be met. Each time Sazonov replied no. Pourtalès handed him the text of the German declaration of war against Russia and then broke into tears.

Europe at War

The rest was formality, preordained by the terms of alliances and of military plans. When the news of the German State of Danger of War reached Paris, General Joffre had demanded the calling up of reservists. After receiving and disregarding the German ultimatum, France had ordered general mobilization at three forty-five on the afternoon of Saturday, August 1, two hours before the Germans had declared war on Russia. At seven in the evening on Sunday, the German Minister at Brussels handed the ultimatum to the Belgians in accordance with previous instructions. Twelve hours later the Belgian rejection had been delivered; the Germans declared war on France that day, and on the following morning invaded Belgium. The British sent an ultimatum of their own to Germany demanding assurances that German forces be withdrawn. The reply was unsatisfactory, and at the expiry of the time limit, midnight on the night of Tuesday, August 4, Germany and Great Britain were also at war.

The course of events that led to this general war are perfectly clear, though the motives and in some cases the timing are not.

Austria-Hungary, at the urging of its ally, Germany, undertook strong measures against Serbia in order to protect its existence and its position as a Great Power. The exact purpose of these measures was not clearly agreed upon in Vienna, but they were of a sort to convince the Russians that Austria intended to extinguish Serbian sovereignty and to establish Austro-German predominance in the Balkans. To prevent this, and perhaps to frighten Austria into a more reasonable frame of mind, the Russians adopted military measures. The Germans felt absolutely obliged to stand by their ally, and they believed, from the moment of the assassination, that the safest course of action for Austria-Hungary to adopt would be a quick, decisive one, a *fait accompli*. They were prepared to incur the risk of fighting Russia, although they believed that it could be avoided. They urged—fruitlessly, most of the time—speed and decision in Vienna, and they continued to urge it after the Russian reaction to the ultimatum had showed that the risks were very serious. The Austrians responded by speeding up the declaration of war against Serbia; the Russians reacted, according to schedule, by mobilizing. Military considerations made it expedient that their mobilization be general, and this constituted a direct threat to Germany that could be met only by German mobilization. The French felt absolutely obliged to stand by *their* ally; it would almost certainly have been impossible for them to abstain from participation if they had wanted to, since the Germans almost certainly would have attacked them anyway as part of their plan for war against Russia. But the French did not consider abstention; instead, they gave the Russians unchanging, and sometimes provocative, assurances of their loyalty. German mobilization meant French mobilization, and German war against Russia meant a war between France and Germany. And since war between France and Germany involved the German violation of Belgium, it meant, too, war between Germany and Great Britain.

In this summary of events, stripped of the fruitless proposals for negotiation, may be discerned several elementary facts.

First, the vital interests of Germany and of France required loyalty to their respective allies; betrayal, or even a suggestion of weakness, would have incurred charges of treachery and led to a vulnerable and invidious isolation in a dangerous world. *The strength of their allies was part—an essential part—of their own strength and safety;* the preservation of that strength was deemed to demand not only loyal support but assistance in executing the policy of the ally. Prestige was part of strength; the Germans feared, rightly, a diminution of Austro-Hungarian authority; the French feared a diminution of Russian authority. Neither believed that the two were wholly incompatible, but they had very different views as to the minimum requirements of their allies' needs.

Second, the safety of each Power depended upon the execution, within very narrow time limits, of a very complicated and unalterable military plan. Not only could the plans not be changed; they must be put into effect as rapidly as possible to prevent grave military disadvantage, once the threat of war became serious.

Third, the Russians were absolutely convinced that Austria had sinister plans in the Balkans seriously menacing to their own interests, and they were convinced that the sovereignty of Serbia, however much of a nuisance they thought that nation might be, was indispensable to their own security and dignity.

Fourth, the Austrians were convinced that the sovereignty of Serbia was a serious and permanent threat to their own existence.

Fifth, the irretrievable steps were military measures, and these were taken in most cases at the urgent behest of the chiefs of staff and their advisers. The generals appear in a very unfavorable light in most narratives of events. There is no doubt that some of them —most conspicuously, Conrad—inclined to rabid bellicosity. But none of them acted except when ordered by civilian ministers. And the advice of most of them, of Janushkevich, of Moltke, of Joffre, was given as a matter of duty when facts drove them, correctly, to the conclusion that they could not safeguard their countries without preparing for war. This had nothing to do with their views as to whether war was or was not wise. They, like the ministers they advised, were merely performing their necessary function. As Winston Churchill was to say some twenty years later, "The responsibility of ministers for the public safety is absolute and needs no mandate."

But this is not to suggest that the course of events was preordained or that nothing could have been done to prevent its developing as it did. There are hundreds of suppositious changes that might have prevented the war from taking place when it did and on the terms it did. To discuss them is profitless, but to suggest a few possibilities, chosen at random, may be instructive.

For one thing, the French Ambassador at Saint Petersburg, Maurice Paléologue, repeatedly pressed on Sazonov the need for a "firm policy." His position was very influential—both because he represented Russia's ally and because, since his chiefs were inaccessible, it was necessary for him to act on his own responsibility. He was, for a time, *making* French policy toward Russia, and the policy he made was incitement to war. A different ambassador might well have altered the course of events. Paléologue went far beyond the terms of the alliance, beyond the need to show diplomatic solidarity, beyond the limits of previous French policy. His actions and influences offer a precise counterpart to those of Tschirschky in Vienna.

To take another example, it has frequently been said by both sides that a clearer stand by Sir Edward Grey would have saved the peace. If the Germans had been told, early and with conviction, that Britain would take part in the war, they would very probably have averted instead of encouraging the Austrian ultimatum and declaration of war. There is strong evidence for this; some Germans have even taken the weird moral stand that Grey was responsible for starting the war because if he had made his position clear the Germans would never have permitted it to start. The ethics of this attitude are not convincing, but the facts are. A less fastidious, conciliatory, and correct statesman might have acted more effectively. A modest measure of duplicity, such as many diplomats regard as a proper tool of their trade, would have permitted him to make much stronger representations much sooner than he did. No absolute commitment was necessary; he could have told both Lichnowsky and his own Ambassador at Berlin that Great Britain *did* regard the Austro-Serbian problem as of European and British concern (that would have been a matter of judgment, not of propriety) and that if war broke out Great Britain would almost certainly take part in it on the allied side. This would have been tricky, in both senses of the word, but experienced diplomats of the utmost rectitude like Nicolson and Eyre Crowe were urging something like it. Sir Edward suffered from an excess of scruples and perhaps an insufficiency of grasp; his case is a demonstration for the argument that there is at times nothing so dangerous as pacific punctilio.

If either Sazanov or Berchtold had behaved differently, on any of several occasions, the course of events would certainly have been different. A less volatile and more judicious statesman than Sazonov, and one surer of his own ground, might not have reacted with so much emotion and so little regard for political realities as he did on hearing of the Austrian ultimatum. A smaller concern for Russia's prestige and his own might have prevented his urging the Serbs to reject the ultimatum, and it might have delayed the Period Preparatory to War and given time for fruitful negotiation. A less indecisive statesman than Berchtold, and one with a clearer vision of the future, might have formulated concrete demands for Serbia that would secure Austria's ends without leaving so much scope for uncertainty, even apparently in his own mind, about what really was intended as an objective. The problem of Austria-Hungary was in some ways comparable to that of Great Britain: there were too many disagreements and cross-currents and deterrents to clear-cut action. But a different sort of statesman in either country might have overcome them and produced a definite and rapid solution to the difficulties.

Most important, there were in Germany many occasions when different events would have followed if even slightly different decisions had been made. At all times the Germans treated the prospective war as if it were a rather inviting prospect. From July 5 on, the Germans behaved unwisely in regard to Austria; they first pressed for decisive action and, when it was not forthcoming, continued to press for it without regard to changing circumstances. They seem to have been wildly optimistic about the chances of French and British pressure being exerted at Saint Petersburg. They were certainly wildly irresponsible in acting on the belief that they could win a European war if one broke out. Such unwisdom was an understandable but not a necessary component of German policy. If the German leaders had not been widely dispersed around the middle of July, if the Emperor had returned a few days earlier from his cruise, if Bethmann-Hollweg and Jagow had not been caught up in the established policy that a *fait accompli* was possible, Austria-Hungary might not have rejected out of hand the Serbian reply, might not have broken diplomatic relations with Serbia, might not have declared war, might not have provoked the Russian mobilization.

All these involve reproaches to the statesmen for deficiencies in their stature. But the basic reproach must be the failure of imagination; the statesmen were thinking of the defense of visible interests that seemed vital; they failed to discern that invisible and much larger interests were involved in their decisions. There were, in Russia, those who foresaw a threat to the regime in the war, but the defense of the regime seemed to Sazonov and the Emperor Nicholas to demand not peace but prestige. No one, let it be said again, realized that the war they were consciously risking would be the first World War.

Two things happened to turn war into cataclysm. First, the breakdown of the German strategy in France and the establishment of stable lines in early September, 1914: instead of a decision there was an indecision, made perennial by the peculiar equilibrium of military technology. Second, the accumulated tensions and conflicts of the European State System, long repressed or stabilized, all broke out the moment that war was a fact; the war could not be ended until they were resolved. Most of these tensions had nothing to do with the events that caused the war to break out;

they were buried at the bottom of the rivalries and the institutions that made it possible. There was Alsace-Lorraine: once a Franco-German war had started, France could not make peace until Alsace-Lorraine was restored, except after a military disaster; without a military disaster, Germany would never concede the loss of the provinces. There was the Anglo-German naval rivalry: once war had started, Great Britain would not make peace until the threat of a strong German Navy had been permanently dispersed. There was Constantinople: once war broke out, the Russian government could not make peace until it was assured that the centuries-old ambition for Constantinople would be satisfied. There was Germany's encirclement: once war broke out, Germany could not, short of military disaster, make peace until the encirclement had been broken, which meant the decisive crushing of both France and Russia.

These needs and ambitions had underlaid the tensions of Europe and had shaped the alliance system and the policies of the Powers. But they none of them had led to actions that produced war. They were either negotiable or repressible. The one problem that was neither negotiable nor repressible was that raised by threats to the integrity of Austria-Hungary. The composition of the Habsburg Monarchy made it fatally vulnerable to the activities of the Serbs; at the same time, it made it difficult to eliminate those activities by rapid and resolute action; and it made it difficult for the government of Austria-Hungary—or its ally, Germany—to retreat, to equivocate, to delay, once the decision to take action had been made, ill defined and unsatisfactory as the decision was. It was this problem that caused the war which became the first World War.

A Note on the Bibliography

THE LITERATURE on the crisis of 1914 and the events leading up to it is probably more voluminous than on any other period of the past. The narrative of diplomatic events has been studied under an assortment of microscopes—and through telescopes and periscopes as well. The documentary sources, and the diary and memoir materials, are as nearly complete as they could well be. Still, the literature has grave defects for the contemporary reader. For one thing, its very profusion is not only an aid but also an obstacle; a thorough acquaintance with the published works would require a lifetime of polyglot reading. Moreover, most of the secondary works, and almost all of the memoirs, suffer from the error of retrospection: the first fourteen years of the twentieth century, and sometimes the last decades of the nineteenth, are too often seen solely as prologues to the first World War, and the selection of materials is consequently badly distorted. By now so false a focus should be (but is not) as conspicuously dated as are the histories of the United States published in the early thirties which conceived the American past as a preface to the Great Depression and the social revolution that seemed to be taking place; or as wartime histories of Germany that conceived the sole significant tendencies in Germany's past as those that pointed toward Hitler. A most important element in this approach is the crippling preoccupation with war guilt; scarcely less important, in many cases, has been the tendency to isolate diplomatic narrative (along with a few other topics: the press, military history, and commercial rivalries) from the main domestic tendencies and problems of the time. The isolation of events that seemed to be causes of the War and the problems of guilt and vindication have frequently converted history from its proper role as an inductively reasoned thesis into the improper one of a prosecutor's brief or a tragedian's diagnosis of impending doom.

For anyone not a specialist who is concerned to form an independent judgment on the history of Europe up to the outbreak of the first World War, the best advice on reading is to begin, not with diplomatic histories or even with documents, but with a thorough general history. Even though the treatment be superficial in the extreme, a textbook that touches on domestic history, and particularly on social, economic, and intellectual history and upon world developments too, is a fairer and a safer beginning than the specialized—and therefore tendentious—diplomatic studies. There are several good general histories; one of the best is Maurice Bruce's *The Shaping of the Modern World* (1958), Vol. I.

The diplomatic narrative of the years from 1870 to 1914 has been repeatedly written. The books generally suffer from the defects noted above: a preoccupation with what the author conceives to be the causes of the war isolated in some measure from their context; a preoccupation with the shadow of Nemesis. One of the most sensible and up-to-date of general diplomatic histories is René Albrecht-Carrié's *A Diplomatic History of Europe* (1958), which covers a much longer period but deals with this one with some detachment and in fair detail. Less reliable, but superbly written and highly imaginative, is A. J. P. Taylor's brilliant but often controversial *Struggle for the Mastery of Europe* (1954); it should be read only in conjunction with a more sober work. Very much older and outdated in many details, but still surprisingly solid, are the first volumes of S. B. Fay's *The Origins of the World War* (New York, 1928) and Bernadotte E. Schmitt's *The Coming of the War* (1930). The corresponding introductory volume of Luigi Albertini's great work, *The Origins of the War of 1914* (English translation appeared in 1952), is less satisfactory than his treatment of the crisis itself; it deals with Italian diplomacy (naturally enough) in prodigious detail, and in other respects its balance is open to question. But Albertini, unlike many other historians, has seen the inchoate nationalities of southeastern Europe as a vital source of Europe's instability, and it is an excellent antidote to the myopic emphasis upon the West which historians have usually provided to English-speaking readers. In this respect, a most valuable and perceptive essay, which in very brief compass does more to explain the essential problems of Europe than most of the previous writings of British and American historians put together, is Hajo Holborn's *The Political Collapse of Europe* (1957). Holborn's little book is purely interpretive; a complement to it, now old but still very useful as an introduction to the facts, is Bernadotte Schmitt's compact book, *Triple Alliance and Triple Entente* (1934).

There is an endless library of works on practically all particulars of international relations after 1870. The following, arbitrarily selected, seem worth mentioning because of their reputation, brilliance, or readability: Erich Brandenburg, *From Bismarck to the First World War* (1927); E. J. Helmreich, *The Diplomacy of the Balkan Wars* (1938); W. L. Langer, *The Diplomacy of Imperialism* (2d ed.; 1951); A. F. Pribram, *Austrian Foreign Policy, 1908–1914* (1923); B. E. Schmitt, *The Annexation of Bosnia* (1937); R. J. Sontag, *Germany and England* (1938); and E. L. Woodward, *Great Britain and the German Navy* (1935). It will be noted that all of these were published between the wars, when 1914 and subsequent horrors were still fresh in the minds of writers. It is historiographically significant that comparatively few books of this sort have been written since 1945. There are, however, a few that deserve particular attention. The distinguished German historian, Gerhard Ritter, has made a definitive study of German strategic planning; the English version, *The Schlieffen Plan*, came out in 1958. In 1964, George Malcolm Thompson published *The Twelve Days*, a finely written and evocative recreation of the atmosphere of the crisis. In 1970 appeared Zara S. Steiner's *The Foreign Office and Foreign Policy 1898–1914*, a superb work of scholarship and a striking revelation of the ways in which fundamental changes in the structure and role of the Foreign Office influenced the conduct of affairs in London.

On the other hand, one really central topic, the history of the Habsburg Monarchy, has flowered, historically speaking, since

1945. The following works, among many others, have been published in the last two decades and give us a much more lucid and just picture of Austria-Hungary, its neighbors, and its problems than was possible in the twenties and thirties, when the major diplomatic works were being written. W. S. Vucinich's *Serbia Between East and West* (1954), frequently cited in the text, is the most important work in English on Serbian policies and activities. Of general interest and importance are: R. A. Kann, *The Multinational Empire* (1950); Arthur May, *The Habsburg Monarchy* (1951); and Z. A. B. Zeman, *The Break-up of the Habsburg Empire* (1961). Of particular interest is the brilliant, thorough, and fascinating book by J. Remak, *Sarajevo* (1959). The most important book on the assassination and its background to appear in recent years is Vladimir Dedijer's *The Road to Sarajevo* (1966). Dedijer had access to Serbian sources hitherto unavailable, and as indicated in the text his very detailed account becomes, now, the cornerstone for any further study of the assassination, of Serbian and Bosnian politics, and of Austro-Serb relations. Dedijer is frankly anti-Habsburg, but he is also unsympathetic to the Belgrade government, and his data seem irreproachable, although his line of argument is not always wholly convincing.

For the 1914 crisis(and for varying periods before it) the most important literature consists, of course, of the documentary collections. They are the basis of all serious historical work in the field. Documents, however, do not themselves supply truth; they merely set limits to error. The collections are highly selective, and in some cases the criteria of selection are known to have been political instead of scholarly. *Die Grosse Politik der Europäischen Kabinette, 1871–1914,* usually known by the first three words of its title, was the earliest and remains the largest and most important. It is a forty-volume collection of German Foreign Office documents, edited by German historians and published in the mid-twenties. A few suppressions and distortions were made by the editors for reasons of contemporary political expediency, and these became known when the German archives fell into Western hands after World

War II. Still, *Die Grosse Politik* is both monumental and fundamental. It has not been translated into English. But German documents dealing with the 1914 crisis had been earlier collected by the Social Democratic scholar and statesman, Karl Kautsky, and published in 1919. There is an English edition called *The Outbreak of the World War.*

The multivolume French collection, *Documents diplomatiques français, 1871–1914,* which began to appear in 1929, is likewise unavailable in English. The *Austrian Red Book,* in four volumes and dealing entirely with the 1914 crisis, first appeared in 1919 and was published in an English translation a year later. Ten years later, the Austrians published nine volumes covering the period back to 1908, but no translation is available. The eleven volumes of *British Documents on the Origins of the War 1898–1914,* began to appear in 1926. The Soviet regime has published a number of collections from imperial archives, including the invaluable and dramatic diary of Sazonov's chief assistant in the Foreign Office, Baron Schilling. An English translation by Cyprian Bridge was published in 1935 under the title *How the War Began,* but it is said that the English version is not altogether reliable.

These official collections of documents form, however, only an infinitesimal part of the materials concerning 1914 and events leading up to it. There are many other official records now available. There are the contemporary periodical sources. There is also the huge body of writing formed by the memoirs, diaries, and autobiographies of participants in the events—several hundred at least. A volume of essays describing the materials that became available in the 1920's was reissued four times, with extensive supplements, to form one of the important bibliographies in English—there are dozens, in all languages. It was written by one of the editors of *British Documents,* G. P. Gooch, and is called *Recent Revelations of European Diplomacy* (4th impression; 1930).

The memoirs vary widely in interest, importance, and reliability. Some, like Maurice Paléologue's *An Ambassador's Memoirs* (1924), are shown by comparison with the docments to be notable chiefly for suppressions and fabrications. Viscount Grey's *Twenty-Five Years, 1892–1916* (1925) seems to contain no intentional perversions of truth; but it reveals its author's high-minded naïveté and his extremely smug self-justification. Most of the statesmen were naturally at pains to exculpate themselves (sometimes at the expense of accusing their colleagues) of any irresponsible attitude toward possible war. Not so the soldiers. Some of them—most dramatically the Austrian chief of staff, Franz Conrad von Hötzendorf, in *Aus meiner Dienstzeit* (1921–25)—vituperatively charged their civilian colleagues with an insane and irresponsible devotion to peace. Conrad, like the German General Friedrich von Bernhardi and, in a much milder form, Moltke himself, revealed a belief in the efficacy of what they called "preventive war."

The following are a few additional autobiographical works available in English, chosen largely at random: Karl Max Lichnowsky, *Heading for the Abyss* (Eng. trans., 1928); the German Ambassador at London was the leading example of a memorist bitterly denouncing the morals and the competence of his own government. Winston Churchill, *The World Crisis* (London, 1928), Vol. I; Theobald von Bethmann-Hollweg, *Reflections of the World War* (1920); Sergei D. Sazonov, *Fateful Years* (1928); Bernhard von Bülow, *Memoirs* (1931); Sir G. Buchanan, *My Mission to Russia* (1923).

Secondary works on the 1914 crisis are no less numerous. For many years a trio of works, covering much the same ground but differing largely in interpretation, led the field. They were Fay's *The Origins of the World War,* and Schmitt's *The Coming of the War,* noted above, and Pierre Renouvin's *The Immediate Origins of the War* (1928). There were dozens of others, but these three were usually regarded, in America anyway, as constituting the peak of scholarship. Fay was famous for his persuasive argument for Germany's relative innocence, and criticism of Russia and Austria; Schmitt and Renouvin were much less sympathetic to the German position.

A NOTE ON THE BIBLIOGRAPHY

Those three have been replaced by the much more massive treatment of Luigi Albertini. The second and third volumes of *The Origins of the War of 1914,* published in Italy after 1942 and in English beginning a decade later, give much the most detailed account of the crisis yet compiled. While interpretations may change, it is unlikely that much new information will be added to Albertini's huge accumulation.

The most important study of German policy written since Albertini is Franz Fischer's *Germany's Aims in the First World War;* it appeared in Germany in 1961 and in the English version six years later, and has been discussed in the introduction. The treatment of the crisis is brief, but it adds to our knowledge of the German scene through a careful reading of new documents from the German and Austrian archives, and it occasioned enormous interest and considerable discussion through the evidence it gives of a consistent and sinister German effort to push the Austrians to war, regardless of consequences and in the interests of German aggrandizement.

Index

Aduwa, Battle of (1896), 109, 110
Aehrenthal, Baron Alois von, (Austro-Hungarian Foreign Minister), 149, 170, 171; co-architect of Bosnian Crisis, 151-61
Afghanistan, 136
Albania, 144, 175, 177, 178, 183
Albanians, 70, 145. *See also* Ghegs; Tosks
Albertini, Luigi (Italian politician), 20, 233, 247
Alexander, Prince, of Battenburg, 100
Alexander II, King of Serbia, 87, 142, 143, 144; assassination of, 141
Algeciras Treaty, 129-30, 134, 167, 168, 196
Alsace, 37-40, 52, 174. *See also* Alsace-Lorraine
Alsace-Lorraine, 42, 204, 268; civilians shot by German officers, 204. *See also* Alsace; Lorraine
Anatolia, 200
Andrassy, Count Julius (Austro-Hungarian Joint Foreign Minister), 95, 211
Anglo-French Agreement of 1904, 136
Anglo-Russian Agreement of 1907, 136
Armenians, 70
Arms and the Man (play), 101
Austria, decline of, 56-59; unification of, with Hungary, 60
Austria-Hungary: World War I, responsibility for, 19; formation of, 60; national composition of, 63-69 (in 1870), 82 (in 1914), *also* 102, 268; source of strength, 72-74; religions within, 74; eco-

nomic development in, 74-76; political forces within, 77-82; annexation of Bosnia, 151-63; "Second Sick Man of Europe," 152, 180-85; encirclement of, 185; assassination of Archduke Francis Ferdinand, its impact on, 204, 209; failure of to demonstrate Serb complicity in, 205, 222; contemplates solution to South Slav problem, 204-12; anti-Serb feeling, growth of, 209; consults Germany, 214-16; note to Serbia, delivery of, 217-19, contents of note from, 225-26; breaks off diplomatic relations with Serbia, 235; begins mobilization against Serbia, 236; declares war on Serbia, 241; general mobilization in, 258. *See also individual treaties and ethnic groups*
Austrian Red Book, 18
Austro-German Alliance (1879), 96-98, 101

balance of power, 33
Balfour, Arthur (British statesman), 125
Balkan nations, 46, 47, 184
Balkan Wars, 169-78
Ballin, Albert (German shipping magnate), 240
Belgium, 40, 104, 198, 252, 260; as invasion route to France, 198-200
Bengazi, 168
Berchtold, Count Leopold (Austro-Hungarian Foreign Minister), 184, 236, 239, 241, 243, 244, 245, 251-53, 258, *passim;* vacillates during Second Balkan War, 170-179; joins war party, 210; reacts

INDEX

to assassination of Archduke Francis Ferdinand, 214–18; indecisiveness of, contributory to war, 266
Berlin-Bagdad Railway, 228; accords, 201
Berlin, Congress of (1878), 91, 92, 93, 94, 99
Berlin, Treaty of (1878), 153, 158, 159
Bethmann-Hollweg, Theobald von (German statesman), 174, 194, 201, 215, 233, 238, 239, 241–44, 246, 255, 261, 267; duplicity of, 250; works to avert war, 251–53
Bienvenu-Martin (French Minister of Justice), 230
Bismarck, Prince Otto von, 28, 30, 38, 40, 43, 45, 51, 55, 87–88, 91, 112, 114, 116, 120, 121; diplomacy of, 86, 95–99, 110; and its breakdown, 100–02; dismissed from office, 102
Black Hand (pan-Serb terrorist organization), 150, 180, 226; assassination of Archduke Francis Ferdinand, responsibility for, 204–207
Boer War (1899–1902), 104, 108, 110, 122, 125, 139, 140, 186
Bohemia, 59, 63
Bosnia, 88, 92, 93, 95, 144, 166, 170, 172, 179, 180, 181, 183, 185, 208, 225; annexation of by Austria, 151–59
British Blue Book, 18
British Empire, 105, 194
British Fabian Society, 193
Buchanan, Sir George (British Ambassador to Russia), 220
Bukovina, 68
Bulgaria, 50, 81, 93, 101, 145, 147, 154, 157, 161, 166, 167, 169, 177, 211, 215; "Great Bulgaria," 89, 90, 92; annexes Southern Rumelia, 100; resists Austrian alliance, 181–82, 184–85
Bulgars, 46, 70, 166
Bülow, Prince Bernhard von (German statesman), 117, 159, 161, 162; arranges Moroccan crisis, 127–30

Cambon, Jules (French Ambassador to England), 231
Canada, 194
Carinthia (Austro-Hungarian province), 58
Carniola (Austrian province), 70
Carol I, King of Rumania, 182, 184
Cavour, Count Camillo (Italian statesman), 28
Central Powers, 99, 227. *See also* Germany; Austria-Hungary
Chabrinovich (would-be assassin of Archduke Francis Ferdinand), 204
Chinese Empire, disintegration of, 134
Christian Socialist Party, 78
Churchill, Winston, 189, 197, 201, 240; orders British fleet to battle bases, 259
Ciganovich (pan-Serb conspirator), 226
Concert of Europe, 32–34, 53, 91, 130
Conrad von Hötzendorf, Baron Franz (Austro-Hungarian Field Marshal), 152, 162, 172, 181, 185, 220, 236, 241, 243, 245, 251, 258; urges attack of Serbia, 157; leads war party, 210, 211–12, 215, 217
Constantinople, 50, 69, 169; Russian aspirations toward, 44, 88, 89, 94, 101, 136, 153, 228, 268; German interest in, 158, 200–203; Greek claims to, 166
Crimean War (1854–56), 45, 90
Crispi, Francesco (Italian statesman), 109, 127
Croatia, 70
Croats, 69, 70, 71, 82, 94, 179. *See also* Serbo-Croats
Crowe, Sir Eyre (British statesman), 132, 260
Cyrenaica, 168. *See also* Libya
Czechoslovakia, 50
Czechs, 63, 68, 70, 71, 76, 94
Czernin, Count Ottokar (Austrian diplomat), 183

Daily Telegraph, The, episode, 117, 161

INDEX

of in Austria-Hungary, 60–63; oppression of minorities by, 69, 70, 71; resistance of, to change, 79–80; anti-trialism of, 94; anti-Slavism of, 95, 211. *See also* Hungary; Austria-Hungary
Manchuria, 108, 134, 135
Marx, Karl, 35
Masin, Draga. *See* Draga Masin
Mazzini, Giuseppe (Italian patriot), 29
Mill, John Stuart, 35, 142
Modena, 58
Moltke, General Helmuth von, 22, 23, 162, 189, 194, 200, 212, 215, 216, 238, 240; urges instant German mobilization, 251, 253, 256, 258, 261; recommends general mobilization to Austria-Hungary, 261
Montenegro, 46, 47, 148, 150, 154, 170, 176, 183, 185, 211; ethnic groups within, 50, 69; leader in Serb nationalist movement, 149; makes war on Turkey, 166, 167, 169
Moravia, 59, 63, 155
Morocco, 124, 126, 168; 1905 crisis, 127–31
Mun, Albert de (French monarchist), 193
Mürzsteg Punctation (1903), 146

Napoleon III, 27, 29, 32, 39
Narodna Obrana (pan-Serb secret society), 163, 179, 180, 181, 205, 226
national states: emergence of, 28; theoretical equality among, 29; unity within, 29; advantages of, 51–52
Naumann, Friedrich (German politician and historian), 118
Naumann, Victor (German publicist), 213, 214
Near Eastern Question, 140, 162. *See also* Eastern Question
Netherlands, The, 108
New York Times Magazine, The, 21
Nicholas, Grand Duke, of Russia, 228
Nicholas I, Emperor of Russia, 45

Nicholas II, Emperor of Russia, 103, 137, 171, 208, 212, 220, 227, 247, 252, 267; wavers in decision to order mobilization, 254–57
Nicholas, Prince of Montenegro, 149, 150
Nicholson, Sir Arthur (British diplomat), 136, 160, 236, 260
Nietzsche, Friedrich, 193
North China, 134
Novibazar, 92–95 *passim*, 144, 148, 154, 170

Obrenovich, House of, 142
Obrenovich, Milan, Prince of Serbia, 93, 94, 98
Orange Free State, 107
Ottoman Empire. *See* Turkey

Palacky, Frantisek (Czech national leader), 82
Paléologue, Maurice (French diplomat), 221, 227, 259; French policy, responsibility for, 265
Pan-German League, 118, 119
pan-Serbism, 147, 150, 209, 210; leads to Sarajevo, 204–06
pan-Slavism, 101, 119; evolvement of, 49–50; Russia encourages, 89; growth of, 166–67
Pashitch, Nikola (Serbian statesman), 146
"People's Defense, The." *See* Narodna Obrana
Persia, 136
Piedmont, 58
Pig War, 147–48, 150, 173
Poincaré, Raymond, President of France, 212, 221, 237, 239, 258; character of, 174
Poland, 42, 43, 44, 57, 194
Poles, 50, 68, 70, 71, 72, 73, 94
Port Arthur, 134
Portugal, 41
Potsdam Conversations, 215
Pourtalès, Count Friedrich von (German Ambassador to Russia), 221, 237–38, 251, 255–56, 261–62
Prague, Peace of (1866), 58
Princip, Gavrilo, assassin of Archduke Francis Ferdinand, 204